TERROR TOWN, USA

THE UNTOLD STORY OF JOLIET'S

NOTORIOUS SERIAL KILLER

BESTSELLING AUTHOR OF *WRECKING CREW*

JOHN FERAK

WILD BLUE
PRESS

WildBluePress.com

TERROR TOWN, USA published by:
WILDBLUE PRESS
P.O. Box 102440
Denver, Colorado 80250

ISBN 978-1-952225-68-0 Trade Paperback
ISBN 978-1-952225-67-3 eBook

Cover design © 2021 WildBlue Press. All rights reserved.

Interior Formatting/Cover Design by Elijah Toten
www.totencreative.com

TERROR
TOWN, USA

PROLOGUE

I was ten years old and growing up in Joliet, Illinois, an industrial, blue-collar Midwestern city that had a Caterpillar plant with 7,000 jobs. That summer, my life revolved around Little League baseball games at St. Joe's Park off Theodore Street and keeping up with the busy Mass schedule as an altar boy at St. Mary Nativity Catholic Church on Broadway Street. I grew up in a two-story, white-sided house with a horseshoe driveway at 1028 Gardner Street, along Route 52. When I wasn't playing second base on the Little League diamond, one of the neighbor kids and I tossed a red rubber ball in our long, gravel driveway, and we made up our own baseball game.

Family was always around our house, and when relatives weren't gathered on Gardner Street, we were over at my grandparents' house. They lived in the same neighborhood, two streets behind our house. I could run from my yard to my grandparents' house on Retta Court in less than a minute.

The summer of 1983 was memorable for me, first because of the intense heat. Summers near Chicago are always hot, but 1983 was a historic scorcher. Temperatures were in the 90s and triple digits for weeks on end, and there was hardly any rain. I remember the Fourth of July. Oh, what a night. Family and some of the neighbors gathered on lawn chairs in my parents' backyard, and one of our guests brought over a bag of fireworks, which may have been illegal back then.

One of the bottle rockets whizzed into the air, as expected, and then made a hard landing in the backyard right behind my house. That man's backyard looked like a pile of straw because of the drought. Sure enough, an orange glow appeared. Under the dark sky, the bottle rocket had started a small grass fire. A couple of my uncles leapt from their lawn chairs and did their best Carl Lewis imitation, sprinting as fast as they could to stamp out the fire with their gym shoes. It worked. Crisis averted. There was no need to call the East Joliet Volunteer Fire Department.

I wish I could say the errant bottle rocket was my scariest moment that summer, but it wasn't. Even though I was only ten, I kept up on the news and took an interest in reading the daily Joliet newspaper, mainly because I was a sports junkie, and I was obsessed with reading the Major League Baseball box scores and the players' statistics. Even though sports consumed my life at ten, I couldn't miss the agony and tragedy splashed across the front page of my parents' newspaper. And if I missed it at home, I was certain to see it spread across my grandparents' kitchen table two streets away.

A crazed madman, like Joliet had never seen, was on the prowl, maiming and torturing along the way. All of his victims were losing their lives in truly wicked ways. About two weeks before I returned to start fifth grade at St. Mary Nativity, one of the summer's gruesome killings hit close to home. Ed Garland, the owner of our friendly and dependable neighborhood full-service gas station, lost one of his children during the serial-killing spree. About a week later a quarter-mile up the street from my yard, the Will Coun Sheriff's deputies had converged upon a two-story hous along Mills Road where an older widow lived all alone. Th Will County Coroner's Office arrived to take away her bod

Another Joliet Township murder victim, what in the world was going on?

Growing up in Joliet was no longer about keeping up on the wins and losses for the Chicago White Sox and the Chicago Cubs or trying to find my favorite Topps baseball cards when I tagged along with my parents to the grocery store. Up to that point in my life, death was a foreign topic to me. I hadn't lost any immediate family members, yet. And the idea of murder, someone being killed for no apparent reason, was unfathomable. But now here it was. The newspaper kept running stories about a killer on the loose, and his tally of victims kept mounting, month after month, that terribly hot summer. Even though I was only ten, I could not escape or avoid the terror and panic all around me. It was no longer a wise idea to leave your house unlocked or throw your keys on the front seat of your car or truck, as people around Joliet commonly did back then.

Ten years later, I was a sophomore in college studying journalism at Eastern Illinois University. That summer of 1993, I returned to Joliet, my hometown, as a newspaper reporting intern, where I had a chance to hear first-hand stories from well-known Joliet *Herald-News* columnist John Whiteside and many other seasoned journalists who covered the 1983 summer of terror as well as the ensuing murder trials.

After college, I disconnected with my hometown and worked in newspapers across the Midwest, including Indiana, Wisconsin and nearly a decade in Nebraska. But as the newspaper era was dying, other opportunities arose and online journalism was booming. In 2017, I returned to Joliet as reporter and editor for Patch. The first few months, I spent a lot of time re-familiarizing myself with Joliet given how much it grew. When I was a kid, Joliet had nearly 80,000 people. Now, it was 150,000. I spent a lot of time getting to know the key people I'd wind up writing about, from time to time, covering Joliet politics, local businesses or the Will County Courthouse since Joliet was the county seat.

One time, I met up for lunch at Jameson's Pub on Black Road with attorney Frank Cservenyak and several members of his Joliet law firm, Rathbun, Cservenyak & Kozol. During lunch, Cservenyak remarked that I should consider writing about Milton Johnson, Will County's most notorious serial killer, as one of my next true-crime books.

One of Cservenyak's law partners, attorney Stephen White, was intricately involved with the case.

And so began my research into one of the country's most terrorizing mass murderers, who just happened to be from my hometown. Around Illinois and across the nation, the names of John Wayne Gacy and Richard Speck are regarded as two of the most terrifying serial killers on the planet, but as many long-time residents of Joliet and Will County know, there's another raging madman whose sadistic nature rivals that of Gacy and Speck.

Some people refer to them as serial killers; others call them spree killers or mass murderers.

Attorney Stephen White has his own insight into Milton Johnson.

"Milton Johnson was a situation killer," White told me when we crossed paths inside the new Will County Courthouse in February 2021.

There have been numerous books, television mini-serie and movies depicting the lives and unspeakable crime committed by suburban Chicago clown-killer John Wayn Gacy and Chicago nurse killer Richard Speck.

The same can't be said for Milton Johnson.

And yet Johnson's crimes are as frightening as those committed by Gacy and Speck put together.

That summer of terror, 1983, took a heavy toll on Joliet, from grandparents to parents to police to politicians to clergy to business owners to waitresses at coffee shops. The killing spree even weighed heavily on the minds of children. I know, because I was one of them.

AUTHOR'S NOTE

Mary West and Tonya Little are pseudonyms used in the book to protect the identity of two sexual assault victims.

The following account is derived from past newspaper articles, trial and court transcripts, Will County Coroner's Office inquest records, investigative police reports generated by the Will County Sheriff's Office, Cook County Sheriff's Office and interviews conducted by the author.

CHAPTER 1

PILCHER PARK

In the Land of Lincoln, the main roads, waterways and communities leading toward Chicago are dominated by semi-trucks, shipping barges and freight train box cars. Urban sprawl created demand to build more homes, apartment buildings, factories and industrial business parks. The construction boom witnessed in many northern Illinois towns and cities on the outskirts of Chicago signaled the demise of family farms and tens of thousands of acres across the Prairie State.

Rolling hills, wetlands and open fields that stood the test of time for generations were gobbled up by tenacious developers and investment partners who had one thing on their mind: the almighty dollar.

During the early 1900s, Robert Pilcher made his fortune in the paper mill industry. But in his later years, Pilcher began to realize the sacredness of the many gifts bestowed by Mother Nature. Pilcher and his wife, Nora, owned several hundred acres of majestic beauty on the eastern edge of Joliet, Illinois, a tough-as-nails, blue-collar industrial city forty-five miles southwest of Chicago.

'ilcher's property was a sight to see. The hardwood forest onsisted of thousands of giant maple trees affording the erfect shade for the squirrels, rabbits, raccoon, beaver, possum and fox. The wetlands attracted red-winged blackbirds, mallards, Canada geese and colorful wood ducks. The great blue heron was a regular visitor to the area of Hickory Creek that flowed through Pilcher's land.

In 1920, Robert and Nora Pilcher donated 327 acres to the city of Joliet. The generous land donation was later shifted to the care and ownership of Joliet's Park District, a completely separate local government. The land once known as the Forest of Arden was renamed in honor of the donors.

It became Pilcher Park.

A century later, Pilcher Park remains a popular destination for outdoor enthusiasts. Every week, hundreds of people walk through the forest along its many hiking trails. Others prefer to stand along the banks of the Hickory Creek to try their luck at fishing. A bronze statue of a life-like Robert Pilcher in a sport coat, slacks and bow tie towers over the nature center. The engraved statue dedicated to Robert Pilcher reads: "Sturdy Pioneer, Loyal Citizen, Lover of Nature and His Fellowmen, A Dreamer Whose Dream Held."

The inscription along the bottom of the statue noted that the Pilcher Arboretum was dedicated on July 31, 1920.

One unusual attraction featured within Pilcher Park was called the Flowing Well. Tucked in the back of the forest, the Flowing Well featured pure artesian mineral water. Many Joliet area residents believed the mineral water was healthy and better tasting than their kitchen faucet tap water. On many days, several cars lined up along the secluded forest road as people filled their plastic jugs with mineral water from the Flowing Well to bring home for consumption.

If they were still alive today, Robert and Nora Pilche would be pleased to know the Joliet Park District has don a fantastic job making sure that their generous donation scenic woodlands remains off-limits to land developers, century later.

On the other hand, the Pilcher's would be repulsed to discover that their well-intentioned land donation aimed at bringing good into the world also became a magnet for evil and wickedness.

**

Over the years, the Joliet Park District added amenities to Pilcher Park, including a greenhouse with hundreds of beautiful flowers and a nature education center for visitors to appreciate the local wildlife. Pilcher Park remained open year-round. During warmer weather, families and groups of friends picnicked and wandered the woods for a refreshing nature walk.

After sunset, Pilcher Park took on another persona, becoming known as a lover's lane. The forest's giant trees and meandering roads offered plenty of hiding spots for romantic couples to park. These roads were exceptionally narrow. There was barely room for one vehicle to pass.

On Feb. 15, 1970, Lee Chandler and his girlfriend drove to Pilcher Park even though temperatures remained in the teens. On this particular occasion, the dating couple parked on one of the back roads toward the Flowing Well. They chose this location figuring nobody would bother them. After all, during the frigid winter, Pilcher Park was hardly overrun with people.

A half-hour after their arrival, the young lovers noticed a car driving the wrong way through the forest.

"It stopped and it backed up and pulled in right behind us," Lee Chandler would later testify in court.

Moments later, the Joliet area teenagers heard tapping on their passenger window.

Chandler's girlfriend, Mary West, rolled down her window.

"Am I going the wrong way?" the stranger asked.

"Yes," she replied.

"Thank you," the voice responded.

The stranger walked back to his car, only to return a few minutes later.

He knocked on the teenage couple's passenger window a second time.

"How long are you going to be here?" the voice inquired.

"About ten minutes," the girl responded.

Suddenly, a shotgun barrel was pointed into their car.

"Bitch, open the door!" the stranger screamed.

As West complied, the intruder climbed into the backseat.

The shotgun-carrying creep asked the terrified teens how much money they had.

Lee had $20. Mary had $5.

"He told me to lay on the front seat and look down toward the brake pedal and stuff and not turn around," Chandler said.

The trapped teens tried to appease their captor. After all, he held a loaded shotgun and seemed not afraid to use it.

The gunman ordered the eighteen-year-old woman to disrobe.

"Broad, get in the back seat," he commanded.

After she took off some of her garments, the man's lustful eyes gazed upon her body.

"He turned around and looked at her and asked what that was. She said it was her slip," Chandler explained.

But because Mary West did not do exactly as her captor demanded, he punched her.

"I told you everything," the stranger hollered.

Next, the angry stranger wanted to know what brought the teenage couple to Pilcher Park on such a cold winter night.

"What were you doing here?" he inquired.

"Nothing," they both repeated.

Displeased by their response, he smacked the girl a second time.

"What were you doing here?" he demanded.

Mary West made up an answer, hoping to placate their captor.

"We were fucking," she claimed.

The man turned toward the scared young woman in the backseat with him.

"I'm going to fuck you," he told her.

The local teen was repulsed by the beast staring at her body.

"Shoot me first," she begged.

Angered by her response, the man smacked her hard as Lee Chandler crunched into a ball on the driver's side floorboard.

He sensed danger. Their car shook. His girlfriend cried.

Lee Chandler later recounted that the kidnapper announced, "Tell Lee exactly what we're doing and she says, we're making love."

But those weren't the right words, so the sadistic rapist punched her.

"We're screwing," she responded.

"No!" the rapist disagreed, hitting her again.

"OK, we're fucking," she admitted.

That was the right word choice.

"Okay," he agreed with satisfaction.

Deep inside the dark forest, Lee Chandler heard his girlfriend's attacker order her to "Kiss me and stick your tongue in my mouth."

"I heard her going, kind of mumble, moan-type thing," her boyfriend explained.

Then, the rapist announced, "Tell Lee what you're doing now."

"I'm sucking his dick," the helpless girlfriend responded.

The oral sex lasted a few minutes, but did not go well.

"Dumb broad," the rapist roared. "You don't know anything. Lay over on your stomach and spread the cheeks of your ass."

As Mary West was being humiliated and violated, her boyfriend feared that any slight movement on his part might provoke the foul-mouthed captor into killing them both.

Suddenly, he heard his girlfriend make a loud painful noise.

"They sat up and he says, 'Now, tell Lee what you're doing now.' She said, 'I'm jacking him off.'"

A few minutes later, the gunman asked his victims if they smoked cigarettes. Chandler answered no, but his girlfriend directed the rapist to her box of cigarettes on her dashboard.

"At that time, I felt like he was reaching over me and took the cigarettes. And he took the keys out of the ignition at the same time," Chandler observed. "I heard a sizzling noise, and I heard (her) screaming. It smelled like something burning."

The backseat rapist used the front seat cigarette lighter to torture his victim.

"He pushed it in to get it hot," the boyfriend recalled. "Then he took it out, and he told her to keep her hands still and not to move them, and he burned her a couple of times with the cigarette lighter. I could hear the sizzling more, and it was more like a hair burning, and she was screaming and crying."

The sadistic rapist began smacking the girl for no apparent reason.

"My jaw's broken. I heard it snap," she cried.

The Pilcher Park bogeyman turned his focus to the helpless boyfriend.

"At this time, I felt him reach over and pull a wallet out of my pocket," Chandler recalled.

The time had come for the shotgun-wielding rapist to decide whether to kill his prey or let them survive.

"Get out of the car," he snapped at Chandler. "Look down on the ground, and if you look at me I will kill you."

Wanting to live, the boyfriend complied.

"And he stayed far enough away from me where I couldn't grab the gun or anything, and he walked over to his car and shut the car door," Chandler remarked.

When the shotgun-toting rapist returned, Lee Chandler remained face down on the ground in the sprawling forest with no one around to help.

"OK, let's get back in the car," the stranger commanded. "Lay down on your stomach."

But before Chandler got back inside, the madman wanted to know whether Chandler had followed his orders.

"Yeah," he agreed.

What about his girlfriend?

"Yeah, I think she did," he answered.

"OK," the perpetrator relayed. "I want you to open the driver's side of the car now because I want the shotgun blast to go through when I kill both of you."

Lee Chandler was not ready to die a lonely and agonizing death at the hands of this cruel and tormenting madman.

As he opened the driver's door, Chandler made a daring dash into the dark forest.

"As soon as I got out of Pilcher Park, I stopped at a motel there, a pay phone there, and that's where I called them from," Chandler said.

Panicked, the rapist climbed behind the wheel of his victim's car. He drove her about a mile up the road to Silver Cross

Hospital, a mammoth six-story, concrete building perched high on a hill along Route 6 and Draper Avenue. The towering 302-bed, Joliet medical center traced its origins to the early 1900s.

At the east-side hospital, doctors realized the Plainfield, Illinois, teenager suffered cigarette lighter burns to her vagina. Her rapist bit through one of her breasts and smashed her jaw.

"Plainfield Girl Critical After Attack In Park," read the next day's newspaper headline.

An 18-year-old Plainfield girl was reported in critical condition in the intensive care unit at Silver Cross Hospital after she was savagely beaten, tortured and raped late Sunday night in Pilcher Park," read The Joliet Herald-News article from February 1970.

"The worst beating I've ever seen," Joliet Police Detective Sergeant Leroy Everson was quoted by the newspaper.

**

Joliet police evidence technician Reynold Rossi investigated the barbarous attack at the city's otherwise peaceful Pilcher Park.

Inside the Silver Cross Hospital trauma center, Rossi encountered Mary West as she lay dazed in bed recovering from the brutalizing attack.

Within a few hours, two of the Joliet Police Department's most-respected officers at the time, Dave Farmer and George Hernandez, made the arrest of nineteen-year-old Joliet resident, Milton Johnson. He was a high school dropout who lived with his mother and stepfather in Joliet's Forest Park area.

According to the 1970 newspaper accounts, the rapist "was so shaken by the girl's condition that he drove her to the hospital himself."

According to the local police, the Pilcher Park torture rapist was a sexual voyeur. Milton Johnson liked to troll desolate roads and out of the way parks in search of young lovers sharing affection. That way, he could watch and fantasize for a while as they remained oblivious to his presence hovering in the background under the cloak of darkness.

Indeed, he was no ordinary Peeping Tom.

"This is just an evil person who truly gets off on the joys of brutality," remarked now-retired Will County State's Attorney Ed Petka.

Sadly, Mary West never escaped the agony and emotional trauma that shattered her youthful innocence inside the wilderness of Pilcher Park. On the night of Feb. 15, 1970, she and her boyfriend had no inkling they were being watched by a methodical and deviant monster hiding in the woods, preparing to slaughter them.

Years later, the ex-boyfriend was asked in court to recall the sizzling sounds coming from his girlfriend's flesh.

"He told her to put her feet up on the roof of the car, and then he proceeded to take the cigarette lighter and burn her on her vagina," Chandler explained.

The atrocity inside Joliet's Pilcher Park transpired during a chaotic time in Richard Nixon's presidency as tensions escalated involving the Vietnam War. Fortunately for everyone, the sundown attack appeared to be an aberration. As the years passed, Joliet residents became less frightened of the wicked and ruthless monster that terrorized Pilcher Park on the bone-chilling night of Feb. 15, 1970.

Over time, people were no longer scared of a bogeyman lurking behind a tall tree or crouched beside a row of thick bushes, watching them as if they were unsuspecting animals of prey.

After a thirteen year absence, Milton Johnson returned to town. That year, 1983, happened to be the same year Joliet would be shaken after the supermarket tabloid, *The National Enquirer*, branded the city as "Terror Town U.S.A."

The shocker tabloid headline left city leaders outraged, but deep down, nobody could deny its accuracy.

CHAPTER 2

CLOSE CALL

On the hot summer night of June 17, 1983, Theresa McKeen returned to her car near Silver Cross Hospital. She and her fellow Elgin, Joliet and Eastern Railway employees used the overflow parking lot from the mammoth Joliet hospital near Route 6 and Draper Avenue. The railroad company was another spoke in the wheel for Joliet's blue-collar economy.

EJ & E train engines lugged freight boxcars and loads of steel, coal, coke and iron ore across a 175-mile stretch known as Chicago's outer belt. Around Joliet, people simply referred to the eastside railyard as "The J." When The J prospered, Joliet prospered. When The J struggled, Joliet struggled.

On this night, McKeen left the parking lot around midnight. She lived about five miles east of Silver Cross Hospital.

As the young woman passed Joliet's outdoor movie theatre, the Hill-Top Drive-In, she noticed a vehicle pulled to the side of Route 6 with its dome light on. Seconds later, the driver began to follow her.

"I then saw a truck on the side of me," she later testified in court. "He had been on the left-hand side trying to pass me. He stayed there for a long time."

But, the truck would not pass her. Rather, the mystery motorist tried to keep pace.

As McKeen pushed the brakes to her 1976 Mercury Marquis, a loud noise rang out.

"I thought kids threw a rock at me, and my whole window shattered and fell into my lap," she recounted.

For the first time, McKeen got a good look at the passing vehicle.

"It was a truck," she recalled.

After shooting out the woman's window, the gunman sped up, gaining distance. Eventually, the truck pulled into one of the side roads north of Route 6.

As she raced toward home, McKeen faced another harrowing encounter.

"It was blocking the other lane of traffic one-hundred percent," she observed. "When I'm approaching it, I see a man getting out of the driver's seat."

The man was Black and looked to be about six feet tall.

"He was yelling," McKeen recalled, "but I don't know exactly what he was saying. But I knew he wanted me to stop."

The angry man tightly gripped his gun.

The Joliet railroad worker feared her life was in grave danger. But would she make it home?

"I accelerated then and went past him," she explained.

The man fired off four more gunshots at the fast-moving Mercury Marquis, but he missed.

McKeen caught a glimpse of his truck. It looked black. She only saw one person standing at the truck, but when asked by police to recall her near-deadly encounter, her mind played games with her.

"I always knew there was another person there," she suggested. "I feel like I could see another person."

After two brushes with death on the same deserted stretch of Joliet Township road, McKeen was not about to let the crazed gunman hunt her down and kill her in the middle of the night.

She had to get home.

"I accelerated to its maximum. I had my foot pressed down all the way," the Will County resident remembered.

The midnight stalker was not about to let her get away without another chase.

"He was right behind me," she recalled.

McKeen tried to keep calm even though her life was in danger. At the rural intersection of Cedar Road, she turned and realized she was in the clear. The madman in the black truck chose to back off and gave up the chase.

Once home, she grabbed her phone book and dialed the police. In 1983, 911 did not exist.

On-duty Illinois State Police Trooper Robert Rogers drew the overnight call of investigating the aggravated gun discharge. His face-to-face interview inside the distressed woman's rural Joliet house lasted nearly an hour.

Between 1 and 2 a.m. Trooper Rogers began to search for the menacing shooting suspect terrorizing Joliet's rural roads. The state trooper was under the impression he needed to look for a two-person team.

As most of Joliet was sound asleep, Rogers retraced the railroad worker's travels along Route 6. He concentrated on the far eastside of Joliet, a mostly rural hillside.

The section of Route 6 between Joliet and the next neighboring town to the east, New Lenox, was mostly country, plenty of cow pastures and horse stables. One of Joliet's oldest cemeteries, Ss. Cyril and Methodius, was nestled along Route 6 as was The Hill-Top, the giant outdoor movie theater.

"I had left the victim's home and was in the process to go back to the scene and inspect the scene for any physical evidence," Rogers would testify. "I was told that it was a pickup truck involved."

When Rogers approached the rural intersection at Cedar Road and Route 6 in Joliet Township, he saw a suspicious pickup, navy blue or black in color.

"There was a subject standing outside the driver's side area," Rogers noticed.

First, he jotted down the truck's license plates. From there, Rogers asked the man standing near the truck for his driver's license.

"It came back to a Milton Johnson," Rogers noted.

Earlier, McKeen insisted there had to be two people in the truck that shattered her driver's window and fired four more bullets at her.

The man stopped for questioning by Rogers, Milton Johnson, was all alone. Following his brief interaction with Johnson, Rogers returned to his police car and got back on the road. There were no written incident reports of the encounter with Milton Johnson.

In time, Trooper Rogers fielded questions pertaining to McKeen's car damage complaint. The person asking the questions wanted to know whether the Illinois State Police trooper stopped anybody else besides Milton Johnson following the shooting call on Joliet's east side.

"Not in the time frame from the time I left, to the time I encountered the vehicle, no," Rogers responded.

After speaking with Johnson along Route 6 in the middle of the night, the Illinois State Police trooper let him go.

Rogers would eventually be asked the following question: "Now, after you spoke with Mr. Johnson, did you take Mr. Johnson back to Mrs. McKeen's house for her to view him or identify him?"

"No, sir, I did not," Rogers answered.

When asked whether Milton Johnson was cooperative during questioning near Route 6 and Cedar Road, the state trooper answered, "Somewhat."

Rogers' instincts led him to believe that Milton Johnson was not the culprit who shot at McKeen's car along Route 6. After all, having a pickup parked on the side of the road did not constitute a crime.

Based on his intuition and training, Rogers didn't believe he had a legitimate reason to arrest Johnson during the early morning hours of June 17, 1983.

"You never placed Mr. Johnson under arrest for an assault on Mrs. McKeen, did you?" someone asked Rogers.

"No, I did not," Rogers responded.

"You were not present at any lineups in which Mr. Johnson was involved in, where Mrs. McKeen observed him, did you?"

"That's correct."

CHAPTER 3

FIRE ON ROSALIND

Joliet Township's area of Rosalind and Briggs streets was reminiscent of a bygone era, where life moved at a slower clip and people appreciated the wilderness. Several acreages dotted a portion of Rosalind Street, featuring large lots where people raised horses. Signs warned motorists to be on the lookout for horseback riders. The region consisted of riding trails and hundreds of acres of farmland that remained outside the city limits of Joliet. The people on Rosalind enjoyed their solitude and valued their privacy. Many had lived here for most of their lives and had no intentions to move elsewhere.

Honora (Blum) Lahmann, sixty-eight, lived in a modest house at 1720 Rosalind Street. More than thirty acres of farmland surrounded her property and posted signs warned hunters to stay off the land. Prior to retiring eight years earlier, Lahmann taught grade school for almost forty years.

She spent twenty-eight years in the Homer Township school district including eighteen years at the Goodings Grove School. Then, she spent her final ten years teaching with New Lenox School District 122. She retired from public education in 1975. She and her husband married in the 1950s and had no children before he died prematurely. After her husband's death, Lahmann chose to live by herself along the rural stretch of Joliet Township, northeast of city limits.

Even though Lahmann was a widow, she had close family nearby. Her younger sister, sixty-six-year-old Zita Blum, lived in the ranch house next door. The two sisters had practically spent their entire lives on Rosalind Street. It's also where their parents raised them.

"They were wonderful. Nora was a retired school teacher," remarked Jean Haas during a 2021 interview with the author. Haas lived more than a quarter mile down the road from the Blum sisters.

One time, Nora Lahmann returned to her house and saw a man attempting to steal her lawnmower in broad daylight, the neighbor remembered. "Nora gets out of her car and yells, 'Now you put that back and he did and he left," Jean Haas recalled. "If something wasn't right, she would tell you. Nora would not tolerate anything that was bad."

The Blum sisters were devout Catholics. They were parishioners at Joliet's St. John the Baptist Church on Hickory Street, according to Jean Haas.

Haas's husband, Pete, was a Will County Sheriff's sergeant assigned to the criminal investigations unit in 1983.

"Pete always told Nora and Zita you need a burglar alarm, and you got to have several weapons, and that was just before this happened," Jean Haas said. "They said it was too expensive. They just felt confident that they would take care of everything here."

On June 24, 1983, Pete and Jean Haas decided to leave their seventy-acre farm and go get ice cream. As they drove past Nora Lahmann's house between 6 and 7 p.m., the Haas' honked their horn. The Blum sisters were outside washing their car.

Later that same Friday night, Jean Cagwin was one of the area residents who heard gunshots from her cow pasture in the vicinity of Oak Avenue and Farrell Road. The gunfire seemed to be coming over her fence line. Around dusk, the Joliet Township resident heard even more gunshots. In both instances, she did not call the Will County Sheriff's Office. Gunfire was a common occurrence in the area. A number of country dwellers, including sheriff's Sergeant Pete Haas, had shooting ranges for target practice in their backyards.

After sunrise the next morning, the neighbors noticed danger, prompting them to call the East Joliet Volunteer Fire Department.

Jean Haas remembered that one of the newspaper delivery carriers pulled into their driveway and began honking her horn. "The paper lady said, the two ladies down the road, their house was on fire."

Jean Haas remembered rolls of dark smoke billowing out of the southwest corner of Honora Lahmann's house on Rosalind.

"It was early," Jean Haas explained. "So, Pete woke up, put his clothes on and went in the house. It was smoldering very bad, and he called the county sheriff's department and East Joliet Fire Department."

While her husband went inside the burning house, Jean Haas said she went next door to alert Zita Blum to the fire at her sister's house.

"At Zita's house, the back door was kicked in, the whole frame and they had a dead bolt on it," Jean Haas explained.

Zita Blum was nowhere to be found inside her house. Jean Haas then ran next door where she encountered her husband.

"He told me don't go in there," Jean Haas said. "He went in and found them."

Several fire trucks arrived by 8:20 a.m. The East Joliet firefighters contained the damage to one of the back bedrooms.

When the smoke cleared, the firefighters and Will County Sheriff's deputies were aghast.

Now retired, Will County Sheriff's Investigator Dave Simpson remembered one of the volunteer firefighters told him, "Hey, we've got something to show you. I went into the building, and it was bizarre," Simpson said. "The black stench of burnt stuff is really overwhelming."

Inside the burned out bedroom were the charred bodies of homeowner Honora Lahmann and her sister Zita Blum.

The older sisters were savagely beaten before their lives were taken with a bullet at close range. The killer went to great lengths to desecrate their bodies, setting them on fire, burning them to a crisp. The intense heat deformed the legs and arms.

Investigators discovered Zita Blum's house was the original crime scene. There was plenty of blood spatter inside her house. Jean Haas suspected the terror happened during the early morning hours that Saturday. After Blum was severely beaten or killed inside her house, the killer carried or dragged her body next door, where her sister also met the same cruel fate.

"Zita was a quiet one. Zita was quiet," Jean Haas said. "She let Nora take care of everything. To just terrorize them like that, maybe he had an encounter with Nora, knowing her nature. He was probably coming or driving by and seeing them a lot by themselves."

At the time, police wondered whether one of the women angered someone driving along Rosalind Street. On the contrary, the idea of a family squabble or inheritance dispute didn't seem likely. Neither sister had any immediate family.

"One of them was pretty spunky, and she would holler at people," Simpson recalled.

Will County Coroner Robert "Bobby" Tezak announced that dental records were necessary to positively identify both victims.

In the first-floor back bedroom, the two sisters were stacked on top of each other in a sexual position.

"The two were there inverted, a sixty-nine position," Simpson remembered. One of the victims had a turkey baster shoved into her vagina, he said.

"That was something I certainly wasn't expecting," Simpson said. "It was violent, degrading. You don't think of seniors in a sixty-nine position. One was shot when they were put in that position and the room was set on fire. It was engulfed. It had burned partially through the wall and partially through the ceiling. With that intense of temperature, everything gets destroyed and wrecked."

The torture and torment inflicted on the two older women was something Simpson carried with him the rest of his career at the Will County Sheriff's Office.

He saw the bodies of two older women, their faces burned beyond recognition and one of them was violated with a turkey baster.

"People are not wired to handle that or to see it," Simpson said.

The killer ransacked Zita Blum's house, making his entrance through a back door. He pried open a wooden storm door with such great force that the door jamb separated from the wall.

Elsewhere in the house, a floor fan was toppled, and the telephone headpiece had blood stains. Police found the dentures for one of the sisters on the kitchen counter and several newspapers strewn across the living room floor.

Honora Lahmann suffered three stab wounds to her neck, and she was shot, her autopsy revealed. She also suffered a skull fracture. The fire burned away her entire right leg plus her left foot. Her face was charred, and nearly all her hair burned away. A foreign object was protruding from her vaginal area.

Her younger sister, Zita Blum, took a bullet to her abdomen.

Authorities were certain the Blum sisters were set on fire after their slayings, not before the killings occurred.

The following week, extended family and grieving friends congregated at Joliet's St. Bernard's Catholic Church in the nearby Ridgewood area to mourn their slayings. Nobody fathomed that the Blum sisters would die in such a grisly and gruesome manner.

The sisters were laid to rest a few blocks down the hill from St. Bernard's church at Joliet's Mt. Olivet Cemetery along Cass Street. The senseless killings near Joliet's Forest Park area made newspaper headlines, but the Will County Sheriff's Office did not have any immediate leads or prime suspects. Intimate crime scene details about the body positions and the torture aspect of the killings were withheld from the newspaper articles published that last week of June in 1983.

Still, people around Joliet struggled to understand why two women in their retirement years were victims of such a ghastly murder and set on fire. What kind of twisted criminal did such a dastardly act?

The killer had used knives and a gun to bring misery and death to Zita Blum and Honora Lahmann on Rosalind Street. Was the double murder meant to send a sign to the Joliet community that more terror and agony remained ahead?

"There were seven driveways on the street at that time, and they picked that one," Jean Haas said. "Why that one? I was worried that the killer might come back, but my husband, Pete, said, 'Well, Jean, you know the perpetrator never comes back to the crime scene, so it's probably the safest place in Joliet.'"

In 1983, Joliet resident Eric Johnson was in his twenties trying to find his place in life. He just found a steady job at the Andrew Corporation in nearby Orland Park, where he worked 3 to 11:30 p.m. Andrew Corporation manufactured antennas, cables, amplifiers, repeaters and transceivers.

When Johnson finished work July 1, 1983, there was a heavy downpour. That Friday night, Johnson got into his red, Chevy pickup truck and headed home, making it back around midnight. His nephew was still at his house, watching Johnson's little boy, whose one-year-old birthday was the next day. As for Johnson's wife, Terri Lynn, she went out with one of her girlfriends, the babysitter relayed. Johnson and his nephew stayed up another three hours before going to bed around 3 a.m. When Eric Johnson awoke on Saturday morning, July 2, his twenty-year-old wife still had not arrived. By noon, Eric Johnson began driving around Lockport, the small historic port city where his wife worked and often socialized at various bars. The frantic husband found his wife's blue Dodge van across the street from the Lockport Moose Lodge. But where was Terri Lynn?

Next, Eric Johnson drove to his mother's house where he enlisted the help of more relatives to find his missing wife. Around 5 p.m., he filed a missing person's report and informed Will County Sheriff's deputies that his wife's disappearance was out of character. Besides, Saturday was a special family occasion, the birthday party for their one-year-old son. Johnson told sheriff's deputies that he did not always keep close tabs on his wife's whereabouts. He was putting in lots of hours at the Andrew Corporation, where he wanted to go full-time.

Johnson remained clueless as to where his wife went or with whom. He told police she was unfaithful to him in the past. He had caught her cheating on him about two years earlier and that led to a brief separation. Furthermore, Johnson expressed doubts as to whether he was the biological father of their one-year-old son. He contemplated getting a blood test to determine whether he was the boy's father, but ultimately chose not to do it.

His missing wife, Terri Lynn Johnson, was five-foot-four, 120 pounds, with long, dark brown hair and hazel eyes. People knew her as a familiar face at the White Hen Pantry convenience store in downtown Lockport. She had been a store clerk since she was sixteen years old.

As the young mother remained missing, a former Lemont Police Department officer began looking for her after her blue van turned up near the Lockport Moose Lodge. He, like many others, knew Terri Lynn by her alias. She often went by Athena McCall or Athena Johnson.

At one point, Eric Johnson remarked to his friend that if someone abducted his wife from her van, her purse and shoes would be left behind.

"Hey man, did you off your old lady?" the former the small-town police officer asked his friend.

"I couldn't do that," Eric Johnson replied.

Johnson suggested to the former officer that if he had killed his wife, he would put her body in the Des Plaines River canal or another waterway.

As to the whereabouts of Terri Johnson, AKA Athena McCall, the former Lemont police officer believed he saw her traveling through downtown Lockport around 7 a.m. on Saturday, July 2, which would have been the day after she disappeared.

However, when the witness honked his horn, the driver of the passing blue van did not honk back. The former officer turned machinist remembered that his wife thought the blue van belonged to Athena McCall, and she was probably going somewhere after finishing her shift at White Hen Pantry.

**

Sharon Hartley, age twenty-nine, worked at the Lockport Assessor's Office and had a part-time job as secretary and invoice clerk for the Midwest Tankerman Barges on East Ninth Street in Lockport. The small port city along the Illinois and Michigan Canal system was roughly thirty miles southwest of Chicago.

Midwest Tankerman was founded six years earlier, in 1977, and the upstart barge company near Joliet prided itself as being experts in loading and unloading crude oil, chemicals and other products from barges to docks. The company's motto became, "Never leave product on a barge."

At Midwest Tankerman, Kenny Chancellor, age thirty-three, became a part-owner, and he was a valued dock man. Being a dock man kept him constantly busy at several locations along the Des Plaines River where tugboats made deliveries or pulled away with precious cargo.

Hartley knew Kenny Chancellor and his wife, Anna, for about ten years. Kenny Chancellor was known to be a womanizer.

"She (Hartley) has known for a long time that Kenny was seeing other women as did most everybody except his wife, in her opinion," according to police. "She advised that she often received phone calls at work by girls asking for Kenny … They never gave names and usually never left messages."

Police were curious if Hartley knew Athena Johnson, but she didn't. Upon being shown a photograph of Athena Johnson, Hartley immediately recognized her as one of the clerks at Lockport's White Hen Pantry. Still, Hartley was positive Athena Johnson had not visited the Lockport barge company.

Hartley told police that "Kenny often joked about girls he had been with but never really mentioned any names. She further stated that Kenny used to send flowers to different girls on a regular basis, and she would get the bills across her desk … She paid them and asked no questions … The bills were always from Lucky's Florist in Lockport."

The invoice clerk at Midwest Tankerman told police that Kenny Chancellor frequented the Sundancer on Illinois Route 53, just north of Interstate 55. Every Thursday, the lounge bar in nearby Bolingbrook held a ladies night, and Kenny Chancellor was a frequent patron on those nights. In fact, Chancellor used to brag about how he met a lot of women at the ladies nights, Hartley told police.

The investigation into Terri Lynn Johnson's disappearance brought police to the Denny's restaurant in the same area, near I-55 and Route 53. One of the Denny's employees had fathered a three-year-old child with Johnson. The two never married, and the Denny's worker broke off their relationship. The man told police that Johnson never asked him for child support.

He last spoke with her toward the end of April in 1983 when she told him she was seeing a Greek businessman who owned three restaurants in the Joliet and Will County area. The father of Johnson's oldest child remembered that his ex-girlfriend said the restaurant owner was taking great care of her. The Denny's worker also knew that Johnson was married, but he never met her husband.

On the weekend approaching the Fourth of July, the Will County Sheriff's Office remained preoccupied with solving the Terri Lynn Johnson mystery, plus the disappearance of Kenny Chancellor, the dock man at Midwest Tankerman.

**

Long before Weber Road became a major thoroughfare for north and south traffic between the Chicago suburbs of Joliet and Naperville, plenty of farms and acreages dotted the landscape.

Kenneth Chancellor and his wife lived along Weber Road between Renwick Road and Division Street, and theirs was a Lockport rural route mailing address. On Friday, July 1, the thirty-two-year-old wife went out for ride with another young woman. Around sunset, the two pulled into the driveway on Weber Road as Kenny Chancellor was backing out in his wife's 1979 black Pontiac Bonneville. He opted to leave his pickup truck in their driveway.

Anna Chancellor asked her husband where he was going.

"For a ride," he told her.

After realizing that her husband was going out that Friday night, Anna Chancellor and her friend drove around for another few hours to look at houses. The two returned to the Chancellor house around midnight and stayed up talking until 1:30 a.m.

When Anna Chancellor awoke on July 2, her husband was still gone. Anna Chancellor fumed and stormed out of her house. She went shopping at the Louis Joliet Mall on the far west side of Joliet, near I-55 and Route 30.

By evening, Kenny Chancellor was nowhere to be found. Most unsettling, he wore a business pager, and he was known to faithfully respond to messages, whenever anybody paged him. On July 1 and July 2, Anna Chancellor made multiple attempts to page her husband without success.

The worried wife called a number of friends. All of her phone calls met the same results. Nobody had seen or heard from Kenny Chancellor. Unsure about her husband's safety, Anna Chancellor called the Illinois State Police headquarters near Lockport, along Route 53. The state police, in turn, urged her to speak with the Will County Sheriff's Office in Joliet.

That Saturday night, she met with sheriff's deputies and filed a formal missing person report. Authorities entered information about her missing Bonneville into a computer database shared by numerous police departments. A quick breakthrough developed.

A police license plate check revealed the Cook County Sheriff's Office had notified Freddy's Towing in Tinley Park to pick up the Chancellors' black Pontiac Bonneville.

By the time Anna Chancellor and one of her friends arrived at the Freddy's Towing along 177th Street and Oak Park Avenue, the business was closed. From the perimeter, Anna Chancellor peered through the fence. Her car did not show any damage. This puzzled her. Why did her car end up at a tow lot in the southwest suburban Tinley Park, of all places? And where was her husband?

The drive from her house in rural Lockport to Tinley Park was roughly thirty minutes. After leaving the tow yard, Anna Chancellor and her friend drove to the area of 179th Street and Wolf Road because this was where police said the tow occurred.

Back in 1983, the area was extremely off the beaten path. It was a remote stretch of wilderness in Orland Township. For two hours in the dark, Anna Chancellor and her friend walked the area near the railroad tracks. In the distance, they saw several people gathered around a small campfire at a nearby house. The nearby residents, however, were of no help. They had not seen Kenny Chancellor, they told her.

Wondering whether her husband visited the nearby taverns, Anna Chancellor entered the Night Gallery Lounge on Wolf Road. She and her friend provided the bartenders and the bouncers with a photo of Kenny Chancellor. Nobody at the bar recognized his face.

By 3 a.m., the two exhausted women still didn't know what had happened to Kenny Chancellor. Anna Chancellor got a few hours of sleep on her friend's couch in Lockport, before resuming the search to find her missing husband on Sunday morning.

By 8 a.m., on July 3, the two women resumed their search, enlisting additional help from Anna Chancellor's brother and his live-in girlfriend, who were also founders of Midwest Tankerman.

First, the foursome returned to the Freddy's tow service in Tinley Park where an employee gave them access to the car.

"Open up the trunk, I want to see if he's in there," Anna Chancellor hollered.

The tow truck driver obliged, but Kenny Chancellor was not inside the trunk. Instead, the trunk contained Kenny Chancellor's duffel bag of Levi cutoffs, various men's toiletries and a large unopened box of condoms.

Inside her Pontiac Bonneville, Anna Chancellor discovered a card written to her husband by someone named Athena. The back of the card contained droplets of blood.

The car's floorboard also contained bloodstains. In the backseat, Anna Chancellor found her husband's jacket and car keys.

CHAPTER 4

MIDNIGHT MADMAN

Freddy's Towing in Tinley Park gave Anna Chancellor and her small circle of friends a lift to the spot where her Pontiac Bonneville was found along the railroad tracks shortly before midnight, two days earlier. The area along 179th Street and Route 6 consisted of high weeds and pesky mosquitos. After sundown, the area was known for being a lover's lane.

As the searchers scoured the roadside and pushed through the tall weeds, a shirt turned up near the railroad tracks, but that's all they found. Frustrated and tired, the little search party drove to a coffee shop on Wolf Road. An Orland Park police sergeant managed the business. After speaking with the distressed wife of Kenny Chancellor, the off-duty policeman agreed to help look for her missing husband.

This time around, the off-duty policeman and Kenny Chancellor's brother-in-law made a gruesome discovery within the tall weeds about seventy feet west of the Norfolk and Western Railway tracks.

On the south side of 179th Street lay Kenny Chancellor's slain body positioned on his back as he wore ankle-high boots, black Levi's jeans, a white shirt with blue stripes and a brown belt. His head faced west and feet pointed east. Rigor mortis had set in. His fingernails turned blue. Tiny maggots covered his eyes and nose.

That Sunday afternoon, a large police presence swarmed Orland Township, a tenth of a mile east of U.S. Route 6 and a half-mile west of Wolf Road. An ambulance was summoned to bring the Lockport man's body to the Palos Community Hospital for medical examiners to conduct an autopsy.

The discovery of Kenny Chancellor's body, along with the recovery of his overnight travel bag containing the large box of unopened condoms, prompted police to ask more probing questions of his wife.

Detectives inquired whether she knew her husband was going out with other women. She answered by saying, "she had had suspicions in the past but didn't really know or want to know. However, she in the last couple days had been told by her friends and relatives that this was the case. She further added that she knew of no one who would want to harm him that she knew about."

Although the Will County Sheriff's Office handled the missing person report, the Lockport man's body was found within Cook County, a very short distance from the boundary line for Will County. As a result, homicide detectives at the Markham, Illinois, headquarters for the Cook County Sheriff's Office took over the homicide investigation.

About thirty hours had elapsed from when Freddy's Towing hauled away the abandoned car to the discovery of Kenny Chancellor's body in the same general area.

Crime scene technicians recovered six keys on a round key ring and a medallion from Kenny Chancellor's left front pants pocket. A second key ring in his same pants pocket contained four keys plus a dime. His right front pocket and back pocket were empty. The young man's Motorola pager remained strapped to the belt on his right hip.

Because Kenny Chancellor's body had been in the weeds the past two days, detectives surmised the abrasions found on his back likely came from insects. His body showed no defensive wounds.

After the body was taken to the morgue, two Cook County sheriff's detectives visited Freddy's Towing in Tinley Park for a better look at the Pontiac Bonneville. One item of physical evidence became the humorous card addressed to "Ken" by someone named "Athena."

Chancellor's brother-in-law told detectives that Athena was the young woman who worked at the White Hen Pantry in Lockport. In fact, Chancellor planned to go out with her Friday night, July 1, the last night anybody saw them alive.

"It was common knowledge to a lot of people that Ken was seeing Athena without his wife's knowledge," noted one of Cook County's investigators.

When the towing service hauled away the Bonneville, the driver's side tires were parked inside the railroad tracks while the passenger tires were outside the tracks. The driver's window was cracked open at least an inch and the seat was wet. Around the time of the tow, a tremendous downpour brought flash floods to the area's roads.

That particular Friday night, the Mokena Emergency Services and Disaster Agency was out in full force because the dangerous storms left many motorists stranded in high waters. Then, around 12:45 a.m., an older woman driving a green pickup truck notified one of the ESDA coordinators of a car parked along the train tracks on 179th Street near Wolf Road. The emergency services coordinator alerted radio dispatchers to summon a tow truck because of the imminent danger that the car posed for an oncoming freight train.

The tow operator didn't notice any suspicious people or vehicles at the time he hauled away the Lockport couple's Bonneville. The only car he remembered was a blue Camaro with its hood up and a guy and girl inside. The tow truck driver figured they had car trouble after trying to navigate the local roads during the severe thunderstorm.

Even though Cook County took the lead on the case, the Will County Sheriff's Office remained intricately involved because Kenny Chancellor was from Lockport, and Will County took the initial missing person's report.

**

The discovery of Kenny Chancellor's duffel bag of clothes in the trunk led detectives to canvass several area hotels in search of a breakthrough. Police visited the Vista Motel at 159th Street and Wolf Road, but there were no records indicating Chancellor was on the guest list Friday night, July 1. None of the employees remembered a black Pontiac Bonneville in the parking lot, either. Detectives showed the hotel manager a photo of Kenny Chancellor, but she did not recognize him.

Next up, Cook County investigators visited the Virginia Motor Court at 159th Street and LaGrange Road. Nobody at that hotel had any records for Kenny Chancellor registering as a guest, either.

Finally, closer to Chancellor's home, the police tried the Haven Motel in Lockport along Route 6, but nobody at the motel knew or recognized him.

"To the knowledge of the above managers, Kenneth Chancellor has never registered in their motel at any time," a Cook County police officer stated.

By the Fourth of July, police questioned Gail Prince, one of the founders and business partners at Midwest Tankerman in Lockport. She credited Kenny Chancellor's knowledge of the barge business as keeping their company profitable.

She remembered seeing him around 9 p.m. July 1 as she and her fiancé pumped gas at Lockport's Clark station at 19th and State streets. She was positive Kenny Chancellor was behind the wheel as he drove past, but she wasn't sure if he was alone or had somebody with him.

That Friday night, Gail Prince and her male companion visited a friend's house until 11 p.m. She later learned from Chancellor's wife that he was not answering his work pager.

Back at Midwest Tankerman, Prince recalled someone left a message with Chancellor's answering service at 7:18 p.m. on July 1. The caller identified herself as Athena and mentioned she would be visiting the Brew & Chew bar and restaurant on the outskirts of Lockport.

At the Brew & Chew at Bruce and Farrell roads, detectives showed the bar owner furnished photographs of Athena Johnson as well as Kenny Chancellor. He recognized Athena as being a past customer who visited several times, often showing up with another woman. The bar owner also knew that Athena worked at the White Hen Pantry in town. She once told him she was divorced.

One of the regular bartenders, a twenty-five-year-old man, remembered Athena Johnson came to the Brew & Chew by herself around 5:45 p.m. on Thursday, June 30. She ordered a screwdriver and played a game of pool with the bartender. Around 6 p.m., she used the public pay phone. About an hour later, a man showed up and joined her at the end of the bar. She kept drinking screwdrivers while he consumed a Bacardi and coke. Johnson and the man left the Brew & Chew around 10:15 p.m.

When detectives showed the bartender photographs of Johnson and Chancellor, he confirmed they were sharing drinks and socializing on Thursday evening June 30. When asked if the couple ordered any food that night, the bartender replied he didn't think so. He was the only bartender on duty, and there were only about five people in the bar that weekday evening.

Subsequent efforts to lock down the whereabouts of Athena and Ken Chancellor prompted police to visit Al's Steakhouse at 1990 West Jefferson Street in Joliet. Additionally, police visited three more Lockport establishments: First and Last Chance at 1605 South State Street, Uncle Richie at 112 East 9th Street and Jacks Tap, 823 South State Street.

All of these places insisted the pair were no shows at their respective businesses on Friday night, July 1, when they disappeared.

**

Around 5:40 p.m. July 2, a young couple from Mokena saw a purse on the road near 179th Street and Route 6, so they pulled over.

The purse contained the driver's license for Terri Lynn Johnson along with a checkbook from the Lockport Heritage First National Bank for her and her husband, Eric Johnson. The purse contained lipstick and makeup. A Mokena police officer took possession of the purse and tried calling the phone number for the Johnsons, but no one answered. When the officer tried calling again around 10:50 p.m., another adult at the house told the officer that Terri Lynn Johnson was missing.

Meanwhile, July 4 marked a national holiday and a day off work for most people, but not for several deputies at the Will County Sheriff's Department. That Monday, police intensified their efforts to find Terri Lynn Johnson, the young married mother of two small children, who vanished three nights earlier.

Police continued to comb the area where Kenneth Chancellor's car and body were found. The shirt that turned up in the weeds the previous day did not belong to Kenneth Chancellor. It was hers.

Back at Route 6 and 179th Street, Will County Sheriff's Investigator Jim Fetzner again interviewed the Mokena boyfriend and girlfriend who found Terri Lynn Johnson's purse two days earlier. The young woman said they were driving when her boyfriend noticed a tan purse on the east side of the driveway, about twenty feet south of 179th Street. Just to the right of the purse was a tan shoe. The Mokena couple retrieved both items and brought them to Mokena's Police Department.

Next up, Sheriff's Investigator Fetzner interviewed a woman who worked at the White Hen Pantry with the missing woman. The coworker remembered Terri Lynn received a bouquet of flowers at the White Hen Pantry the previous week. The coworker did not know who sent the flowers. She did, however, make it clear to sheriff's detectives that she was not fond of Terri Lynn Johnson's husband, Eric.

The Lockport employee "stated she received a call at the White Hen Pantry from Eric Johnson on Saturday night between 5 and 6 p.m. and he asked where (she) and Terri Johnson were at … she told him that she had no idea where Terri Johnson was and Eric Johnson further stated that (his wife) left the house at approximately 7 p.m. and had not returned home yet, and there was supposed to be a birthday party for one of the children on 7-2-1983 and she had not returned yet."

The coworker told Fetzner she saw Terri Lynn Johnson with a man who was not her husband about ten days ago. The white man had dark hair and sported sunglasses. He was clean shaven and had medium to long hair above his shirt collar.

Fetzner learned Terri Lynn Johnson talked about having marital problems, but the coworker did not have any first-hand knowledge of arguments involving the married couple.

More than a year earlier, Terri Lynn Johnson had traveled to Florida, where she had a boyfriend. "The reason Terri Johnson went to Florida was because Eric Johnson had beaten her up," a police report stated.

Later, Fetzner interviewed a Joliet woman who considered herself a dear friend of the missing woman. She advised that her friend often used the name Athena McCall, inventing the alias when she ran away from Florida at age fifteen or sixteen.

After Terri Lynn married Eric Johnson, she had a daughter. The young parents moved into Eric Johnson's mother's house in rural Lockport.

The last time the Joliet woman saw her friend was between 5 and 6 p.m. July 1. The friend learned Terri Lynn was throwing a birthday party for her one-year-old son on July 2, followed by a much larger party, July 3, in which the Joliet woman and her husband were invited.

**

Will County Sheriff's Sgt. Tom Hernandez was unable to spend Independence Day with family and friends sharing hotdogs, laughter and adult beverages. Instead, he walked along the Will-Cook boundary line investigating the disappearance of the White Hen Pantry worker, who lived on the outskirts of Joliet.

Hernandez searched the wooded area along 179th Street, about two blocks west of Route 6. A row of trees flanked both sides of the road and behind the trees were grass and tall weeds.

At 1:06 p.m., the intense three-day search for Terri Lynn Johnson, otherwise known as Athena McCall, came to a somber end.

Sgt. Hernandez found Terri Lynn Johnson's body covered with mud and insects inside a roadside drainage ditch. She was on her back and her legs spread apart. Her left arm was bent at the elbow and her hand covered her left breast.

She wore a buttoned shirt, a tube top, nylon stockings and slacks. Her shirt was yanked above her breasts and her tube top was pulled below her breasts. The left sleeve on her shirt was torn. Her pants were unbuttoned, but the zipper was closed.

Sheriff's deputies escorted Eric Johnson to the drainage ditch. He confirmed the remains were his missing wife.

By 2:40 p.m., Cook County's Medical Examiner staff arrived in Orland Township to take the twenty-year-old's body back to the morgue. It marked the second straight day someone turned up dead in the same area.

On July 5, a forensic pathologist discovered a bullet hole through the victim's chest and the bullet exited her right breast. A bullet hole penetrated her blouse and tube top.

Besides the bullet wound, the doctor counted eleven lacerations to the top and left side of her head. Terri Lynn Johnson suffered a skull fracture and two smaller fractures on the back of her skull. Moreover, the autopsy detected a small abrasion to her middle finger and a bruise to her left cheekbone.

A number of bites to her back and shoulders were attributed to insects.

Johnson's death was ruled a homicide. The pathologist wrote that "the victim died from the gunshot wound through the back. That wound had a trajectory of back to front slightly to the right and slightly upward."

The same pathologist completed the autopsy on Kenneth Chancellor. A startling observation was made: "the bullet recovered from the body of Kenneth Chancellor had first passed through Terri Lynn Johnson. The mushrooming effect on the projectile was caused from striking both victims."

The bullet penetrating Chancellor's right upper chest traveled in a downward trajectory, piercing his heart before lodging in his left hip.

A July 6, 1983, newspaper headline referred to the lover's lane slayings along the deserted stretch of 179th Street and Wolf Road as the "Double Death Bullet."

The so-called double death bullet was either .38 caliber or .357-caliber ammo that came from a .38 or .357 revolver that had lands and grooves consistent with a gun made by Colt.

Two Joliet area families that didn't know one another now shared a common bond of unspeakable grief.

The free-spirited White Hen Pantry clerk had hooked up with the Lockport barge company worker for a late night summer rendezvous. Now, they were dead.

The pair met their violent end at a dark and secluded spot. They thought they were alone sharing affection, but someone was watching them. Someone hunted them down. The double murder bore scary similarities to the Pilcher Park torture rape from thirteen years earlier.

In that crime, Milton Johnson startled the parking couple, tapping on their window, clutching a shotgun and later promising to kill them with one single blast that would tear through both of them.

But that crime didn't go as planned when the boyfriend darted into the woods, causing Johnson to panic. Nobody was murdered on the night Feb. 15, 1970, in the Pilcher Park woods, though Johnson went to prison that November.

Johnson lost the next thirteen years of his life to the Illinois Department of Corrections until his release in March of 1983.

Now, in the summer of 1983, Johnson had the chance to fulfill his dark fantasy. Two lovebirds parked along a deserted and unlit road were slain. And only one bullet was used.

Near Route 6 and 179th Street, the killer dragged the lifeless bodies of Kenneth Chancellor and Terri Lynn Johnson through the drainage ditch, where he discarded them. They would be baked by the scorching sun and suffer the infestation of maggots.

In the coming days, investigators cleared Terri Lynn's husband and Kenneth Chancellor's wife in connection with the double murder.

Terri Lynn Johnson, known to others as Athena, left behind a grieving husband and two little children, ages one and three.

"I would hope there aren't several maniacs out there," her widower told the Joliet newspaper. "My wife was killed on my son's first birthday, and I have two things to think about every year on that date. It will always leave me very confused. I just don't understand. She was so sweet."

Eric Johnson told the newspaper how his three-year-old keeps asking for her mother.

"She's asking and it hurts me," he said. "What do I say to her?"

To recap, the Will County Sheriff's Office discovered the burning bodies of the two older Blum sisters at the rural Joliet house during the last Saturday in June.

One week later, came the scary Friday night killings of Kenny Chancellor and his female companion, Terri Lynn Johnson.

"Both were married, just not to each other," Will County Sheriff's Investigator Dave Simpson remarked. "I think they were trying to find a quiet spot to park. It was completely open and forest. The couple, they're not looking out the window and not looking around when Milton Johnson stops his truck, gets out, walks down the railroad tracks and goes up to their car. They're paying attention to each other, not that stupid bastard hunting and stalking, and that's kind words for that guy."

The lover's lane murders occurred several miles up Route 6 from Theresa McKeen's agonizing midnight encounter with a diabolical madman just two weekends prior.

Fortunately, the bullets that shattered her window didn't strike McKeen as she managed to maintain control of her car and keep driving home. The EJ & E employee became one of the lucky ones during the summer of terror that wreaked havoc on the people around Joliet, Illinois, who weren't accustomed to such ruthless random violence.

CHAPTER 5

BACKROAD MANIAC

Despite back-to-back summer weekends of double murders, most Will County residents did not let fear and fright alter their lifestyle. During the second weekend that July, Ann Shoemaker attended a party at a farmhouse northeast of Joliet.

That Saturday night, the nineteen-year-old from suburban Darien, Illinois, left the gathering to go on a walk with one of her friends. Suddenly, a dark pickup truck whizzed past them from out of nowhere. The truck kicked up gravel dust as it sped west along Bruce Road as the girls walked in the opposite direction.

Among its distinctive features, the truck had a cap on the back and the cap's rear door was wide open. Shoemaker surmised there was only one person in the truck. As the truck zoomed past, the driver eased off his gas pedal. Then, he accelerated. Surely, the driver saw her and her friend, Shoemaker thought.

When the two young women reached the neighboring farmhouse in Homer Township, the pair sat down in the driveway under a bright illuminating street light. Shoemaker had just broken up with her boyfriend, so she wanted moral support from her friend. Now, the romantic breakup became an afterthought. Off in the distance, the young women saw the menacing truck turning around at one of the rural subdivisions.

The truck was heading back their way, but why?

Under the cloak of darkness, the girls ducked for cover within the tall patch of weeds along the ditch. The driver did not stop.

Not sure whether it was safe to emerge, the two stayed hidden in the thick weeds. Finally, after a few minutes, Shoemaker and her friend ran for it, darting back to their party house. Just moments before they reached their destination, they spotted the same truck turning around at Gougar and Bruce Roads.

The thought crossed Shoemaker's mind that the mystery motorist was not a creepy prowler. Perhaps it was a mischievous friend pulling a late-night prank on her and her friend. Shoemaker set out to unmask the possible prankster by getting in their car and following it.

Out on the road, the two college-age girls panned the farm land and saw the truck at the stop sign for Bruce and Cedar roads. When the truck turned, the girls remained behind at a safe distance.

Eventually, the girls pulled into a driveway in Lockport Township. They shut off their lights and turned off the ignition. There, they waited, wondering if the dark truck would circle past. When it didn't, their patience wore thin. The girls pulled out of their hiding spot and proceeded east on Division Street.

In the midst of this exhilarating adrenaline rush, Shoemaker spotted the truck pump its brakes under the night sky as it went over a hill along Old Bell Road. Trying to be sneaky, Shoemaker pulled into a side street for Deboer Woods, a Homer Glen subdivision, south of 159th Street.

At the rural subdivision west of Will-Cook Road, Shoemaker turned off her ignition and the headlights. After a few nerve-wracking minutes, the truck failed to reappear. Shoemaker turned on her lights and got back on Old Bell Road.

Within a few minutes of driving toward 167th Street, she realized she had company.

As Shoemaker passed a hill, she saw the truck's headlights. Now, the truck was going faster and faster. This worried her. Thinking fast, she knew a safe spot. Shoemaker pulled into a familiar driveway of three male acquaintances near 167th Street. The girls started telling the boys about their terrifying close encounter, but the conversation ended prematurely when the pickup truck approached and slowed. As the driver squealed his tires, the nose of his truck dipped toward the road. Then, he raced off.

At that point, Todd Walsh and two other young men piled into a car, following Shoemaker and her friend back to the party along 167th Street. As the girls approached Bruce Road, that's when they saw him.

He was a Black man, five-foot-nine, weighing more than 200 pounds. He wore a red and black flannel shirt.

Todd Walsh's description differed slightly. He thought the man was five-foot-eight and approximately 180 pounds. Walsh guessed the truck was a mid-1970s model.

"The hood was up and the driver was standing on the passenger side of the truck and leaning on the side of the truck on his hands," Walsh later told police.

He described the pickup driver as a Black man in a red and black flannel shirt, no hat and a short Afro.

"Also, Walsh advised when they pulled up alongside the pickup truck, the driver was standing close to the hood hinges, and it was difficult to see the subject," Will County Sheriff's Investigator Jim Fetzner reported. "This is all Walsh could offer at this time."

Shoemaker made a mental note of the truck's distinctive features. The silver rear bumper looked to be heavy-duty, perhaps made of diamond plate. The bumper bore a specially designed area for the back license plate. As the stocky man leaned on the passenger's side window ledge, the truck's headlights were off, Shoemaker noted.

However, since her windows were rolled up and it was dark, the young suburban woman didn't get a good look at the pickup driver's face.

But she studied his truck all right. On a tiny piece of scratch paper she found in her purse, she jotted down the words: *"blue, black Chevy."*

She even wrote down the license plates: *889930B.*

Shoemaker's scary encounter on the backroads of Homer Township was not relayed to the Will County Sheriff's Office until after the events of the next weekend.

The following weekend marked another scorcher as the thermometer reached the low 90s. The long summer heatwave was creating drought conditions throughout northern Illinois.

But friendly conversations amongst family and neighbors about the summer scorcher became an afterthought once Joliet area residents awoke on Saturday, July 16, 1983.

"It makes me sick," remarked Jerry Reeder, a Homer Township supervisor. "Generally speaking, Homer is not a violent area. It's quite calm except for a few robberies and break-ins."

CHAPTER 6

AMBUSHED

Denis Foley embraced life, devoting full attention to his family's needs. He had a strong work ethic and a deep admiration for keeping people safe.

Foley had proudly served his country in the U.S. Army. After his military service, Foley spent twenty-seven years with Consolidated Freightways in Chicago, where he became division manager. On weekends, Foley served as a volunteer safety patrol officer at the Will County Sheriff's Office in Joliet.

A fifty-year-old Lockport resident, Foley was starting his fourth year with the sheriff's agency. His wife died the previous year, leaving behind five grown children.

On July 15, 1983, Foley partnered with someone more than half his age: Steven Mayer, age twenty-two. The young Joliet man was furthering his education at Joliet Junior College, studying criminal justice. Mayer worked a steady job at the Service Merchandise store in the Hillcrest Shopping Center just outside Joliet in neighboring Crest Hill. In addition, Mayer worked a part-time job as a police dispatcher for the Willow Springs Police Department, a western Chicago suburb.

The summer of 1983 was eventful and brought him great joy.

On June 25, Steven Mayer and Ami Michelle Shields exchanged wedding vows before a large crowd of dear friends and proud family inside Joliet's St. Patrick's Catholic Church, 710 Marion St. The newlyweds traveled to Florida to soak up the sun for their honeymoon. When July rolled around, Mayer was back to work.

But having two regular jobs was not enough.

Like Foley, Mayer was now part of Will County's auxiliary division. Auxiliary officers were volunteers who assisted with crowd control at community festivals and helped with traffic control following crashes. On weekends, auxiliary officers often drove around at night providing an extra set of eyes to keep Will County safe. Without the likes of Denis Foley and Steven Mayer, hundreds of area subdivisions and businesses were otherwise vulnerable to late night vandals, trespassers and prowlers.

Indeed, the young Mayer had a bright future ahead in his police pursuits. His father, Edward Mayer III, was a well-liked sergeant on the Will County Sheriff's Department. Now the elder Mayer was watching his recently married son aspiring to become a full-time police officer, following in his footsteps with Will County.

Ed Mayer recalled talking with his son that Friday evening.

"He called me and stated he was waiting for his partner to pick him up. That must have been six o'clock on the 15th," Sgt. Ed Mayer said.

Oftentimes, the Will County Sheriff's auxiliaries encountered a stranded motorist either from an engine failure or a flat tire. In rural pockets of Will County, it was not uncommon for police to find a pair of young lovebirds pulled to the side of the road for a late night rendezvous.

During the early morning hours of July 16, 1983, Richard "Dewey" Paulin, age thirty-three, and Cathy Norwood, age twenty-five, parked their little red Chevy Chevette in the grass where 147th Street and Gougar Road meet. In the 1980s, the deserted area consisted of gravel roads and no overhanging street lights.

Paulin worked in Chicago at Stewart Dean Metal Refinishing on North Milwaukee Avenue. In the summer of 1983, he spent time in the hospital.

"He had a back operation," Paulin's father recalled. "He had two discs removed from his back, and he was drawing workman's compensation."

Paulin's father remembered his son planned to be out that Friday night, July 15, but he was not sure where.

"He just walked out. He said, 'I'll see you later.'"

"Dewey" Paulin met up with a younger woman, who was married. Both of them lived about a dozen miles north of Joliet, in the older community of Lemont, population 5,000.

Around 3 a.m., Will County auxiliary deputies Foley and Mayer came across a man in the road gesturing for them as they traveled the gravel roads of Homer Township. Presuming they encountered a broken down motorist, Foley and Mayer slowed their squad car. They exited, figuring the man needed their help.

Will County Sheriff's deputy Pat Lombardo was on patrol during the overnight shift.

"I was in my squad, and I heard someone calling for help, car 301A, and I notified the county that they were trying to get through to them … I started heading north, at which time I heard somebody say, 'Send help, please! So myself, Deputy (Bob) Pedersen and Sgt. (Marilyn) Dixon started moving toward Homer Township," Lombardo would later testify. .

**

At the scene, Will County Sheriff's Sgt. Sigurd Hjemvick saw Foley on the ground near the passenger side of Will County auxiliary car 301A. Another deputy was giving him urgent medical attention.

West of Foley's squad car, a red Chevette was backed into the entrance of the adjacent farm field. The time was now 3:30 a.m.

The county sergeant approached the small car and peered inside. Dewey Paulin was sprawled across his backseat, fatally shot through his back. The gunfire penetrated his lungs, liver and lower lip.

As for Cathy Norwood, the Lemont woman's body lay across the grass, just beyond the passenger side door. She, too, was the victim of close range gunshots. A bullet penetrated her back, lungs and larynx.

For the third time in four weekends, the Will County Sheriff's Office encountered a crime scene with multiple murder victims.

This time, there were more than two dead bodies.

South of the little red Chevette, authorities saw the bullet-riddled body of auxiliary deputy Steven Mayer.

Mayer came to his final resting place in the ditch along the gravel road, south of Will County Sheriff's auxiliary car 301A. Near Mayer's body was his flashlight, a baton, a comb and a long trail of fresh bloodstains.

His gun and wallet were missing.

"The door on the passenger's side, I remember was open," Sgt. Hjemvick observed. "I don't recall if the door on the driver's side was open when I arrived."

Denis Foley, although shot in the face, was clinging to life.

Even though a bullet tore through his mouth, Foley managed to use his police radio to plea for help. In all, Foley suffered five gunshot wounds to his face and abdomen. After being shot, the father of five played dead, hoping the ambush killer wouldn't notice him or wouldn't care.

The grim tally reached four gunshot victims, but there were more to be found.

When he first learned of the chaos on the garbled police radio, sheriff's deputy Pat Lombardo raced toward the Stately Oaks subdivision in Homer Township.

"I went up in that location and checked around," Lombardo said, "and that's when I heard Sgt. Dixon say she had the squad car at 147th and Gougar. And I was returning back to that location when I found Miss Troutman in the field on State Street."

Blood covered Laura Troutman and drenched her clothes as the terrified twenty-one-year-old raced to one of the farmhouses. She awoke the property owners in the middle of the night, yelling hysterically that she was shot.

At 147th Street and Gougar Road, the young woman from Lockport offered to show Lombardo where the Chevy Suburban station wagon crashed about fifty yards into a bean field.

"I went up and checked the vehicle and found George Kiehl in the front seat and he appeared to be dead," Deputy Lombardo remembered.

Accordingly, Lombardo took to the police radio. He summoned the coroner's office plus more sheriff investigators. And he needed an ambulance for Troutman, and fast.

"She was badly injured," Lombardo recognized.

As for Troutman's slain boyfriend, the twenty-four-year-old Lockport man worked at his father's business, Kiehl Body Shop. George Kiehl and Laura Troutman had spent their Friday night out with friends. On their middle-of-the-night drive home, Kiehl and Troutman encountered a clean-cut white man darting toward them along the dark road. He acted as if he needed help.

Just as Kiehl slowed his station wagon along 147th Street, several gunshots rang out. The bullets shattered his window, mortally wounding him. Other bullets struck Laura Troutman's left shoulder and abdomen.

As George Kiehl gasped his final breaths, his station wagon veered out of control. The Chevy Suburban continued another three-fourths of a mile before crashing into the soybean field. Kiehl's wounded girlfriend, unbelievably, managed to escape the wreckage, but she had to live with the horror she just witnessed.

Back at his squad car, Deputy Lombardo tried to bandage Laura Troutman's gunshot wounds and apply First Aid.

"Please don't shoot me," the young woman begged.

"Miss Troutman appeared to be going into shock," Lombardo relayed. "Due to the victim's condition (I) did not question the victim."

Yet, moments earlier, Troutman claimed she and her boyfriend were shot by a Will County sheriff's deputy. That didn't seem plausible, however.

All in all, it was hard to make heads or tails out of Troutman's account at the chaotic crime scene.

Homer Township paramedics strapped her to a stretcher and the ambulance rushed her to the emergency room at Joliet's Silver Cross Hospital near Route 6 and Draper Avenue.

"I believe she said briefly that they had been flagged down by an individual and that she had been shot," Deputy Lombardo recalled.

Lombardo was later asked if Troutman told him that the person who flagged her down was the same officer she believed who shot her.

"She didn't indicate," the deputy explained. "All she said, she had been flagged down. What she believed to be a police officer, and she was then shot by an officer."

The Will County Sheriff's Department faced a daunting task of determining the sequence of events and how all these Homer Township killings came to be.

There was one general crime scene: 147th Street and Gougar Road, but three separate homicides along these gravel roads. One crime scene involved the red Chevette with the slain Lemont couple.

Will County Sheriff's squad 310A marked another crime scene as both auxiliary officers were shot multiple times after exiting their car.

The third crime scene consisted of George Kiehl's lifeless body in his station wagon that crashed into the bean field.

The unanswered question: how much faith would Will County detectives give to Laura Troutman's version of events? Did one of the venerable auxiliary deputies, in a fight for survival, dash toward the Lockport couple's station wagon, take aim with his pistol and blast multiple bullets into the bodies of two innocent people?

If one of the auxiliary deputies recklessly fired his gun into the Chevy Suburban, why was that same officer dead in the ditch and his police-issued gun missing from the crime scene?

This was more than a killing spree. The overnight assassin swooped down on his prey, picked apart his dead and gravely wounded for any valuables and money.

The guns, ammunition and wallets from both Will County auxiliary officers were taken. Homicide victim Cathy Norwood's purse was missing. The wallet belonging to her late night companion, "Dewey" Paulin was gone.

"4 DIE IN MURDER SPREE," declared *The Herald-News,* Will County's daily newspaper of record, on Sunday, July 17, 1983.

Overnight, Will County gained six more shooting victims. The sheriff's office speculated that robbery appeared to be the motive.

"We don't know what other motive there could be," Will County Sheriff's Chief Deputy Ted Kelly told the newspaper.

Kelly estimated the entire killing spree lasted no more than fifteen minutes. He called the scene "pretty gruesome," and admitted the murder site "is still sketchy."

In the aftermath of the senseless bloodshed, hundreds of employees at the Will County Sheriff's Department held out hope that auxiliary deputy Foley would pull through. The middle-age gunshot victim remained in critical condition at Silver Cross Hospital.

As for Troutman, she progressed.

Silver Cross listed her in fair condition. Her gunshot wounds were not considered life-threatening. Apparently relying on Troutman's account from the scene, Joliet's newspaper informed its 50,000 readers that police were looking for two shooting suspects. One was described as a clean-cut, young white man, in his twenties or early thirties with short hair and a slim build.

However, that description closely resembled Steven Mayer, the young auxiliary deputy gunned down in the ditch, whose gun and wallet were stolen.

The second murder suspect was described as a Black man in his mid-thirties with short hair, wearing a dark shirt, according to the newspaper.

Will County offered a $1,000 reward for information "leading to an arrest and arraignment of the two suspects."

Unbeknownst to the newspaper, two reliable witnesses would emerge. Daniel Birmingham and Burt Thompson were walking along 143rd Street during that hot, muggy summer night early July 16, 1983.

Around 3:45 a.m., they heard emergency sirens blaring off yonder. Moments later, a dark-colored truck, perhaps a Ford or Chevy, zoomed past them along the unlit rural road. The truck sped east along 143rd Street.

The two eyewitnesses did not get the license plates; after all, the truck moved along the backroads at a pretty fast clip, plus, there were no overhanging street lights. But the truck had one distinct feature, it bore a cap on the back, the witnesses assured police.

The massacre on Homer Township's backroads had all the trappings of a random crime spree. There were no signs that a jilted ex-lover of Cathy Norwood was hiding in the bean fields, waiting to slaughter her and her male companion as they parked along the dark and deserted road.

Likewise, no evidence suggested that the two conscientious auxiliary deputies were being stalked by a crazy gun-wielding loon who had a vendetta against the Will County Sheriff's Department.

On the contrary, police investigators discerned that gym shoe impressions belonging to Converse brand All Stars were evident at several locations around the killing spree.

Three of the killer's shoeprints turned up near Dewey Paulin's red Chevette near the farm property. Two more identical shoeprints turned up near Will County squad car 310A. There were no other distinct shoe impressions found at the crime scene, just the ones resembling Converse brand All Stars, a high-top basketball shoe.

When it comes to crime scene investigations, size doesn't matter. Sometimes the tiniest evidence can lead to a breakthrough in an otherwise perplexing murder investigation. And every so often, an obscure clue surfaces, a clue that at first blush appears innocuous, but it's a remarkable diamond in the rough.

Underneath auxiliary deputy Steven Mayer's slain body in the roadside ditch was a sales receipt. The receipt was not faded by the unbearably hot summer heat, though.

This was a fresh new clue.

"I just picked it up because I didn't want the wind to blow it away," explained Jim Fetzner, the now-retired sheriff's investigator. "Maybe it was piece of paper thrown on the road.

"It turned out to be a good lead."

That sales receipt came from a Joliet area fish and bait business known as Walt's Tackle Shop.

The slip of paper was addressed to someone named Sam Myers. He and his wife, Dolly, lived on Joliet's east side, in an older Forest Park Neighborhood a few doors up the street from the two-story, brick building at the corner of Draper and Woodruff now known as the Forest Park Community Center.

**

Barely thirteen hours after the Homer Township massacres left six people shot, more noteworthy clues emerged.

A canoeist spotted two wallets and one purse along the shoreline of the shallow DuPage River near the community of Shorewood, just west of Joliet.

The wallets and purse turned up down below an I-80 overpass, just west of I-55. The wallets belonged to the two Will County Sheriff's auxiliary officers who were shot, Foley and Mayer. The purse belonged to homicide victim Cathy Norwood. The recovery of their personal artifacts was significant.

The mass murderer discarded the dead woman's purse and the wallets from the auxiliary deputies after rummaging through them for money or valuables.

These clues surfaced about twenty-five minutes away from the Homer Township massacre. It became obvious to police that the elusive killer was comfortable utilizing the major interstates around Joliet.

About seventy-five volunteer firefighters from nearby Troy Township, Rockdale, Plainfield, Channahon and Minooka helped drag the lazy Du Page River in hopes of finding additional clues from the Homer Township massacre. But the secondary search was not a success.

Back at the Will County Sheriff's Department on Joliet's Laraway Road, the men and women dedicated to protecting and serving the county's citizens were hurting.

Auxiliary Deputy Foley remained in bad shape at Silver Cross Hospital with gunshots to his jaw and abdomen. His nighttime partner, Steven Mayer, the young man who just got married, lost his life from five bullets that tore open his chest.

"Steve and fellow officer Foley stopped to help a stranded motorist," Joliet Catholic Priest Vytas Memenas explained at the time. "They thought somebody needed help."

In June of 1983, Father Memenas served as pastor of Joliet's St. Patrick's Catholic Church and as chaplain for Joliet's Police Department. The beloved Joliet priest from Lithuania got to know Steven Mayer as the husband-to-be prepared for the Holy Sacrament of Matrimony. Part of their conversation centered on Mayer's hopes of making his mark in the field of law enforcement, following in the footsteps of his father.

"I talked to him just before he was married less than a month ago. I asked him, 'Is that what you want to do with your life?' And he said, 'Yes, because I would like to help people,'" Father Memenas said.

The overnight killing spree in Homer Township shocked the conscience of Will County. People across Will County became sad, bitter and angry. The grandmother of Lockport homicide victim George Kiehl told Joliet's newspaper that crime was spiraling out of control.

"I'm afraid people will take things into their own hands," she said. "I try to be a Christian woman, but I have evil thoughts when I think about this. It's really sad. It's horrid."

What motivated the titan of terror to toss the wallets and purse over I-80 like they were some useless candy wrapper or empty soda bottle?

Was he careless, lazy or perhaps trying to taunt the police?

That same night, after sundown, Will County's weekend killer was itching to inflict more carnage. After Saturday's skies grew dark, he set out to roam the boondocks and unlit roads for his next rampage.

CHAPTER 7

INTERSTATE 55

Modern day Joliet is the fourth largest city in Illinois, with a population around 150,000. It is home to the largest inland port in North America. Amazon, IKEA, Target, Mars candy, appliance maker Whirlpool and dozens of other major companies have opened large distribution centers in Joliet. The community's motto is "City of Champions."

Many outstanding professional athletes have come from Joliet, and the city boasts an uncanny number of state high school championships in athletics. Green signs along the main roads leading into the city inform motorists that Joliet Catholic Academy has a record-setting fourteen state championship titles in high school football.

One of Joliet's most famous gridiron stars was a gritty, undersized young man named Daniel Ruettiger. His rags to riches underdog story as a walk-on football player at collegiate powerhouse Notre Dame University in South Bend, Indiana, and sacking the quarterback in the final game of the season, became immortalized in the iconic Hollywood feel-good movie, *Rudy*.

And although one notable student-athlete named Lionel Richie tossed his tennis racket aside and never made it to Wimbledon, the Class of 1967 graduate from Joliet East High School went on to become one of pop music's all-time greatest singers-songwriters. Richie's hits included "All Night Long," "Stuck on You," "Hello," "Dancing on the

Ceiling," "Say You, Say Me," "Truly," and "Three Times a Lady."

Indeed, Joliet and stardom go hand in hand. Built in 1858, there is a giant limestone fortress that stretches several blocks along Joliet's Collins Street. This property is known as Old Joliet Prison, and it's become world-famous thanks to actors John Belushi and Dan Aykroyd, who starred as Joliet Jake and Elwood Blues in the 1980 musical comedy directed by John Landis, *The Blues Brothers*. Besides the "City of Champions" motto, Joliet has another slogan: "Crossroads of Mid-America."

Joliet is one of the destination cities along America's iconic Route 66. Every year, thousands of international tourists visit Joliet as they make their east-west journey that starts in Chicago and ends on America's West Coast. I-80 runs east and west while I-55 runs north and south. Both major interstates intersect on Joliet's far western edge.

If you drive I-55 south toward St. Louis, much of the terrain remains flat as a board. Miles and miles along I-55 are flanked by frontage roads, farms and prairies. Traffic becomes less dense the farther you drive south of Joliet.

Avid boaters, campers and fishermen know that some of the best places to enjoy the majestic beauty of Mother Nature are south of Joliet. Along the I-55 corridor are several large lakes and rivers valued for their tasty catfish, trout and bass. One popular fishing spot is around the community of Wilmington, which is bordered by the wide mouth of the Kankakee River.

In the summer, Wilmington held "Catfish Days," an annual small-town, community festival to celebrate its outdoor recreation heritage. One way to reach Wilmington from Joliet was heading south along I-55. The other was traveling the old U.S. Route 66 corridor, which has since been renamed Route 53.

**

Ray Tusek lived in Lockport, the old port and railroad community settled in the mid-1850s along the east banks of the Des Plaines River, just north of Joliet.

By 5 a.m., July 17, 1983, Tusek hit the road, driving through Joliet.

"I was going fishing in the Kankakee River to meet a friend of mine at approximately 6 o'clock," Tusek explained.

About twenty miles south of Joliet, Tusek worked as a Pullman. He handled sheet metal at the Braidwood nuclear generating station. The power plant originally built by Commonwealth Edison, provided electricity across the entire Chicago area for decades.

During the Lockport man's Sunday morning drive toward his favorite fishing hole, one portion of Route 53 took a major dip along the southern lanes. Tusek happened to be one of the few motorists on the road shortly before 5:30 a.m.

"As I came up out of the dip, I looked in the mirror," he recalled. "I really couldn't believe what I seen, but I thought I seen a hand above the high weeds."

Calling 911 was not an option in 1983. Cellular phones were unavailable, and police did not have 911 systems for dispatching help to local emergencies at a moment's notice.

The motorist on a mission to go fishing could have dismissed what he thought he saw and kept on driving. But he didn't.

His instincts told him to return to the grassy median along Route 53. That's what he did.

He was thirteen miles south of Joliet.

"Well, I got out of the car, walked maybe eight feet, and I seen this person ... she was looking up at me," Tusek explained.

"I asked her if she could talk. She said yes, yes, she made sounds ... I asked her if she could stand. She tried to. She couldn't. About that time, I heard an approaching car coming. Because it was early in the morning, and I was down in the hollow, and I was parked partially on the road, so I knew I had to do something.

"I stepped around the back of the car, and I waved down an oncoming car for help."

And that's when David Sims Jr. stopped.

"He says, 'What's up?' I said, 'I need help,'" Tusek relayed.

"We went over to the scene, which would be a few feet away, and I says, 'Well, we're going to have to do something. About that time, I heard another car coming, and I mentioned to him to flag this oncoming car down, so we all wouldn't get in an accident, which he did."

Sims, a Black man from Joliet, worked as a youth counselor supervisor at the Illinois Youth Center, known as IYC, in Kankakee.

"I got dressed, left for work, traveling on Route 53. That is the route I usually take every morning," Sims remembered. "I was going south on 53, and ... an elderly white gentleman flagged me down on the highway. I pulled off behind his car, we walked across the street, and we seen a young white Caucasian girl in the bushes."

The two passing motorists, who had never met before, men of different races, lifted the badly injured woman off the grassy median, where someone put her to die.

"We picked her up and put her in back of my car. I had a four-door car," Tusek recalled.

"There was blood, and to my own recollection, I thought there might have been gunshot wounds over her eyes ... I had to do something, so we put her in the car, closed the door. I told this man if he knew where the police station was at in Wilmington to drive as fast as he could and tell them to get an ambulance because I know they have a volunteer rescue squad and so forth."

Time was of the essence.

"She was in real serious condition," Sims pointed out. "Well, I told him to drive on. I was going ahead and to notify the Wilmington Police that he was coming with her."

The two brave men loaded the incapacitated woman into Tusek's car and away they raced in separate cars.

They sped toward the Wilmington Police Station a few miles up the road. The gravely injured woman they had stumbled upon was on death's doorstep. There was no telling whether she would survive her trauma.

Sims accelerated on his gas pedal as he neared Wilmington.

Sure enough, he drew the attention of an Illinois State Police trooper posted by the Johnson & Johnson manufacturing plant off Route 53, on the lookout for speeders.

"He threw on his lights, but I didn't stop," Sims said. "I drove all the way into Wilmington to the police station. He pulled up behind me, and I went in and I told them that there was a gentleman coming with a girl that was seriously hurt."

At this stage, fishing was the last thing on Ray Tusek's mind. The Lockport man concentrated on delivering the badly injured young woman to the small-town fire and rescue squad in Wilmington.

"On the way in," Tusek explained, "she was in bad shape."

**

A new recruit, Douglas Brown was wrapping up his first year of public service with Illinois State Police. He happened to be on duty that unforgettable Sunday morning, July 17, 1983.

"I had received a radio dispatch from headquarters to meet a subject in that area on Route 53," Brown recalled. "It was a citizen's report of a young female lying near the roadway."

Brown activated his squad's blue and red flashing lights. He floored the gas pedal, zipping toward the dip in the road along the rolling hills of Route 53.

About halfway there, Illinois State Police radio dispatchers notified him of a change in plans.

"She had been picked up by a passing motorist and transported to Wilmington Police Department," Brown said. "At that point, I turned around and went to Wilmington Police Department."

When he arrived, the situation looked bleak.

"There was an ambulance crew on the scene, and there was also a silver older model Dodge," Brown remembered. "There was a young girl seated in the back of that car."

After Wilmington's emergency crews loaded the unidentified woman into their ambulance, they began first aid. Then, paramedics shut the back door and sped toward Saint Joseph's Medical Center in Joliet, twenty miles away.

Before he got to the hospital, Trooper Brown stopped along Route 53 where the two Good Samaritans first spotted the incapacitated woman. The site was about three quarters of a mile north of Hoff Road, near a small creek and the GM&O Railroad tracks.

Once he made it to the hospital emergency room, Brown met with Illinois State Police Special Agent John Meduga, who came to interview the victim.

"Officer Meduga had a conversation with her," Brown recalled. "I made some brief conversation, but she was fairly incoherent at the time."

According to Brown's police reports, the injured woman "informed me that she had been on her way back from Marriott's Great America and went to sleep alongside the road. At that time, she said she heard gunshots and assumed the person with her had been shot. She had been taken from the vehicle put into another vehicle and driven around for an unknown period of time and dumped out alongside the road."

By mid-morning that Sunday, Brown left the Joliet hospital. He drove south on I-55 away from Joliet. He stayed singularly focused.

"I was looking for a car that she had said contained her boyfriend. I was looking for a gold Plymouth at that time," Brown said.

Along the way, Brown passed the mammoth ExxonMobil Joliet Refinery along I-55 and Arsenal Road. He crossed the four-lane steel bridge situated high above the Des Plaines River where large freight barges often anchored to the docks.

With both hands clutching his steering wheel, Brown panned I-55's southbound lanes for the elusive gold Plymouth.

Sure enough, he saw it.

The rookie state trooper spotted the Plymouth about a quarter mile north of the I-55 exit ramp for Wilmington, near the wide banks for the Kankakee River.

"It was on the shoulder of the road, appeared to be abandoned, engine was not running," Brown observed.

As cars and semitrailers kept whizzing by, Brown parked his squad car along the interstate shoulder.

He was all alone, without backup. He didn't know what to expect.

"I approached on the passenger side, gun drawn," Trooper Brown remarked.

CHAPTER 8

GREAT AMERICA

Operating in Chicago's northwest suburbs, Great America Amusement Park became a humungous summer time attraction. In 1983, the park featured the world's tallest and fastest wooden rollercoaster, The American Eagle.

Great America was replete with scores of rollercoasters, carousels, log rides and performing acrobats. Costumed characters from the Looney Tunes wandered the grounds, posing for memorable keepsake photographs with countless guests.

On muggy, summer days, Marriott's Great America drew crowds in the several thousands. On Saturday, July 16, 1983, Tonya Little and her boyfriend Tony Hackett made the three-hour journey from their tiny hometowns in central Illinois, halfway between Springfield and Bloomington. Once they paid their admission tickets, the teens entered the amusement park around 2 p.m.

Hackett, eighteen, was a 1982 graduate of a tiny, consolidated school district, Hartsburg-Emden Community Unit School District.

During high school, Hackett worked at the local Hardee's fast-food restaurant to earn spending money. After high school, he landed a full-time job in the state capital of Springfield. He worked for the Illinois Secretary of State's Office in the Vehicle Services Department.

Now that he had a steady job, Hackett looked forward to his daylong excursion north of Chicago. He got to spend the day with the person who mattered most: his high school sweetheart.

Tony Hackett's father taught school in Lincoln, Illinois. He did not have a chance to speak with his son prior to the Great America trip.

"Well, I wasn't up," his father later testified. "My wife and he spoke. Him and his girlfriend had planned on going to Marriott's Great America to spend the day and come back home in the evening after it closed, at, I believe 10 p.m."

At Great America, the teenage couple enjoyed themselves, held hands, as they wandered the spacious amusement park and did several rollercoaster rides, bumper cars, buying snacks and souvenir t-shirts. A trip to Great America was a memory-making event.

The small-town teens stayed at the amusement park for eight hours. One of Tony Hackett's last purchases was the furry Looney Tunes character known as the Tasmanian devil. When he paid cash for the stuffed animal, an amusement park employee gave him a paper receipt that he stuffed into his wallet.

After a tiresome day at Great America, the downstate teenagers weren't quite ready to head home. The Wisconsin border was just a couple miles up the road. In 1983, it remained perfectly legal in the Dairy State to buy alcohol at eighteen years old rather than at twenty-one.

The long, exhausting day under the scorching sun left Tony Hackett thirsty. The temptation to buy beer was too strong to pass up for the eighteen-year-old boy.

That Saturday night, he and his girlfriend rolled into a small Wisconsin town where Hackett purchased six bottles of beer. He and his girlfriend returned to his car intending to drive home. They had several hours of travel ahead. Plus, it was getting late.

Making matters worse, they got lost. After driving about an hour, the teenagers wound up in the Windy City, after heading in the wrong direction.

On Chicago's interstate system, the two found their way back to I-55 and they drove south toward Kankakee. About forty minutes later, fatigue became a factor. Hackett and his girlfriend pulled over along I-55 and switched positions.

"She informed me that approximately at 1:30 a.m. they had switched drivers and that would have been somewhere north of Bolingbrook, and she had driven down to the location where the incident occurred. I would assume sometime after 2 a.m.," Illinois State Trooper Brown noted.

Tonya Little eased her boyfriend's gold Plymouth to the southbound shoulder of I-55, near Wilmington's exit ramp.

On the interstate shoulder, the teenagers desired to get a restful sleep. They planned to wake up after sunrise to resume their two-hour drive still ahead.

Instead, an intruder emerged. Tony Hackett never had a chance to defend himself or to flee.

After pumping Tony Hackett's body full of bullets, the gun-wielding stranger took Hackett's girlfriend captive.

"I was told to get in the truck and stay on the floor and keep my eyes closed," she recalled.

She crouched on the floorboard of the stranger's truck. Where was he taking her? What did he plan to do with her?

The eighteen-year-old feared she would die if her kidnapper realized she had looked at his face. Instead, she tried to make swift, quick glances at his features in hopes of committing those haunting and painful images to her long-term memory.

Now behind the wheel of his pickup, Tony Hackett's killer ordered the terrified teenager to sit beside him on the vinyl front seat of his truck cab.

Little found herself kidnapped in an unfamiliar town, trapped and tormented by an evil, vicious monster more disgusting than a toilet bowl brush. And yet this venom of filth controlled her destiny. He determined whether she lived or she died. She knew he had a loaded gun and that he had already used it once, right in front of her eyes.

With his kidnap victim sitting next to him, the I-55 killer turned his ignition key and got back on the highway. They drove around for a while, perhaps at least two hours.

After realizing it was still dark, she asked her kidnapper the time.

It was 4:30 a.m., he remarked.

Several minutes later, the man slowed his truck.

"He stopped along the shoulder of the highway and put a rag in my mouth, not a full rag, and he covered my eyes with the rest of it," Little remembered.

She could partially see through the rag as her abductor resumed his driving.

He kept his eyes on the road, contemplating where to dump his next victim. He found a rural section of four-lane highway. Hardly anybody was on the road at this early morning hour, still before sunrise.

When he pulled over, he was about a dozen miles south of Joliet.

The pick-up truck driver had already made one overnight kill. It was time for his second.

"He stabbed me. I lost consciousness," Hackett's girlfriend said.

At that moment, the truck drove off.

Like a bloodthirsty vampire, he intended to make a safe getaway before the sun rose. In this case, before any police cars hunted him down.

The man used both a gun and a sharp knife to harm his victims.

The wicked stranger ripped a hole through Little's chest a matter of hours after pumping bullet after bullet into her defenseless sleeping boyfriend.

Little recognized she was bleeding badly as she collapsed in the highway median, in the middle of nowhere, with nobody in sight, and the skies were still dark.

How much longer did she have to live? Was she about to meet the same tragic fate of her boyfriend?

**

When the young state trooper approached the gold Plymouth, he saw a young white man stretched across the front floorboard.

The victim's head faced the passenger door.

"It was cold, stiff, and there was a lot of dried blood in the front seat area," trooper Brown gleaned.

Broken glass landed inside shooting victim's car. The car was at mile marker 242.5 in Wilmington Township.

On the pavement near the passenger door, the Illinois State Police trooper spotted patches of brown fibers. The fibers likely came from a pillow cushion. A pillow would muffle the noise from a semi-automatic handgun.

The abandoned car had Illinois license plates.

"I ran that license number, and it registered out of a city down south, last name was Hackett," Brown explained.

Tony Hackett suffered three bullet wounds to his chest and another bullet through his brain. He resided in Emden, Illinois, a little town roughly 130 miles south of Joliet between Bloomington and Springfield.

As for Hackett's girlfriend, tubes connected to both her arms while another tube went through her nose that Sunday morning. She recuperated at Joliet's Saint Joseph Hospital off Glenwood Avenue.

When Illinois State Police Special Agent John Meduga arrived that morning, the teenage stab victim was incapacitated on an emergency room table. Meduga was a composed and even-keeled, ten-year veteran with the state police, who mostly investigated homicides. Before that, he spent eight years at Chicago's Police Department where he responded to more than his fair share of deadly shootings across the city.

He feared the teenage girl might not survive the brutal roadside attack along Route 53. If she died on the surgery table, her insight of the killer would be forever lost.

"She could barely talk," Meduga noted.

Not wanting to lose any precious time, the persistent state police investigator tried to draw out clues, any clues, from this brave young survivor. According to Illinois State Police reports, the rapist was a Black man, perhaps six-foot to six-foot-two. He bore a potbelly and looked medium to heavy set. He had terrible body odor.

Besides his lingering objectionable wicked smell, there was something else distinctive, something Tonya Little would never forget.

Even though the random attack transpired during one of the absolute hottest summers on record for northern Illinois, the cold-blooded roadside killer wore a long-sleeved, blue-colored, plaid flannel shirt.

He also wore blue jeans and white gym shoes, she noticed.

Over the coming week, as Little remained in critical condition, Meduga and other state policemen visited her Joliet hospital room.

"We felt it was a good idea to … draw a composite, not knowing if she would live or die," Meduga said. "She would talk for a few minutes and close her eyes and she would fade off and then she would come back for a minute, close her eyes again and fade off. She would constantly come in and out."

For crime evidence technicians, the obscure out of the ordinary clues often capture their attention.

What was the unusual clue inside Tony Hackett's gold Plymouth?

"A Tasmanian devil doll," Meduga said.

Police found the stuffed animal underneath the teenager's body.

**

By 1983, Melvin Trojanowski had fifteen years with the Illinois State Police including his past three as a crime scene technician assigned to the Joliet Crime Laboratory.

On July 17, 1983, near Wilmington, he met up with three state police colleagues at the two-door, 1974-model Plymouth Grand Coup Fury.

He photographed Tony Hackett face down on the car's floor, with his arms tucked under his chest. Other photos captured the victim's blood splashed across the entire front seat.

In this ghastly crime, the killer approached the passenger side of the car and fired several bullets into the sleeping teenager's body. Who on earth would commit such a dastardly crime?

As they wrapped up their work along I-55, officers taped the windows and doors shut. They put locks on the trunk. A tow truck brought the murder car back to Illinois State Police area headquarters across the road from the Stateville Correctional Center.

After completing their meticulous work along I-55, the police could not call it quits for the day. A second scene needed processing.

The Illinois State Police regrouped at the grassy median along Route 53 where the eagle-eyed motorist from Lockport spotted the badly injured teenage girl left for dead.

The distance from the I-55 murder scene to Route 53 was six miles.

At Route 53, police found smeared blood near a guard rail. The blood trail led into the ditch, just west of the guardrail, near a bunch of large rocks and thick tall weeds. One of the troopers spotted an empty aluminum Miller Lite beer can.

"He gave it to me, I packaged it in this package and subsequently transported it to the Joliet Crime Laboratory," Trojanowski said.

As for the furry Tasmanian devil doll from Marriott's Great America, the stuffed animal remained inside the murder car for at least a month.

Then the Illinois State Police chose to get rid of it.

"We destroyed it by burning because it was full of blood and body fluids and insects," agent Meduga pointed out.

Bear in mind, this was 1983.

People in police work knew practically nothing about DNA forensic evidence in the early 1980s.

**

Dr. Clyde Dawson became the key surgeon responsible for saving the downstate Illinois teenager's life in the emergency room at Joliet's Saint Joseph Medical Center.

Six years earlier, in 1977, Dr. Dawson obtained his medical degree from the University of Illinois in Chicago. From there, he did a two-year residency in general surgery at Wayne State University in Detroit.

By 1981, Dr. Dawson came to Joliet where he specialized in general and vascular surgery. In layman's terms, Dr. Dawson performed surgical operations on all parts of the body.

During the 1983 summer, the St. Joe's hospital emergency room surgeon faced the daunting task of saving eighteen-year-old Tonya Little.

Dr. Dawson remembered she was resuscitated from shock by the emergency room physicians prior to his arrival that eventful Sunday morning.

"I got there about thirty minutes or forty minutes after she came to the emergency room," Dr. Dawson recalled. "She was still in dire straits, but her blood pressure was OK. She was slightly incoherent because of the stress, and she had multiple injuries."

Joliet's emergency room doctors and nurses already put several large catheters into her veins along with large amounts of fluid to bring back her pulse and blood pressure.

"She had a pale face, and she had multiple injuries to her head, including two blunt cuts to the scalp of her head from a blunt object," Dr. Dawson described. "And, she had a slice behind her ear from some type of sharp object."

One stab wound pierced the right side of her chest.

"Right above over where her heart is," the Joliet surgeon noted.

After observing the stab wounds, Dr. Dawson went forward with surgery.

"I found that by opening the abdomen, that the stab wound went through the chest wall into the pericardium, which is the sack surrounding the heart," Dr. Dawson explained. "It passed through that sack, but missed the heart itself. It then went through the diaphragm, which divides the belly from the chest cavity and then, after entering the abdomen, it went into the liver."

The knife had plunged into a ligament between the girl's stomach and liver. The wound penetrated her pancreas, extending from the front of her body to her backside.

Dr. Dawson answered in the affirmative when asked whether her life was in danger at the time of her surgery.

"I base it on the fact that she had no pulse and blood pressure when she came into the emergency room and, if she had not been resuscitated, she would have died there," he predicted. "And the types of wounds that she had, if she didn't have treatment for these, they would have led to death sooner or later, within days or weeks, but eventually she would have died from those wounds."

As the Illinois State Police hunted for a psychopathic monster whose identity remained a mystery, the time had come to enlist the help of a capable long-time Joliet hypnotist.

Perhaps Dr. George Honiotes could unleash the true killer's identity during a hypnotic session with the kidnapping victim who was pushed out of the killer's pickup with an expectation she would bleed to death in the grassy median.

CHAPTER 9

HYPNOSIS

As Tonya Little recuperated in her Joliet hospital bed, three state police investigators stood nearby to help guide Joliet hypnotist Dr. George Honiotes. The teenager's mother sat in the hospital room to give her badly injured daughter moral support.

To begin the hypnosis, the Joliet doctor made her look at a fixed spot on the wall.

"Just let your eyes get heavier and heavier and heavier," he told her. "Very soon as you begin to let your eyes get heavy, what you want to do then is to begin to let them want to close."

As Little drifted off to sleep, Dr. Honiotes talked in a calm, soothing voice.

"Let yourself get loose and relaxed, OK? Now, I'm going touch your right arm. Let it be nice and loose and heavy as can be. Good girl, that's the way. Let me bring this arm down now and be nice and relaxed. Let it go, nice and relaxed. Good, you're doing just fine … I'd like you to imagine that you're there in your bedroom, OK? What's there?"

"Dresser, drawers," she answered in her trance-like state.

"And where are you there in the bedroom?" the doctor inquired.

"Sitting on my bed," she replied.

Dr. Honiotes wanted his patient to let her memory drift back to the night of her brutal attack from six days ago.

"Now, when I snap my fingers what I want you to do is to be back on early Sunday morning and you're facing a truck," Dr. Honiotes told her. "Is that OK? You're on the ground facing a truck. I'm going to snap my fingers, and I want you to be right there. Snap!

"What do you see?"

"The grill of a truck; the grill of a truck," she repeated.

"What else do you see there?" Dr. Honiotes wondered. "It's like a motion picture, and you can stop that motion picture and look right at it. What do you see?"

"The lights, and the front ... Just the whole front of the truck," she responded.

"OK, tell me everything that you see on the front of the truck. You're right there."

"The lights and the grill and the bumper, it's so shiny," she said.

Dr. Honiotes pressed for more details of the killer's vehicle, but the hospitalized patient responded, "I don't see anything else."

"Is there a license plate on that bumper? Is there a license plate anywhere else?" he asked.

"Uh-huh," she replied.

Realizing he was not making extraordinary progress, Dr. Honiotes tried another tactic.

"I'm going to talk with the officers for a moment, OK?" he instructed. "You just stay there nice and relaxed, OK?"

The hypnotist turned to his three trusted police investigators.

"She's in very good regression right now," Dr. Honiotes assured them. "She's excellent. She's right there. No question about it. You can see this with the flickering and the movements in her eyes. She hears what we're talking about right now, OK?"

When he addressed his patient for the second time, Dr. Honiotes told her to move back farther away from the truck.

"What do you see? Tell me everything that you see," he asked.

She made a murmuring noise he did not understand.

"You're frowning," he told her. "What are you looking at?"

"Nothing else there," she answered.

Dr. Honiotes asked her to describe the lights of the kidnapper's truck.

"They're kind of square with curved corners," she replied.

"Are the lights on or are they off?" the doctor inquired.

"Off," she said.

With that, Dr. Honiotes conferred with Illinois State Police Detective Ed Miller and let the detective ask her a question.

Miller addressed her, saying, "We just want at this point to see if we can get the license plate, OK? Describe the vehicle."

"It's got two colors on it, one of them dark and the other light," she replied.

"Do you know what the colors are?" Dr. Honiotes followed up.

"It was so dark," she answered. "The dark's on top and then there's light and then there's a real thin dark color at the bottom, by the door, well, not that much under the door and across the bottom."

Could she remember anything else?

"It's got a little bit of chrome; think it's the chrome running down the side," she responded. "It's got kind of big square mirrors."

Little estimated the mirrors were five inches long.

She also remembered the passenger door contained a push handle.

However, the police were hoping the courageous young woman remembered seeing the back of her captor's truck.

She shook her head, indicating no.

Dr. Honiotes wanted to know if she remembered markings on the door or windows.

She remembered a numbered sticker, the type you get when your truck underwent a vehicle emissions test.

Dr. Honiotes wondered if she saw any numbers.

"Seven. It's green, dark sticker," she answered.

"Do you see anything else with that sticker?"

"Nope."

"What does the seat look like?" Dr. Honiotes wondered.

"It's a vinyl seat, kind of smooth," she responded.

"Is it light or is it dark?"

"Dark."

"What color is it?"

"You shook your head. You can't tell?"

Next, the hypnotist asked her to remember any other details from the truck.

"Steering wheel," she responded.

"What about it? What about it?"

"It's dark. It is an automatic truck," she pointed out.

"Is there anything else you can see?"

"The ashtray, it is just open a little bit, and there is a jug on the floor, and a Styrofoam cup."

She also thought she saw tools or metal on the floor. "I'm not sure what they are," she professed.

At this point, the Joliet hypnotist focused on the moment Little crawled to her captor's truck.

"Describe the front of the truck. You said there's a grill there. What does that look like?"

"It's not real shiny," she answered. "Like maybe plastic or something, you know. It's kind of rectangular and the corners are curved on the top part."

Illinois State Police Detective Miller asked her about the hood.

"Any numbers on the side of the truck at all?" he wondered.

Again, Miller's question was met with a negative response.

The patient nodded in a negative manner.

"Is there anything else that we can do?" Dr. Honiotes asked the three detectives huddled around him in the hospital room.

"Go back and take one more look at the front of the truck," Investigator Miller suggested. "Tell us what she sees."

Dr. Honiotes agreed to give it one more attempt.

"You're on your stomach, right? Tell me what you see," he inquired.

"The lights and the grill and the bumper, I don't see anything else," she admitted.

"Do you see any numbers at all? Do you see a license plate?"

Little gave another negative response.

"The answer is 'No' and she's there," Dr. Honiotes advised everyone. "I'll tell you that right now."

Finally, Dr. Honiotes asked if she knew the truck's color.

Again, she gave a negative response.

The time had come to end the session.

Dr. Honiotes told Little to keep her eyes closed and stay nice and relaxed.

"Now you did very fine, very well, OK," he assured her. "When I count to three, you're going to be able to open your eyes, and you'll feel nice and relaxed. Maybe from time to time in the next few days you may recall some other details that you'll be able to give to the officers. Your mind will become more and more refreshed. Is that OK? One! Two! Three!

"Hi, there," the doctor greeted her.

The hypnotic session did not unearth any major clues to put the Illinois State Police any closer to catching the killer of Tony Hackett.

As far as police were concerned, every investigative technique, no matter how unorthodox or bizarre, was worth pursuing. After all, a crazed methodical madman continued to troll the local roads and interstates for his randomly selected victims. He showed no signs of backing off his growing appetite for death and destruction in the Joliet area.

Joliet's long and astonishingly hot summer of 1983 was about to get hotter.

That July, Joliet's marvelous medical staff at St. Joe's hospital nursed Tonya Little back to recovery. She was allowed to go home, several days later. As she recuperated at her family's downstate farm, she had plenty of time to replay the nightmarish events in her mind, the deadly shooting of the young man she wanted to marry.

Still, Tonya Little remained the police's best hope for making a positive identification of the I-55 assassin.

CHAPTER 10

CERAMIC SHOP

In July 1983, Marilyn Baers sold her house in rural New Lenox, Illinois, where she lived with her adult son, David, who was in his late twenties. She needed the money for the down payment on a building she just purchased called Lynn's Ceramics in the community of Lemont. Unbeknownst to her regular customers, Marilyn Baers was in the process of closing her Joliet ceramics shop and bringing all her inventory to her new business in the historic business district of Lemont, Illinois.

Located at 1405 East Cass Street, her Joliet store was called Greenware By Merry. Baers kept it open from 10 a.m. to 4 p.m. Monday through Saturday plus 7 p.m. to 10 p.m. Monday and Thursday. After selling her house near New Lenox, Marilyn Baers moved in with her elderly mother who lived in the 300 block of Joliet's North Briggs Street.

Much of Joliet's East Side featured a blend of older affordable homes with small yards along with several blue-collar factories trying to stay afloat in the 1980s.

Others on Joliet's East Side worked at the EJ & E railyard. The constant sounds of lumbering freight trains entering and departing the train yard near Cass Street became a way of life for East Siders. A large concrete overpass bridge separated vehicles from the EJ & E yard down below.

The busy stretch of Cass Street, known as Route 30, included flower shops, fruit stands, car washes, liquor stores, car mechanics and two long-time cemeteries. Oakwood Cemetery and Mt. Olivet Catholic Cemetery served as the final resting place for some of Joliet's earliest settlers.

Just up the street from the two cemeteries, Marilyn Baers operated her ceramics shop, where she developed a loyal following and made several friendships with her customers. On Friday, Aug. 19, 1983, Baers closed her business to attend a daylong pottery convention in Milwaukee, a three-hour roundtrip from Joliet.

The next day, Saturday, the forty-six-year-old Baers opened her Joliet store around 10 a.m. She had $500 cash leftover from Friday's ceramic show exposition that she attended with her son David and a woman from suburban Downers Grove, Illinois, who had a passion for ceramics.

The Joliet ceramic shop was normally a busy place on weekends.

**

Joliet's East Side and West Side are separated by the Des Plaines River canal that includes five drawbridges that lift high into the sky whenever a freight barge is moving back and forth along Joliet's waterway. A resident of Joliet's West Side, Helen Allen had about a ten-minute drive to get to the ceramic shop from her Raynor Avenue house.

When Allen approached the Greenware By Merry store between 11:30 a.m. and 11:40 a.m., she saw a red and white Chevy Blazer in the parking lot but nobody else. The Joliet woman's intuition told her not to enter the store. She figured the owner, Marilyn Baers, would hound her within the store if she was one of the only customers.

Allen preferred to be left alone when she shopped for ceramics. As she stood outside the entrance, Allen saw a silhouette of a man standing inside the ceramic shop toward the front of the store.

She decided not to go inside. Instead, she walked back to her car and drove away from the Ridgewood neighborhood. The older Joliet neighborhood had its share of quirky characters. Allen noticed an older tan-colored General Motors automobile caked in dirt on the driver's door.

At first, the Joliet woman didn't think anybody was in the car parked along Jackson Street, but to her surprise, the car lurched forward a few feet. Out popped a man, and he looked back to the rear, as if he had a flat tire or a mechanical problem with his car.

As Allen drove through the neighborhood, she kept looking at her rear-view mirror. The beat-up brown car moved forward again, another few feet. Eventually, Allen passed through the East-Side neighborhood and went on her way.

Like Allen, Georgene Sopko, age thirty-six, remembered driving past the ceramic shop that same Saturday morning. But when the Harwood Street resident drove up to the store at 10:55 a.m., she saw no cars in the parking lot. Her intuition told her not to go inside, so she drove away. About an hour later, she drove past the ceramic shop, again. When she looked at her watch, the time was 12:05 p.m. This time, there was a red and white Oldsmobile or Buick La Sabre in the parking lot, and it had fender skirts on the wheels, she thought.

Again, she backpedaled and chose not to enter the ceramic shop, figuring she could return another time. She was not positive, but it looked to her like the lights inside the business might be off.

"Georgene was questioned as to how sure she was about the times, and she stated she was very sure about the times due to the fact that she checked her watch both times she went by," Will County Sheriff's Investigator Nick Ficarello's report showed.

Little did these two Joliet women know but their last-minute impulse to stay out of the ceramic shop on East Cass Street may have saved their lives.

**

A lifelong Joliet area resident, Anna Agnes Ryan devoted her career to the New Lenox public schools, teaching twenty-five years at the grade school district east of Joliet.

On Friday nights, Anna Ryan's home was the focal point of a family feast. As many as thirty people gathered at her house for Irish-style family meals. Anna Ryan had lived through the Depression Era, so she always made sure she had enough food. She owned several large refrigerators and three freezers. She turned two of her closets into food pantries at her house in Joliet.

"Mom had Friday nights as something to hold everyone in the family together," explained her son Bob Ryan in an interview with *The Herald-News* at the time. "You had to grab for the food because nobody was going to hand it to you."

Besides hosting family feasts, Anna Ryan baked bread and cookies. She always made enough food so her Friday night guests had some to take home. While many senior citizens became homebodies and kept to themselves, Anna Ryan was not that type as she approached her mid-seventies.

"Mom was always on the go," her son said. "She would leave at 6 a.m. some mornings and not return until 2 a.m. the next morning. She always told us not to worry about her."

On Saturday morning, Aug. 20, 1983, her daughter-in-law, Pamela Ryan, along with Pamela's best friend, Barbara Dunbar, showed up at Anna Ryan's house. Around 11:15 a.m., the three women piled into Pamela Ryan's red and white Chevy Blazer. They planned to spend the next hour looking at pottery supplies inside the Joliet ceramics shop on Route 30.

But by noon, their red Blazer was gone from the parking lot.

About 12:05 p.m. the ceramic shop appeared empty as another Joliet resident, Edna Hauck, pulled into the parking lot. A regular customer, Hauck stepped inside the store and called for Marilyn Baers. The owner did not respond. Hauck returned outside for a moment. Her daughter-in-law and her grandchildren remained back in her car. Hauck wondered if there was a burglary because the ceramic shop door was open, but no one was there.

The Joliet woman hurried toward Cass Street and waived down two passing Will County Sheriff's vehicles.

Working off the premise that Greenware By Merry was burglarized, the sheriff's deputies cautiously entered the ceramic store. After not seeing anyone in the front of the business, the sheriff's deputies walked toward the back of the shop.

Because the building was dark, one of the deputies flipped on a light switch. Sprawled across the floor, lifeless, was a young woman with light brown hair, blue shorts and a pink-colored blouse. She wore gold-rim glasses and had her arms tied behind her back. Blood flowed from her chest and more blood dripped from her mouth.

Not far away, authorities saw a gray-haired woman in a pink-and-purple house dress, a slip and nylons. She was not tied up or gagged. Blood poured from her chest and her mouth bled.

Back on the south side of the ceramic shop, the deputies stumbled upon a third body. The young woman had brown hair down to her shoulders. She wore blue jeans, a red-colored tube top and sandals. Her hands were tied behind her back and someone gagged her mouth. Like the other two victims, her chest bled profusely and blood pooled in her mouth.

A fourth body turned up near the bathroom on the building's south end. The brown-haired woman wore blue-checkered shorts, a plain blue short-sleeved blouse and tennis shoes. She became the third victim whose hands were tied behind her back, rendering her defenseless.

"You can't describe something that gruesome," Will County Sheriff's Sgt. Gae Luchowski told *The Herald-News*.

Sheriff's deputies Warren Miller and Luchowski did a building sweep, including the roof, but found no criminal suspects on site. The Will County deputies summoned evidence technicians, investigators, supervisors and the coroner's office. There were four bodies that needed to go to the morgue for autopsies.

Not all the victims died the same way. Anna Ryan, the retired New Lenox school teacher in her seventies, was the only person shot. A bullet ripped through her neck. However, all four women were stabbed repeatedly in the chest.

None of the victims exhibited signs of sexual assault. All four women were fully clothed.

These were four mortifying murders.

Bob Ryan lost his mother and his wife, plus his wife's best friend.

"These were real people we're talking about," he told the newspaper. "They were always themselves. There were no fronts. More people should be like them. They touched a lot of lives."

Bob Ryan's twenty-nine-year-old wife, Pam, was survived by her stepdaughter, three brothers, a sister and her parents. A 1971 graduate of Joliet East High School, she worked for seven years at Rust Craft, a greeting card printing factory building at the corner Richards and Washington Streets. Her father owned Garland's, a full-service, Mobil gas station and auto repair shop at the corner of Manhattan Road and Richards Street.

Besides taking up sewing, Pam Ryan was a skilled baker. If her family had a birthday or anniversary, Pam Ryan was sure to bake them a cake.

"She loved to make cakes, and she was very good at it," her husband noted. "Pam loved to make everyone else happy."

A resident of suburban Mokena, thirty-eight-year-old Barbara Dunbar left behind her father, a stepmother, three sisters and nine brothers. Like her best friend Pam Ryan, Dunbar worked at Rust Craft, employed twenty years as a clerk. She was a devout Catholic, a member of St. Jude's Church on Joliet's McDonough Street.

"She was like a daughter to me," noted Rose Garland, Pam Ryan's mother. "She and Barb started ceramics about six months ago. Ninety-nine percent of what they made was for someone else. They were very giving people no matter if you wanted material things or emotional support."

The oldest homicide victim at the ceramic shop was seventy-five-year-old Anna (Toepper) Ryan.

Divorced, she was survived by two sons, three daughters, fourteen grandchildren and three great-grandchildren. A devout Catholic, she attended daily Mass at St. Mary's Magdalene Catholic Church on Briggs Street.

Marilyn Baers, owner of Greenware By Merry, was the fourth homicide victim. A Joliet native, Baers graduated from Joliet Township High School in 1955. She and her husband had divorced more than a decade earlier. She had a son and a daughter, both in their twenties. Additional survivors included one grandchild, plus her mother, one brother and one sister.

The ceramic shop slasher was also a thief. He had stolen his homicide victims' purses, and he drove off with Pam Ryan's red and white Chevy Blazer bearing license plates RR 650.

The chilling killings of four defenseless women left Joliet residents terrified. The crimes were especially unnerving for small businesses. Some places wondered whether the rampage killer was one of their customers. Local shops became hypervigilant about their unfamiliar guests.

Tammy Burkhart worked at the Home Cut Donuts shop on East Washington Street in Joliet's old industrial area. One customer who patronized her bakery on the morning of the killing spree gave her an uneasy feeling.

The shaggy-haired white man with a torn t-shirt stepped inside to order coffee. He was unshaven, had dirty blonde hair and wore a dark-colored baseball cap. He had a smaller frame, probably five-foot-nine and 160 lbs.

Burkhart's coworker brought the man his coffee.

When the man left, Burkhart thought she saw blood on his right hand. The man drove off in a light-brown 1970s clunker. She wasn't sure the make and model, but the slope of his roof was similar to the 1969 Buick La Sabre parked near her house.

The suspicious man visited Home Cut Donuts about an hour before the ceramic shop slayings, about ten blocks away. Home Cut Donuts closed at noon that Saturday and Burkhart started her normal clean up duties around 11:30 a.m.

Prior to cleaning up, Burkhart sat at one of the tables with her boyfriend's mother for about forty-five minutes. The waitress was certain that the scruffy young man had already left by that point.

Chris Pyles was the Home Cut Donuts waitress who served the shaggy man. She surmised he was in his twenties, and she thought he had blood on his hands and face. The Will County Sheriff's Office relied on her recall to produce a suspect composite to disseminate to the daily newspaper.

The Home Cut Donuts employee thought the young man had three elongated bloody fingerprints on his cheeks plus dried blood on his hands, notably his knuckles. Aside from his outward appearance, nothing else stood out. She remembered he ordered coffee, paid cash and drove off in an old brown beater.

At the time of their encounter, the two Home Cut Donuts waitresses had no idea that four women up the road were about to be slain.

However, Pyles remembered asking her coworker if she got a look at the odd-looking customer as he left, and Burkhart agreed she did.

Friends, family and coworkers held out hope that Will County Auxiliary Officer Denis Foley would recover from his horrifying gunshot wounds to his jaw and his abdomen during the overnight hours of July 16.

About a week after the Homer Township massacre, the newspaper reported Foley was improving at Joliet's Silver Cross Hospital; however, sadly, a month after the shooting, Foley succumbed to his injuries. He died at age fifty.

The death toll from the Homer Township massacre now reached five.

For the second straight month, hundreds of area police officers gathered for another memorial service to honor one of their own who gave his life while trying to keep the good people of Will County safe.

The summer of terror took its toll as the body count became more than the Joliet area could handle.

CHAPTER 11

BAD COMPANY

Because most murders are committed by someone intimately acquainted with the victims, David Baers became an immediate and prolonged focus of Will County's investigation into the Aug. 20, 1983, mass murders of his mother and her three customers.

The twenty-six-year-old was questioned regarding his activities in the hours leading up to the Joliet ceramic shop murders. He maintained that he and his girlfriend rolled out of bed around 9 a.m. at his new loft floor apartment in downtown Lemont. That Saturday morning, he visited Fritz's Restaurant in Lemont for a coffee. By 9:40 a.m., he arrived at Lynn's Ceramics, the new business he and his mother had bought. One of his business partners arrived at work around 10 a.m.

"Dave stated that he then went to get two more cups of coffee, one for himself and one for Lee," his police interview showed.

A couple of customers visited to buy merchandise around 10:45 a.m. as he and his coworker remained busy in the Lemont ceramic shop until around 1 p.m. when the phone rang.

The caller inquired if his mother was there. When he told the caller that his mother was not there because she was at the Joliet store, the woman on the phone began sobbing.

The caller informed him that Joliet's news radio station, WJOL, was reporting that people were found dead inside his mother's business.

Moments later, a friend called, telling him something terrible happened in Joliet and he needed to go to Joliet. When David Baers pointed out that his car was disabled, the woman and her husband, a Joliet police sergeant, arrived in Lemont about thirty minutes later and brought him to the ceramic shop along Route 30. It was now around 2 p.m. and dozens of Will County and Illinois State Police had swarmed the business as David Baers still didn't know whether his mother was one of the victims. At the crime scene he found one of his aunts. She, in turn, drove him to his grandmother's house several blocks away.

When Will County Sheriff's investigators asked about his Chevy Nova, David Baers explained how his car remained parked in downtown Lemont because it was broken and did not run.

There were no immediate arrests made following the ceramic shop murders.

"These were victims of opportunity," reflected Will County State's Attorney Ed Petka. "I don't think there was any plan of targeting any of the people."

The sharp cutting instrument used in the four killings had to be similar to a bayonet because the knife wounds were deep, Petka recalled. "Those four women were bayoneted in front of each other, evil for evil's sake. Someone just walked right in and killed them." Petka added.

**

David Baers was re-interviewed by Sheriff's Investigator Dave Simpson along with Marty McCarthy of the Illinois State Police a few months later. Their interview stated "he has been injecting heroin approximately twice a day, four times per week, for the last three weeks."

During the interview, Baers identified a man from Orland Park as being his drug connection.

"He said that his drug habit included MDA, LSD, speeders and heroin before his mother was killed, but that he was not using as many drugs then as he has been lately," the pair of investigators noted. "Baers said that although some of these people fronted him drugs in the past, he'd always paid them back, and he wasn't under any pressure to pay off a drug debt at the time of his mother's death."

Meanwhile, the young man's grandmother told police that "Marilyn had considerable problems over the years with raising David in that he has gotten himself into considerable trouble in school and also has been arrested several times for different criminal offenses. One instance came into mind with her stating that he was arrested in Frankfort for burglary and also possibly some type of drug charge."

While the Joliet woman acknowledged her grandson battled a bad drug problem, he seemed to have straightened himself out during the past year, she told detectives. In fact, Marilyn Baers had taught her adult son the tools of the trade involving her ceramics business, and he had taken a liking to it.

And that's how the mother and son became business partners. Marilyn Baers was divorced at the time of her slaying. The ex-husband was present at the Orland Park wedding ceremony for his daughter, which was earlier that year, in 1983. The Will County police surmised that the ex-husband was not a viable suspect in the homicides.

As for David Baers, he acknowledged several past burglary arrests as well as a drug habit. One of his burglary codefendants was a young man from Chicago's North Side who introduced him to drugs.

Sometimes, the drug associate from Chicago traveled to Joliet's East Side to visit the ceramic shop on Cass Street. The drug associate even made one visit to the family's new ceramic shop in downtown Lemont.

Police also asked David Baers about any local acquaintances he maintained from around Joliet's East Side area.

"David Baers states that he has broken off all ties with his friends and acquaintances in the Ridgewood area and that he has not seen any people in the Ridgewood area, which he classifies as people with unsavory characters ... he wishes to help in any way possible with any information that he may have and ... in regards to this investigation."

David Baers was reeling from the gruesome death of his mother and her three customers at their Joliet shop along the busy Route 30 corridor. And yet he remained a focus of Will County investigators as the days passed.

On the crime's one-month anniversary, police again interviewed him inside the sheriff's department along Laraway Road in Joliet. He reiterated how he moved into his new upstairs apartment in downtown Lemont on July 30, which was three weeks before the killings. Since then, he only made two trips back to Joliet. He recalled visiting his mother's ceramic shop Aug. 1 to pick up supplies for his new Lemont store.

He returned to Joliet two days later with his girlfriend, and they visited his grandmother's house on North Briggs Street.

During the remainder of August, he lived above their new ceramic shop in Lemont and managed the business, which stayed open five days a week, but closed Friday and Sunday.

David Baers told police he had a business relationship with someone in Pennsylvania who ran Eddy's Mold Shop. The owner of Eddy's drove a brown van and visited ceramic shops across the country to sell molds that were considered bootlegged.

Even though David Baers had not implicated himself in the killings of his mother and her customers, sheriff's investigators were not ready to eliminate the twenty-six-year-old as a prime suspect.

"David Baers states that at no time did he traffic or deal in drugs," police reports noted. "He maintains that he has been off drugs, which he describes as poly drugs and MDA's, for approximately the last six to seven months. He freely admits to going to a drug rehabilitation center called Crossroads, which was held at the Tinley Park Mental Facilities at 183rd and Harlem Avenue."

Because the polygraph machine was an important tool for solving crimes, Will County detectives asked Baers to take a lie-detector test in connection with the ceramic shop slayings. As a result, he was later cleared as a suspect.

CHAPTER 12

THE GRECIAN

Following the ceramic shop slayings, the phones rang off the hook at the Will County Sheriff's Office. Overworked investigators raced to figure out which tips were valid and which ones sounded crazy. Many of the phone tips required additional investigation to determine their legitimacy. One such tip came from a woman in her twenties who worked at the Kitty Lounge, a seedy bar on Joliet's East Side.

The woman told police that one of the ceramic shop victims, Barb Dunbar, had a relative who had worked at the Kitty Lounge as a musician. Then, after the murders, a local man known as "The Grecian" approached Steve Dunbar and told him he could have the murderer killed for $5,000. The Grecian supposedly knew who committed the ceramic shop murders: It was a Black man who lived roughly three or four blocks away from the ceramics shop on East Cass Street.

When asked why The Grecian had not furnished his information to police, the woman replied he didn't trust Will County Crime Stoppers.

By January 1984, homicide investigators Marty McCarthy and Dave Simpson tracked down the man known as The Grecian, Richard Brooks. He worked at Grecian Motors in Joliet. Brooks, age thirty-one, was questioned about the Cass Street murders and whether he, himself, had participated in a completely different murder in Joliet.

Brooks said he remembered talking with Steve Dunbar inside Kitty's Lounge, but maintained he never made any comments regarding the ceramic shop slayings. Brooks told investigators he was an alcoholic and may have told people he was a hitman while he was drunk at the bar, but he did not remember saying such a thing inside Kitty's Lounge. During the fall of 1983, Brooks patronized Kitty's Lounge a lot because his girlfriend was one of the barmaids, he told police.

Later, Simpson and McCarthy tracked down The Grecian's girlfriend. She claimed that Brooks and the co-owner of Grecian Motors were inside the Kitty Lounge on the night of Nov. 17, 1983, and Brooks proclaimed how he and the co-owner of Grecian Motors just made $5,000 for a murder hit. The girlfriend told police she knew he was drunk at the time he made the claim, but she believed him because she noticed he began spending a lot of money in the coming days.

On the night of Nov. 17, 1983, Brooks was supposed to pick her up from work at 9 p.m. He failed to show up until 12:45 a.m.

The bartender claimed that Brooks and the co-owner of Grecian Motors may have killed somebody near the P.T. Club in Joliet. She told the police that Brooks had a $1,000 a day heroin habit, and she had never heard him make any comments in reference to the ceramic shop killings.

**

Around the five-month anniversary of the ceramic shop killings, Simpson and McCarthy interviewed a Joliet woman who developed a peculiar obsession with the crimes.

The woman, age twenty-nine, rented an apartment on the east side of Joliet where a scrapbook was found and given to police. The booklet had dozens of pages of neatly clipped out newspaper articles. The headlines and articles chronicled numerous Joliet and Lockport homicides from the summer of 1983 and were neatly placed into the photo album.

During questioning, the woman told the detectives she was born and raised in Dover, Arkansas, and her mother still lived there. Prior to moving to Joliet, the young woman had never heard of such violent crime. Therefore, she made the murder photo album from the newspapers and planned to mail it back to her mother in Arkansas.

The investigators realized the woman's obsession with the Will County murders, although bizarre, didn't constitute any crime. Police found no evidence connecting her to any of the slayings. Facing a time crunch and bombarded with more than enough leads and tips to pursue, the lead investigators ended the interview and moved on.

**

Eventually, investigator Simpson again interviewed the bartender at Kitty Lounge who claimed to have inside knowledge pointing to the man known as The Grecian. During her interview in early 1984, the woman who lived on Joliet's Sherman Street claimed that when she was on her porch, she overheard Richard Brooks talking with two others about the previous summer's homicides, and the ceramic shop murders came up. "Well, there's four broads who won't bother anyone anymore," she claimed she overheard Brooks say. She interpreted this as being an incriminating admission to the crime.

While the information seemed like a worthwhile lead for Will County police, in the end, investigators realized it was all a big lie.

Simpson and McCarthy concluded "that all of the information she gave in regards to the murders was fabricated and that she made this information up due to the fact that she was angry with Richard Brooks due to the fact that he was passing bad checks on her account in the Joliet area and that she wished to get even with him."

At times, finding the elusive madman became even more of a challenge for Will County police because some people looked at the crimes as leverage to settle vendettas with people who had double-crossed them in the past.

CHAPTER 13

STRANGE GUEST

As the Will County Sheriff's Office remained slammed with tips about murder suspects, investigators tried to make sure every lead got taken seriously. On one instant, sheriff's deputies sped out to a rundown motel along the busy Route 30 corridor in Plainfield, nearly thirty minutes away from Joliet's East Side.

A maid in her late twenties at the Lakeview Motel told police that one of the guests, Dudley Blake, gave her specific instructions the previous night to come into his motel room and vacuum his rug.

"This was somewhat strange as she was told earlier by Mr. Blake not to come near the room and to stay away from the room," Will County Sheriff's Investigator Wayne Howard noted.

The maid was not supposed to enter the room of motel guests, but she ultimately agreed to enter, bringing along her five-year-old son.

"There was some kind of brown smoke inside the room," she told investigators. "The smoke did not smell like anything she had ever smelled before, and when she opened the door, the smoke did not roll out of the door, but seemed to settle down on the floor."

Inside the smoky room, the maid vacuumed the floor to accommodate her odd guest. Moments later, the maid's little boy summoned her to the bathroom where the sink contained dried blood.

As for the rug, the maid saw particles that looked like ceramic bits, pieces and powder.

The discovery of dried blood, ceramic pieces and the cloud of smoke left the maid uneasy. She retreated to the motel office and alerted her manager. She also noticed Mary Kay cosmetics and children's shirts inside the guest's room. The last time she remembered Blake he was wearing a blue sports suit and white-and-brown golf shoes.

Turned out, Dudley Blake checked into room sixteen at the Lakeview Motel during the same weekend as the ceramic shop murders in Joliet.

Blake drove a light-brown car without license plates. His motel room contained a bloody towel, a switchblade knife, six women's purses and ceramic material. He was described as a skinny white man, with white hair.

Following up on the tip, two Will County sheriff's investigators raced out to interview the Lakeview Motel manager. The manager, who was in his early forties, told investigators that Dudley Blake was an unusual character.

Nine months earlier, in December 1982, the motel manager was visiting the Joliet Public Library with his two children when he encountered Blake for the first time. That same day, a Joliet woman was purportedly stabbed to death in Joliet.

"Dudley Blake told him that he had caught the killer of Marion Brown," the sheriff's investigators wrote. "Dudley Blake stated that the police were too dumb to catch the killer, so he had to do it."

The Lakeview Motel manager remembered his strange conversation at the Joliet library lasted about two hours during which Blake mentioned how Marion Brown's husband "was the dumbest lawyer around, and it served him right and called him, Mr. Brown, all kinds of names."

Over the coming months, the motel manager encountered Dudley Blake a half dozen more times, usually on the streets of Joliet or at the library. Joliet's homeless or street people often congregated at the library.

Then, on the day of Joliet's ceramic murders, someone showed up at the Lakeview Motel on Route 30 inquiring about renting room 1126. The motel, however, did not have a room 1126. Then, the visitor asked for room 116, but the motel did not have a room 116, either. The motel rooms only went up to twenty-six. The guest left the motel office for several minutes only to return later.

This time, the visitor told the manager that room sixteen was fine. He would take it.

"He was very messed up, shirt torn, approximate one day growth of beard, sweating, wet pants, looked like a bum, zipper was open on the pants," the motel manager told police.

Several minutes later, when the disheveled man came back to the office, the motel manager made the connection. That was Dudley Blake.

Upon receiving his room key, Dudley Blake warned the motel maid "to stay away from his room, not to go near his room."

Later that afternoon, Dudley Blake returned to the motel office and spoke "about how he was going to have to stay around and clear up the case where the four women had been murdered."

During his rambling conversation with the motel manager, Dudley Blake claimed that Will County judges Herman Faulkner and Charles Connor called him in to solve the murders, just like Will County Circuit Judge Angelo Pistilli "had called him to solve the Marion Brown murder. He also said he knew who killed the women. He then left and went back to his room."

Another twenty-four hours passed before the motel manager encountered his odd-behaving new guest.

This time, Dudley Blake wore white pants, but no shirt and no shoes. Blake helped himself to some complimentary coffee from the motel office and left.

On Aug. 22, two days after the ceramic shop killings, Blake called the motel from a Joliet tavern on West Jefferson Street. He wanted the manager to go into his room to see if he left his wallet on the chest of drawers.

The motel manager dealt with his share of shady customers, so he asked Blake to hand over the telephone to the bartender. When the manager confirmed that his guest was at Rittof's Tavern in Joliet, he agreed to look for Dudley Blake's wallet back at room sixteen.

First, though, the manager asked his son to accompany him. The manager warned his son "not to touch anything and watch everything that he does because this might be a set up."

The manager opened Blake's motel room with a key, but once inside, he didn't see a wallet. He saw an umbrella opened on the bed.

Upon being told his wallet was not in his motel room, Dudley Blake replied, "That's OK. Just get out of my room!"

After the manager hung up the phone, something else in room sixteen caught his eye – a half dozen purses and cigarette cases.

What possessed the mangy-looking motel guest to have six women's purses? The manager decided to explore other parts of the room. On the stove, a knife with a twelve-inch-blade was covered in dried blood.

"In the kitchenette is a small cubbyhole that is supposed to be a closet. When he looked into it he saw the clothes that Mr. Blake had on when he checked in and he noticed a towel that looked like blood stains on it," sheriff's reports reflected.

After leaving the kitchen, the motel manager entered the bathroom, which had a Norelco electric razor. The room was otherwise clean. It had no blood in the sink. Lastly, the manager inspected each of the six purses, but all were empty.

Elsewhere, the manager noticed women's makeup on a chest of drawers inside Dudley Blake's room plus women's garments including blouses. At that point, the manager and his son headed back to their office.

About an hour later, the phone rang. Dudley Blake called asking whether the motel manager "had told anyone or the police that he was living there." Eventually, Blake returned to the motel, lugging a small suitcase in his hands.

By 10 p.m., the motel manager called his room wanting to know if he would straighten out his bill for staying there. Blake promised to drop by the next morning after he visited the bank. On Aug. 23, the motel manager saw Blake walk out to his car, only to return to his motel room without leaving for the bank. The maid informed the manager that Blake's car had not started, so he ended up walking somewhere. Around 1 p.m., the maid returned to the motel office with an update.

"She stated … that it was funny that after Mr. Blake had stated for her to stay away from his room, he asked her to come in with him to vacuum the rug. She told Mr. Blake the maids are not to go in the rooms with the tenants in them, but he insisted that she come in and vacuum.

"She advised she went in with her small son and vacuumed the rug. She stated her son was in the bathroom and found something in the sink and asked what it was. The maid told (the manager) it looked like blood."

Given the unsettling sequence of events over the past few days, the manager told the maid to stand by the door and watch if Dudley Blake returned. A half-hour later, the motel manager and one of his carpenters, Pablo, returned to room sixteen and went inside. The purses and cigarette cases were gone. So was the blood-stained knife and bloody towel. Dudley Blake was gone, but he left behind footprints on the rug. The manager bent down to inspect the substance, which smelled like ceramic particles.

The manager had familiarity with the product because he used to work in ceramics, he told police.

Even though room sixteen was vacant, a witch's head hung on the east wall of the motel room. A candle and a pile of incense remained on a table. After four days of staying at the Lakeview Motel, Dudley Blake had packed his bags and moved out.

Did he have something to do with the ceramic shop murders? The Will County Sheriff's Office had to find that out.

CHAPTER 14

THE HAND

After the ceramic shop killings, David Smith came to the Will County Sheriff's Office for a hypnosis interview. Before she put Smith into a trance-like state, sheriff's investigator Dianne Seeman began by asking the young man what he remembered.

"I was at home with a buddy of mine, and my dad cooked us breakfast, and I remember looking up at the clock, and it said something like 11 a.m., and we were supposed to go down to Tonkovich's Auto. I was on my way down there, and I was going down Hebbard Street past the ceramic place, and I thought I heard a scream or something, so I turned around and looked to see what it was, and I didn't see nothing. I can't really remember if I seen a Blazer or not, but I think it was there."

David Smith said he remembered a car approaching him on Jackson Street, which is the street behind the ceramic shop.

"There was a car coming up Jackson Street with two Blacks in it that almost hit me, so they just, I guess that's what turned me off the track. I went down to Tonkovich's Auto, I was buying this car. I was paying down for it. I was paying a hundred bucks down on it, and I stayed there for about fifteen twenty minutes, not very long, and then I went back down Cass Street past the ceramic place."

Investigator Seeman wondered if Smith remembered the time he rode his bicycle along Cass Street.

He thought it was around 11:30 a.m.

"You don't remember what you saw?" Seeman inquired.

"Like I really can't remember if I heard the scream going down Hebbard or going past Cass. I know I heard it," Smith answered.

Smith offered to describe the scream in more detail.

"If you ever hold a dog's mouth together, I mean hold his jaws together and kick him, he'd make that real high screech sound, and it'd sound muffled," he advised.

In regard to murder victim Pamela Ryan's red and white Blazer, "I think I did see it," Smith replied. "I thought I seen a car parked there too, another car, but I can't remember what it was."

"OK, and that's when you almost got hit by the two Blacks?" Seeman asked.

"Yeah, they was going up East Jackson and they stopped, they were stopped right in the middle of Hebbard and Jackson, right there on the corner. They stopped right in the middle, and they was, they was yelling at me ... I was going to stop and find out what that noise was, until I almost got hit by that car. I was going to go to Cass."

Then, after riding to Tonkovich's Auto to make his down payment for a used car, Smith hopped back on his bicycle and rode past the ceramic shop a second time.

"I'm pretty sure I looked at it, I can't remember if the door was open," he remarked.

Finally, the sheriff's investigator explained how her hypnosis session would work.

"What I'm going to do when I put you in hypnosis … in your mind you're going to see it all over again, and I'm going to take you all the way through down Hebbard, down to your uncle's and then back up Cass Street," Seeman explained. "And we'll see what we can see. You've never been hypnotized before?"

"No."

"It's not hocus-pocus or anything like that you see on TV, OK?" she told him. "It's just you're very relaxed. If you've ever had a couple beers and you're just about ready to go to sleep or something, that's the feeling. It's just like a real relaxed floating feeling."

To get started, Seeman asked the young man to stare at the funny picture of a skeleton on the wall.

"David, let your eyes go closed, just relax," she said as it took several minutes for him to reach his hypnotic state.

"If you want to smile, go ahead and smile," Seeman suggested. "Or giggle, go ahead and giggle. Take a nice deep breath. Let all those giggle feelings out. There you go, nice and relaxed."

Seeman's interview subject was now under her power.

"Just leave your eyes closed," she urged. "Don't get uptight or tense or anything … And we're going to ride your bike down Hebbard Street and you're going to hear something Dave, and tell me what you hear again? What did you hear Dave? Just like you told me before, what did you hear?"

"I ain't riding down the hill," he responded.

"OK, let's go back to when you started out in the morning. You were having breakfast. Your dad cooked you breakfast in the morning, and you looked up at the clock. Can you tell me what time it is David?"

"Fifteen until 11," the young man announced.

"You had breakfast. Remember what you had for breakfast, Dave?"

"French toast," he replied.

"OK and you're going to ride your bike down because you're going to give some money for a car. I want you to leave the house now, and you're on your bike. Are you with somebody Dave?"

"My friend," he answered.

"Can you tell me your friend's name?"

"Tim. Went down Belmont on both sides, and I took Osage to Elgin. Then I went to Hebbard. I stopped at Hebbard, seen a couple of my friends."

The hypnotized witness was asked if he remembered what time he saw his friends as he rode on his bicycle.

"I don't know," he replied.

"Is Tim still with you, Dave?"

"Yeah, he's right behind me."

"OK, what do you hear?"

"Sort of like a scream, but it ain't a scream."

"Does it sound like a human scream?"

"Sort of, it's been muffled."

"OK, like maybe somebody's holding their hand over their mouth?"

"Yeah."

"Is it just one scream you hear Dave?"

"Just one long one, it's pretty long, not like three minutes long. It was about a minute."

"OK, and you were going to stop and look back, or what did you do then?"

"I looked back and I asked Tim do you hear that? And he just looked at me, and I looked over at the ceramic shop, and there's that red truck there, and he said, 'Watch out!' and I looked to my right, and I looked to my right, and there was that white car."

"With the Black guys in it that almost hit you?"

"Yeah, then I remember a friend stopped up there, he was right there, he stopped right there in the parking lot and then them Blacks stopped there too. They stopped for a couple of minutes, and they was yelling at me. They was in a Chevy, white Chevy four-door small car."

Smith maintained that he kept peddling his bicycle as his friend Tim remained behind at the busy Joliet intersection. When Smith arrived at the used car dealer, he paid the guy and got a receipt. From there, he rode his bicycle toward the 7-Eleven.

"I ain't at 7-Eleven yet. I'm still riding past the ceramic shop again. The door's open," Smith remarked under hypnosis.

"The door is standing wide open?" the investigator repeated. "What do you see in the parking lot?"

"I don't know. For a brief glance, I ain't for sure."

"OK. Let's stop your bike and look at the parking lot real close."

"I see the red Blazer. Then I seen something."

"What did you see?"

"I ain't for sure."

Smith pointed out that he was not riding to 7-Eleven. His actual destination was the popular Deb's Hot Dogs stand along Route 30.

"What do you see David?" Seeman inquired.

"See the red Blazer," he replied. "Now, I ain't for sure."

"What do you think you see? What do you think you saw?"

"Black person," he answered.

"Where at?"

"At the door."

"Was he standing like inside the doorway?"

"Yes."

"OK, why aren't you for sure you're seeing that?"

"It's just brief. It's just real like a flash. It's there, and then it wasn't, looked like he's looking right at me."

The investigator had Smith retrace his bicycle route along Cass Street against traffic.

"OK, you're not for sure if you seen a Black person," she asked. "Could it have been Mexican? Was he just dark complexioned?"

"Black," he replied. "Can't really make out his facial features, I see his eyes though."

"That's OK. Does he look black or white, Dave?"

"Black."

"Are you sure he's black?"

"Not really sure but he's dark."

Then, for one last time, the investigator had Smith retrace his bicycle ride as he rode past the ceramic shop. "You tell me what you see?"

"See a red Blazer. I see the figure in the doorway. His eyes, that's all."

"OK, tell me what his eyes look like?"

"White and just white and blue, looks like he's wearing a wrist watch too, shining."

"OK, look close. Do you see something?"

"The door's open."

"OK, you can't tell if he's Mexican or white?"

"He's like, there's a big shadow over him."

"Was he inside the doorway, Dave?"

"He is inside."

Smith continued pedaling his bicycle until he arrived at Deb's Hot Dogs and ordered a Polish sausage for lunch.

By early afternoon, he dropped off his bike, met up with friends and goofed around before getting a ride in a car to the 7-Eleven.

"And that's when they told us about the ceramic place," he said.

"OK, you went down to 7-Eleven, and somebody told you that somebody had been murdered?" Seeman inquired.

"Yeah, they found four bodies."

The hypnotic session went so well that the sheriff's department asked Smith to return for a second interview days later.

"I see a black or brown hand around the girl's mouth," he revealed. "She's wearing a white dress with flowers on it, black all around it, I think."

"You're doing great, OK?" Seeman assured him. "Is the girl white that you see?"

"Yes."

"OK, now you saw you saw a black or a brown hand on her face?"

"On her mouth."

"Does it look like it might be a black guy, a black hand?"

"That's the scream I heard. That's it."

"Did you see this when you were coming down the hill David?"

"No, I seen it when I was going past it. I didn't hear a scream when I was going down Hebbard. I wasn't going down Hebbard. I was going down Cass."

Smith said when he first heard the scream, he looked across the street into the Mt. Olivet Cemetery, thinking the scream came from the other side of Route 30, which is also East Cass Street.

"And then I turned my head to the left, and I looked around, and I seen that flash," he exclaimed. "The guy's got a hand around her mouth pulling her back right there in the shop. I mean the ceramic place, pulling her back in the door. She was right by the door."

"That's when you heard a scream?"

"Yes, the guy, a black hand, because she was white, and she had kind of brownish hair … dress on it looked like it had kind of like flowers on it with a black belt around it, and she was wearing a knee-high dress."

"But you saw a black hand?"

"Black or brown, he ain't white."

"So it has to be a Black person? Could it be a Mexican?"

"It could be. I can't see his face ... He's got the hand around the girl's mouth, wearing a white dress with flowers or whatever. I'm not sure."

The young woman being harmed wore high heels, Smith insisted.

Seeman was impressed with her witness's recall during the hypnosis.

"You did very good, just excellent, very, very good," she complimented him. "Just stay nice and relaxed, and you tell me when you've passed the ceramic shop, and we'll have you relax for a minute, more, and then we'll have you come up out of hypnosis."

Eventually, Seeman turned off her tape recorder. She included the following notations in her police report.

"After the tape recorder was turned off in reference to the hypnosis session with David Smith, David was asked to look at car books and indicated to this officer a picture of a 1974 Plymouth Fury as being close to the car he had seen in the parking lot as possible. However, he wasn't definite … he also stated that the subject that he had seen pull Pam Ryan back into the ceramic shop had a leather wrist strap on his right wrist.

"When David was asked what he meant by nappy hair, he stated 'a short Afro, close.'"

As Seeman gave Smith a ride back to his house, he told her, 'You know, it wasn't a dress. It was that color top and black slacks or shorts.

"It should be noted in the hypnosis session he stated he had seen the female at the doorway wearing a white and red dress. The undersigned did not tell David that none of the victims had been wearing that type of clothing. When the undersigned had checked the pictures of the victims, she found that Pam Ryan had been wearing a red and white top with a pattern similar to flowers, which was what David had described, and black shorts. Evidently, David heard the scream and had seen Pam Ryan being pulled out of the doorway of the ceramic shop."

As for Smith's description of the helpless woman being pulled back inside the business, "It should be noted that David also stated that he did see facial hair."

Investigator Seeman asked if the killer had a mustache or beard or something else, "and David stated he thought it was a beard."

CHAPTER 15

CAN COLLECTOR

The hot beating sun on Aug. 20, 1983, prompted Peggy Karstens to stay inside her Joliet house until her phone rang around 12:30 p.m. One of her nosey girlfriends with a portable police scanner heard of a homicide at the ceramic shop along Cass Street.

From her house, Karstens could see any police activity at the pottery shop down the street, but she agreed to go outside and call her friend back. The Ridgewood neighborhood resident walked closer toward the ceramic shop but did not see anything unusual toward the back of the building.

As she walked past the car wash between Cass and Jackson Streets, Peggy Karstens noticed the door to the second wash bay remained closed. By late afternoon, helicopters circled over her older Joliet neighborhood. They belonged to Chicago's inquisitive television news stations, covering the latest big crime wave to strike Joliet.

Will County police issued a bulletin to the Chicago television stations asking that television viewers be on the lookout for a missing Chevy Blazer.

Meanwhile, Peggy Karstens and her husband left their house to visit with relatives. After they made it home a couple hours later, Mr. Karstens walked to the car wash to toss a bag of garbage into the large trash bin on the property. Sure enough, he stumbled across important information related to the ceramic shop murders.

Mr. Karstens spotted the red Blazer at the car wash. He was sure it was there for several hours. This was the vehicle Pamela Ryan drove to the ceramic shop, where she, Barbara Dunbar, Anna Ryan and store owner Marilyn Baers were slaughtered. The ceramic shop killer immediately made his getaway in the Ryan family's Blazer, only to have second thoughts about keeping the stolen auto. The mass murderer backed the Blazer into the car wash bay less than a block away, shut the door, left it there and managed to escape without anybody seeing him.

When Mr. Karstens visited the car wash around 3 p.m., he saw an older couple washing their car by hand. "He definitely remembered seeing the Blazer at 3 p.m. when he was talking to the older couple, when he had crossed in front of the car wash," police reports reflect.

**

During the early 1980s, the main entrance road leading into downtown Joliet was a haven for pimps, prostitutes, panhandlers and hard-core drug addicts. South Chicago Street was not a thoroughfare where most people wanted to visit. If you pulled up to the stop light, it was wise to have your doors locked and your eyes focused on the traffic lights.

Modern-day Joliet looks vastly different as the Skid Row buildings and businesses have been demolished as part of a revitalization effort to improve Joliet's southern gateway. In 1983, Jimmy's Pool Hall operated on South Chicago Street, and Obrie Trotter visited Jimmy's seven days a week. Trotter came here to deal drugs and partake in illegal gambling among other transgressions.

As a regular, Trotter knew practically everybody coming and going from the seedy pool hall on South Chicago Street.

The thirty-four-year-old Joliet man vividly remembered the events of Aug. 20, 1983, since that was the Saturday the four women were slain in the ceramic shop. Like everyone else, Trotter saw the TV helicopters hovering over Joliet. Inside the pool hall, people spoke about the ceramic shop slayings.

That afternoon, Milton Johnson had showed up at the pool hall, along with his uncle, Jerry "Babe Ruth" Mitchell, between 2:30 p.m. and 3 p.m.

"Where can a man get a gun?" Johnson asked Trotter.

Trotter told Milton Johnson to speak with Michael Dennison, who was in the pool hall that afternoon. Dennison was a Joliet resident with a long, criminal rap sheet, a convicted cocaine dealer. At any rate, Trotter informed Milton Johnson that Dennison had a reputation of being able to procure weapons for customers around Jimmy's.

In 1983, the twenty-four-year-old Dennison lived with his mother on Joliet's East Side at a house on Marion Street.

Inside the pool hall that ominous Saturday afternoon, Milton Johnson joined Trotter and others for a dice game. Johnson came loaded with cash, approximately $500, all $20 bills. But the dice game went horribly for Johnson. He lost at least $300 to Obrie Trotter.

Eventually, Johnson lost the rest of his money in dice games to other players. He left the pool hall empty-handed between 4:30 and 5 p.m.

At one point that afternoon, Milton Johnson mentioned he was working in Gary, Indiana, doing plumbing.

"Mr. Trotter remembers this due to the fact that Milton Johnson and Mr. Trotter walked out to the Currency Exchange parking lot where Mr. Trotter observed some type of plumbing supplies on the floor of a black pickup truck Milton Johnson was driving," Will County Sheriff's Investigator Charles Malinowski noted.

The afternoon of the ceramic murders marked the last time Johnson visited Jimmy's Pool Hall, according to Trotter. And he would know, since he visited Jimmy's seven days a week.

"Mr. Trotter describes Milton Johnson as a very quiet person and had only seen Milton Johnson in the pool hall on two to three prior occasions, and on those two to three other occasions Milton Johnson only had approximately $20 to $30 in his possession," a sheriff's report showed.

Two days after the ceramic shop slayings, major clues would surface along South Chicago Street, a short distance from Jimmy's Pool Hall.

**

Lee Washington lived in the 400 block of Joliet's South Chicago Street, and he collected aluminum cans for income. On Monday, Aug. 22, the fifty-three-year-old walked along the shallow Hickory Creek and discovered a brown wallet containing identification plus a pair of sunglasses.

Realizing this was something out of the ordinary, Washington approached the I-80 Enterprises business along Patterson Road. When a company worker told Washington they would call the sheriff's department about the mysterious property, Washington left the area.

Malinowski drove to Patterson Road to speak with the employees of I-80 Enterprises. Malinowski learned that the aluminum can collector located a large box with several wallets and purses, and the man thought they might be important. Eventually, Malinowski located the can collector near Patterson Road and South Joliet Street. Washington showed the deputy where he found the items in the Hickory Creek, which was only four inches deep.

Washington pointed to a cardboard box surrounded by purses and several pieces of paper floating in the water. He then approached the north side of the bridge and handed the deputy a brown wallet and a pair of sunglasses he had retrieved from the water using a long stick.

Malinowski opened the wallet saw the name Pamela Ryan on a plastic credit card. Realizing this was crucial evidence connected to the ceramic shop murders, the Will County Sheriff's Department investigation unit was notified of the find. Sgt. Tom Hernandez and an evidence technician took possession of the items recovered from the Hickory Creek.

The cardboard box included three purses with personal effects, plus several miscellaneous papers. Sheriff's deputies waded in the water covering about one hundred yards of territory in the Hickory Creek in hopes of finding additional clues unmasking the killer's identity.

The moneyless purses belonged to murder victims Barbara Dunbar, Pamela Ryan and Marilyn Baers. Still, the purses presented the Will County Sheriff's Office with valuable insight into the mind of the maniac still wandering the streets of Joliet.

"We have to assume the motive was robbery anytime we find money or wallets are taken," Will County Sheriff's Chief Deputy Ted Kelly told local reporters. "However, we still need to find out what was in the purses before they were taken."

Turns out, Anna Ryan's purse was left behind at the pottery store. The shop's cash box, which contained a small amount of currency, went untouched as well. "But both were in places where they either were hidden or could have been overlooked by someone in a hurry," the chief sheriff's deputy explained.

Common threads were developing in Will County's multiple murder investigations.

At the Homer Township massacre, wallets and purses were taken from the victims as were the guns of the two auxiliary officers. The empty purses and wallets were tossed from a moving vehicle along Joliet's I-80, landing along the banks of the Du Page River.

At Joliet's pottery shop, the raging killer maimed and murdered four defenseless women, stealing three of their purses in the process.

Many serial killers develop a signature, perhaps using the same ligature or strangling method, but the elusive Joliet killer was unpredictable.

One of the only recurring traits was that his murders always occurred on weekends, never during the workweek.

Will County's weekend killer always carried a loaded gun and a long, sharp cutting instrument. He used both weapons interchangeably. For instance, after fatally shooting the sleeping teenager inside the car parked along I-55, a knife was plunged into the kidnapped girlfriend's chest a couple of hours later.

At the ceramic shop murders, the four women were stabbed to death, but seventy-five-year-old Anna Ryan also was shot through her neck.

Knives function as the silent killer and are a more torturous murdering machine. While a gun can bring instantaneous death, thrusting a knife through someone's vital organs can bring enormous agony for the inflicted.

Stabbings can bring enormous delight to the wicked warrior wielding the weapon. He can hover over his helpless victim, gaze into their faces as they struggle, gasp for air, float in and out of consciousness before losing oxygen and dying.

With no immediate arrests on the horizon, the people of Joliet were aghast that such a demented and heartless creature lived among them; someone who showed no signs of relenting on his summer killing spree.

**

On the same day, the aluminum can collector found the purses of the ceramic shop victims, a crowd of three hundred fifty packed into the St. Andrew the Apostle Catholic Church in Romeoville to remember Will County Auxiliary Deputy Denis Foley.

Sixty police cars participated in the motorcade as did a semitrailer and two trucks from the Consolidated Freightways in Chicago where Foley was employed for twenty-five years. Foley died in his Joliet hospital bed one month after the Homer Township massacre left four others dead at the scene. Foley's funeral included a large police honor guard and several officers played bagpipes. During the gravesite service, five planes flew out of the Lewis University Airport in Romeoville, and one of the planes left the formation to symbolize a missing pilot.

The four remaining planes returned for a second flyover at the cemetery.

Father Donald Kenny, the former pastor of St. Andrew, returned to his old parish to preside over Foley's funeral mass. Just a year before, the Diocese of Joliet Catholic priest delivered the eulogy when Foley's wife died.

"This is a time of sorrow, but also a time of hope," the priest told mourners. "We share a kind of numbness and disbelief. And we want to say, 'Why?'"

One Joliet man attending the funeral told the newspaper that Foley's death left him feeling mortal.

"I'm a little more frightened than I was before," admitted Tim Schultz. "It makes you wonder when you go out at night. Denis senior was a real nice guy, real generous. How could it have happened to him?"

CHAPTER 16

FIGHTING BACK

In 1983, there was no such thing as Facebook, social media or cell phones to stay connected. Television, local news radio and hometown newspapers kept people informed.

All three were one-way platforms. In other words, the journalists kept you informed, but you didn't have a voice in the process, except in limited circumstances allotted by the local radio stations that created small windows of time for listeners to call and discuss the news of the day. The only way to have your voice heard in the local newspaper was with a pen, an envelope and a stamp: writing a letter to the editor. Even then, the top editors decided whose letter got published in the newspaper and whose letter got pitched in the waste basket.

Around Joliet, *The Herald-News* remained the most trusted source for everyone's news. Daily circulation topped 50,000 subscribers. In most Joliet neighborhoods, there was strong reader penetration. In many parts of the city, adolescent children, often with the support of their helpful parents, delivered the daily newspaper in their respective neighborhoods.

Some older residents requested that their paper carrier put their newspaper inside the front porch. Others wanted the paper left between their screen door and front door. Some residents put special boxes on their porch or plastic tubes at the end of their driveways. A number of paid subscribers preferred the newspaper be left in their mailbox.

On Joliet's east side, between Richards and Gardner Streets, was an older ethnic neighborhood mostly of Italians. The subdivision consisted of more than one hundred homes. The white-sided house this author grew up in along the 1000 block of Gardner Street was built in 1936. The house his grandparents built, two streets over in the same subdivision, was erected in 1951.

There was a sharp elevation along Gardner Street as a long row of houses faced Nowell Park, a large outdoor recreation area owned by the Joliet Park District. Nowell Park had an outdoor swimming pool, an open pavilion, tennis courts, softball fields, plenty of playground equipment including slides, swings and climbing bars.

Nowell Park had some of Joliet's oldest, biggest trees. Just up the hill from Nowell Park was an array of established houses along Mills Road, plus a grocery store, a gas station and a banquet hall. Although the A & P grocery store closed in 1982, Ed Garland's full-service Mobil gas station was still going strong. The Garland family cleaned your windows as they filled your car with gasoline.

Sadly, it seemed as if the 1983 summer murder spree had touched every corner of Joliet. Ed Garland's daughter Pamela (Garland) Ryan was one of the four women butchered inside the ceramic shop.

Less than a week later, another unconscionable crime shook Joliet. This time, it was a two-minute walk from Garland's Mobil station.

**

On Aug. 26, 1983, a father helping deliver his teenager's daily newspapers stopped in his tracks when he reached the white, two-story house at 207 Mills Road.

The previous day's newspaper remained inside the homeowner's front porch delivery box. The woman's front door was ajar.

When the newspaper carrier called for the homeowner, no one answered. The man stopped in his tracks and summoned a neighbor. When the two adults stepped inside, they found the body of eighty-two-year-old Mary Mae Johnson in her living room chair about ten feet from her front door. The Will County Sheriff's Office determined that the widow was killed the previous afternoon.

"This was a brutal death, totally senseless," Will County Coroner Robert Tezak told reporters. "At this point I am not sure what kind of object was used to beat the victim, but it was a blunt object."

Johnson tried to fight off her attacker. Her intruder stabbed her in the head and beat her repeatedly with a large object, Tezak revealed.

Johnson's homicide on Mills Road brought the total of unsolved murders throughout Will County to seventeen since June 25. A couple of those slayings were believed to be gang-affiliated and drug-related, but not the vast majority.

When one reporter asked if Johnson's homicide could be connected to the other recent slayings, Tezak answered: "I am not saying no. I can't remember this many homicides in this short a period of time in my eight years as coroner and ten years as deputy coroner," explained Tezak, whose rising political career as a Will County Republican would implode a few short years down the road in one of Will County's most prolific political scandals.

Tezak would plead guilty in an arson-for-profit scheme involving a Crest Hill bowling alley fire from 1987. Another arson charge, involving a 1987 fire at a downtown Joliet building, was dropped as part of his plea deal with the federal government.

Because the elderly widow's murder on Mills Road occurred outside Joliet's city limits, it called for yet another Will County's Sheriff's Department murder investigation.

Given how the crime scene was brutal, it made sense for police to theorize that the same person who slaughtered the ceramic shop women only five days earlier might be the same culprit.

On the other hand, the widow's murder deviated from the pattern. Practically all the previous killings involved multiple victims and always happened on weekends. Mary Mae Johnson was beaten to death with an object on a Thursday. All the other victims were fatally stabbed and shot.

Additionally, Johnson's attacker sneaked into her house in southeast Joliet Township through a window.

"We never saw a light in the house. She always kept the blinds down and the doors closed. But we never saw much of her," her neighbors told the newspaper.

Mary Mae Johnson was survived by one son, who lived downstate in Pekin, six grandchildren and three great-grandchildren. Her husband Harry had died seven years earlier, in 1976. She had lived in Joliet her entire life and mostly kept to herself.

One of her neighbors recalled a conversation he had with Johnson several months beforehand. He inquired about storing his camper on her property since she had a large backyard.

"She was agreeable and told me it would not cost a cent when I mentioned a charge," Tyler Smith recounted. "When we got ready to move the camper to her yard, I tried to contact her but without success. We even tried telephoning her, but without results. Finally, I gave up and left the camper in my driveway."

The brutal and baffling killing of Mary Mae Johnson meant the dark cloud of evil hovering over Joliet and Will County was spreading like a lethal vapor.

Whether the same killer perpetrated all these crimes was a question the Will County police needed to address. Even if these crimes were the work of multiple killers that would not minimize the sheer viciousness perpetrated against Johnson, a frail woman in her eighties, who was mostly homebound as she lived out her golden years.

The summer of 1983 was unlike any other for Joliet. It was terribly hot and dangerous. Older women weren't safe in their homes. Women of all ages weren't safe at the pottery shop. Romantic couples weren't safe sharing affection in a secluded place to park after dark.

Now, a defenseless elderly widow was the latest Joliet resident hauled away in a body bag. She had found joy from life's simple pleasures, such as reading her daily newspaper, as she lived all alone with no immediate family in the area to look after her.

**

Mary Mae Johnson's barbaric beating death became the tipping point for Joliet. The community would not take any more brutality without fighting back.

None of these victims had it coming. They were business owners, policemen, married mothers, hair stylists, auto shop repairmen, great-grandmothers, printing card factory workers and high school sweethearts who planned to marry.

Cathy (Long) Norwood's boss with Regis Hairstylists in Bolingbrook remembered the twenty-five-year-old Homer Township massacre victim as "a very assertive person who knew where she was going. She had a very pleasing way about her. As a hair stylist, she had the potential to become a great one. She had the desire to learn everything about the business. She built up a clientele very fast, and for her it was not just a job. She worked to do something good for everyone else."

After the slaying of Will County auxiliary officer Steven Mayer, his summer softball team, The Loads, wore black armbands in a show of solidarity. Mayer's parents sat in the bleachers at the Joliet Park District softball game dedicated to their son.

Edward Mayer, a high-ranking sergeant at the Will County Sheriff's Department, told the Joliet newspaper that his son's murder left him rethinking whether his son made the right career choice.

"Maybe my wife is not bitter, but I am," he remarked. "Something is wrong with the criminal justice system. The whole thing stinks. Not just because Steve was killed, but because of this early release program.

"It wasn't that many years ago that we could go to bed with the doors unlocked," Mayer was quoted by the paper. "It's just been bad the last fifteen years."

The non-stop murders led to some high-profile events that were good and bad for Joliet.

On the bad side, the city gained infamy from *The National Inquirer*, the salacious and sensational tabloid known for its outlandish, shocker headlines about people giving birth to aliens or the latest Elvis Presley sightings. The supermarket tabloid made sure its unflattering article about Joliet had a doozy of a headline to capture the attention of everyone standing in line at their local grocery counter.

The National Enquirer branded Joliet as "Terror Town U.S.A."

Sure, *The National Enquirer* was regarded by many as a national laughingstock. But there was no denying the fact that during the early 1980s, before the Internet, the salacious supermarket tabloid sold hundreds of thousands of copies of its weekly rag.

That meant people in Seattle, Dallas and Boston, people who had no institutional knowledge of Joliet, Illinois, were left with the indelible impression that this mid-sized Midwestern city was the armpit of society, one of the worst places on the face of the planet.

Joliet's string of summer murders had indeed tarnished the city's image. Now, a national publication better known for writing outrageous headlines about two-headed extraterrestrials being hidden inside the White House was fanning the flames and hyping the hysteria of Joliet's endless random violence.

Joliet's business leaders, politicians, and even the local press, fumed at the unwanted national publicity.

But everyone stayed determined, bound to make a difference, desiring to make Joliet a better place. Local leaders wanted their city viewed by outsiders as a caring community, a proactive community.

The Mills Road murder of Mary Mae Johnson struck a nerve. Joliet would choose to fight back and use the news media like a cannonball, to blast its message to the masses, far and wide.

"We want the world to know we have a good area, and we will fight to keep the crime element out," remarked Rudy Mahalik, director of Will County's Crime Stoppers program.

The Joliet Herald-News published a front-page headline that read, "Rally Aimed At Stopping Crime."

Several big-name local politicians helped organize the rally. Will County State's Attorney Ed Petka, a Republican from Plainfield, would be the event's main speaker. Other notable attendees included Will County Sheriff John Shelley, a Republican from Joliet; State Representative Leroy Van Duyne, a Democrat from Joliet; and two future Republican congressmen: Jack Davis of New Lenox; and Dennis Hastert of Yorkville.

Meanwhile, Joliet's daily newspaper donated two full pages of free advertisement space to promote a new overly ambitious $100,000 Crime Stoppers reward.

The newspaper urged readers to attend the upcoming rally in downtown Joliet at the Renaissance Center or to make a donation to Crime Stoppers, regardless of amount.

"News of the county murders has been splashed across the nation and abroad," Joliet's newspaper declared. "The newsroom at *The Herald-News* has received inquiries from media throughout the world. Now is the time to show everyone we have a good community. Tuesday's rally should receive lots of publicity from newspapers, radio and television. Be there and show everyone we are standing up to crime and fighting back."

The late August rally drew between six hundred and eight hundred people, according to the newspaper. This was still an impressive feat considering the event took place in downtown Joliet on a Tuesday afternoon. A total of $2,600 in cash donations was collected for Crime Stoppers of Will County. Several businessmen and other dignitaries made large donations of their own, the press reported, including $5,000 from Joliet's Silver Cross Hospital, $5,000 from *The Herald-News* plus $3,500 in free advertisement space to promote the upcoming rally.

Donations of $1,000 came from Lindblad Construction, the Kiwanis Club as well as Will County politician Robert Tezak and Tezak's business, International Games.

The director of Crime Stoppers said that at least $40,000 in pledges and contributions resulted from Joliet's generous spirit.

The rally, if nothing else, gave Joliet citizens confidence. It boosted their psyche; it left them energized, empowered. True, the crazed murderer – or murderers – still lurked at large, but the city had taken a stand. Its residents, police force and politicians were watchful and on guard. Terror Town, USA, was not how they wanted Joliet portrayed across the globe.

Yet, reality and perception are often intertwined. Even though Joliet resisted the Terror Town mantra, many out-of-town journalists embraced the scary label. Out-of-state journalists being asked to write lurid and sensational crime stories about Joliet often had no concept of the city. None of that mattered, what mattered was that *The National Enquirer* had thrown a dart at the board, and it landed on Joliet, Illinois. Other news media outlets scrambled and scurried, thinking they could outperform a lowly grocery store tabloid that most reputable journalists mocked and despised.

As the summer of 1983 wound down, John Whiteside, the respected columnist for *The Herald-News,* offered the following commentary in a piece headlined, "Four Murders Latest in Shocking Violence Trend."

"Has life become so cheap that four persons die for the few dollars they might have in their pockets?" Whiteside asked his readers. "Is this violence a sign of more to come?"

As the most powerful voice in Will County during the 1980s, *The Herald-News* urged subscribers to help the Will County Sheriff's Department do their job. "We support police efforts to find the killers," the newspaper announced. "We promise to do all we can to alert the public to information about the suspects. We ask that people remain calm and cooperate with the police."

The newspaper editorial reminded citizens that all telephone calls made to the Crime Stoppers of Will County remained anonymous. "We, along with police, are determined to see these killers caught and prosecuted fully. There must be punishment for these senseless killings," the newspaper vowed.

From late June until late August, the Joliet area's homicide count in 1983 was unimaginable. The unwanted attention stirred by *The National Enquirer* sparked even more controversy for Joliet.

Fifty out-of-state Guardian Angels arrived in downtown Joliet to mobilize citizen foot patrols in wake of the string of seventeen unsolved summer murders.

Sure enough, tensions intensified and Joliet drew even more national publicity. The Sept. 2, 1983, headline in *The New York Times* declared, "Guardian Angels in Joliet Arrested For Camping."

CHAPTER 17

GUARDIAN ANGELS

Joliet's area remained under enormous duress as the maddening summer heat gave way to autumn. Fatigued police and befuddled politicians began running out of ways to reassure an already alarmed public.

In an era when the daily newspaper ruled the land and competition was fierce, there was a mad scramble to stay ahead of the latest news in the Will County murder saga.

The combination of community paranoia and law enforcement overzealousness contributed to the creation of several newspaper articles that, in retrospect, probably should not have been written in the first place. On the other hand, these articles were a sign of the times, and times were scary for Joliet in 1983.

Four days after the ceramic shop killings, a front-page headline featured a police sketch of a skinny white man described as twenty-four or twenty-five, wearing a baseball cap and having blonde hair past his ears. Will County police said the young man was wanted for questioning after being seen on East Washington Street about 11:15 a.m., driving an old brown clunker as he looked "extremely spaced out."

Although the article didn't connect the dots, the police sketch came as a result of the two waitresses who worked at Home Cut Donuts. Will County would spend dozens of hours investigating the mysterious character that walked into Home Cut Donuts with what the waitresses described as dried blood on his arms and face.

After an exhaustive effort, sheriff's investigators ultimately cleared the man in connection with the ceramic slayings. He and his brother had been busy painting a large house on the Saturday morning of the ceramic shop murders. The bloodlike substance the waitresses thought they saw on his hands and face turned out to be red paint, authorities determined.

Over the course of many weeks, more than a dozen viable murder suspects emerged. All were investigated thoroughly by Will County police. If some of their answers showed deception, they were interviewed again and given a second lie-detector test.

David Baers, son of murder victim Marilyn Baers, was one of the suspects who answered the following polygraph test prepared by Illinois State Police:

"Were you in the ceramic shop on Cass Street when those four women were stabbed?"

"On August 20, 1983, did you stab any of those four women?"

"Do you know for sure who stabbed those four women?"

Baers answered each question with a convincing "No."

Illinois State Police subsequently issued a report advising the Will County State's Attorney's Office, "There were no indications of deception on the suspect's polygraph records."

Another person hauled in for further questioning was David Smith, the bicyclist who rode past the ceramic shop and heard screaming. Smith, it turned out, hung around with a number of dubious characters in 1983, and some of them speculated Smith was the ceramic shop killer.

One woman told sheriff's police "this David Smith subject is having continuous nightmares and keeps hearing screaming and that he is unable to get the sound of screams out of his head and that he rationalizes that if he possibly kills again that that would get rid of the screams."

Sheriff's deputies were told "that this David Smith is also heavy into drugs and is hanging around with a (man) who helped David Smith with the Cass Street homicides."

The tipster told police she feared retribution if Smith were ever picked up for the murders and "that possibly David Smith would come and do great bodily harm to the entire family."

At the advice of sheriff's investigator Dianne Seeman, state police made Smith undergo a polygraph exam. He reiterated his previous statement, that he and Tim O'Donahue rode their bicycles to Tonkovich's Auto Body to make a down payment on a 1968 Cutlass Supreme Oldsmobile. About two weeks after the homicides, Smith said one of his friends, Todd Lewandowski, claimed he found a knife in the Mt. Olivet Cemetery across the street from the ceramic shop near the Jesus Christ statue. Lewandowski did not want to turn the knife over to the authorities because he and Will County police did not get along. Smith agreed to bring the knife to police in the event it was involved in the ceramic shop killings.

The following questions and answers came during Smith's lie-detector test:

"Do you know for sure if the knife you turned in to the police was used to kill the four women in the ceramic shop?"

"No."

"Did you cause the death of any of those four women in the ceramic shop?"

"No."

"Do you know who killed the four women in the ceramic shop on August 20, 1983?"

"No."

"Did Todd Lewandowski tell you he found the knife stuck in the ground by a Jesus Christ statue?"

"Yes."

"Are you withholding any information regarding the death of the four women?"

"No."

The state police examiner advised the State's Attorney not to pursue Smith as a murder suspect moving forward.

"It is the opinion of the examiner based on the suspect's polygraph records that he is telling the truth when he answers the above listed questions."

After Smith was dropped from the suspect list, Todd Lewandowski was questioned in connection with the killings. Police were baffled about this mysterious knife Lewandowski claimed he found in the cemetery across the road from the mass murders.

"Mr. Lewandowski ... stated that a David Smith came over to his house and told his dad that a shiny-bladed knife was used to kill the four ladies in the ceramic shop. The suspect stated that he found the knife stuck in the ground near a Jesus Christ statue in the cemetery across the street from the ceramic shop and that this was about two weeks after the stabbing," the polygraph examiner wrote.

During his lie-detector test, Lewandowski answered "No" to the following police questions:

"Did you cause the death of any of those four women in the ceramic shop?"

"Do you know who killed those four women in the ceramic shop on August 20, 1983?"

"Were you present when those four women were killed in the ceramic shop on August 20, 1983?

On those three specific questions, the examiner deemed his answers truthful.

The final two questions were as follows:

"Did you find the knife that you gave to David Smith by a statue of Jesus Christ in the cemetery?"

"Have you made any false statements to the police regarding this case in any way?"

For the final two questions, Smith answered yes to the first one and no to the second.

Lewandowski lied on the last two questions.

The examiner confronted the young man and told him he had flunked the exam based on his final pair of responses.

"The suspect at this time stated that he had not been telling the truth regarding the knife and that in fact he did steal the knife from a Fred Haywood's house in Joliet," police reports reflect.

A new set of questions were drawn up. This time, Lewandowski's answers were deemed truthful.

After careful examination, police concluded the mysterious knife was not used in the ceramic shop killings. Lewandowski, who had a solid alibi to account for his whereabouts, was later cleared as a suspect.

At least a dozen young men, mostly in their twenties, were questioned and asked to furnish their fingerprints in connection with the Cass Street murders. One by one, they were eliminated as suspects. None of their fingerprints matched the ones found at the murder scene or the fingerprints lifted from Pam Ryan's Blazer that the killer drove to the car wash.

**

Following the I-55 killing near Wilmington, Illinois, police released a different sketch, one for a medium to heavy set Black man in his mid-twenties said to be about six foot.

Not surprisingly, the composite left the police bombarded with a sea of tips that proved to be useless. For instance, the sighting of a man walking along the frontage road for I-55 near Wilmington left one local woman riding a bicycle so unnerved she called the police. She told police she thought the man was concealing a gun underneath his jacket.

Police learned the man was a highway transient who went to a nearby farm asking the owners for food and water. The farmers told him he could use their garden hose and that's it. The farmers were positive the wandering stranger did not mean any harm nor did he have a gun tucked inside the jacket he carried over his shoulder.

Meanwhile, a semi-truck driver notified police he saw a man with a gun hiding under an overpass bridge off I-55. The trucker's tip prompted a pack of squad cars to zip twenty-five miles south of Joliet, toward the exit for Braceville. The tip, however, proved worthless.

On another occasion, well-intentioned Will County deputies drew their guns and ordered an out-of-state man to get out of his camper truck with his hands up along U.S. Route 30 in Plainfield. However, the deputies offered the man an apology after realizing he was not their I-55 murder suspect. The deputies told him he was the second person they had pulled over that day, thinking he might be the elusive weekend murderer.

By late summer, *The Herald-News* published an article headlined, "Manhunt Yields No Leads To Murders."

"Paranoia over the slayings also is evident in the restaurants and shopping malls of Joliet. Often, conversations turn to fears over the murders," the newspaper article read.

As thousands of newspaper subscribers were hungry for more information, some journalists got the green light from their editors to pursue risky story angles. Newsrooms tried to make sense of the senseless killings, notably the massacre in Homer Township.

A week after the Homer Township massacre, *The Herald-News* produced an article suggesting the killer targeted Richard "Dewey" Paulin, the young man from Lemont who drove a red Chevette.

At the time he was gunned down in his car along the lonely unlit road, Paulin was waiting to stand trial on felony heroin charges, the newspaper unearthed. Paulin's codefendant drew a seven-year prison sentence after pleading guilty. However, one month before Paulin's slaying, his defense lawyer convinced a Will County judge to issue another continuance, delaying the Lemont man's jury trial until mid-September 1983. The defense lawyer who sought the trial delay suggested Paulin injured his back at his job as a metal refinisher, and needed to undergo back surgery.

Once September came around, there was no shortage of news stories for ambitious local journalists to chase. New York City's Guardian Angels arrived in downtown Joliet. The Guardian Angels wanted to make sure everybody in Joliet and around the globe knew about their presence.

Four years earlier, in 1979, twenty-three-year-old Curtis Sliwa founded the Guardian Angels after he was a night manager at a McDonald's fast-food restaurant in the Bronx and grew tired of the muggings and violence on New York's subways. The Guardian Angels became a source of controversy as some viewed them as vigilantes and a para-police group.

During a 2016 interview, Curtis Sliwa reflected on the emergence of the Guardian Angels as a major force in New York. He used a vehicle painted with a mural that became known as the Avalanche van.

"And what we did in the middle of the crack cocaine epidemic is we would do drug raids, and I'd load up forty Guardian Angels in that van, and we would hit the crack houses, and we would rob crack dealers in front of everybody. Forty of us would come bum rushing out, slamming and jamming people, we'd steal their money, and then we would bring it to the local soup kitchen, which was run by a church, and then we would destroy the drugs right out in the streets, and people thought that was crazy."

While some locals welcomed the Guardian Angels walking the streets and neighborhoods of Joliet, local politicians and many of the police detested their presence.

Tensions flared and the Guardian Angels quickly made international headlines when *The New York Times* and the

United Press International news wire service published articles about five Guardian Angels being arrested for pitching tents on the lawn of the Will County Courthouse. The five Guardian Angels were charged with disorderly conduct, criminal trespass, resisting arrest and obstructing a police officer.

The UPI article began: "Five Guardian Angels, members of a volunteer patrol who traveled to Will County to ease citizens' fears over seventeen grisly summer slayings were jailed today on charges of disorderly conduct and trespassing."

One of the five arrested was Lisa Sliwa, the wife of Guardian Angels' founder, Curtis Sliwa. UPI reported that fifty Guardian Angels arrived in Joliet in recent days, and they came at the urging of residents of Joliet. Most of the Guardian Angels came from Chicago, Milwaukee, Gary, Evanston and Hammond, Indiana.

The Will County Sheriff's Office arrested the five Guardian Angels after they refused to take down their camp they had set up on the courthouse lawn.

"They were sleeping on the lawn of the county building, sleeping on the war monument," one of the sheriff's lieutenants remarked at the time. "Tonight, we asked them five different times to take the tents down and not sleep on our statue. We don't appreciate it when they want to put tents up, litter our lawns and sleep on our war monuments."

In September 1983, Sliwa's wife and four other jailed Guardian Angels were charged in Joliet with misdemeanor crimes and paraded in front of a Will County judge who set their bail at $100 each.

The five arrests drew outrage within the Guardian Angels organization. UPI reported that Curtis Sliwa was flying into

Chicago and another forty Guardian Angels from New York, Detroit and St. Louis were being sent to Joliet.

A man who held the title of National Troubleshooter for the Guardian Angels had a different perspective. He said the local police were harassing the Guardian Angels as they signed up Joliet volunteers.

"When you speak the truth in a little hick town like Joliet, mention the incompetency of the police department in a public forum, they find the time to find superficial charges to arrest four patrol leaders and Mrs. Sliwa," he told UPI.

The troubleshooter said the Guardian Angels were busy holding a meeting when sheriff's deputies came by and started kicking the stakes out of their tents and began to take apart their tents.

Many around Joliet did not welcome the Guardian Angels for a variety of reasons.

During their extended stay in Joliet, the Guardian Angels had a permit to conduct an open assembly on the city's streets. Guardian Angels took turns patrolling downtown Joliet. And once word of the Guardian Angels presence in Joliet became known, a number of Joliet teenagers began inquiring about how they could join. Several residents brought food and offered shelter in their private homes as a token of appreciation for their efforts to make Joliet safer.

"We're not here for the authorities or the police. We're here for the people," the wife of the founder of the Guardian Angels told reporters. "Whether or not we save anyone or deter a murder is not important. People from the whole county come to downtown Joliet. The important thing is people will feel better, safer, knowing we're here.

"Part of it is symbolic. Part of it is practical, too. We're dealing with psychological terror."

PHOTOS

A bronze statue of a life-like Robert Pilcher greets visitors to the monstrous Joliet nature center that bears his name. The Pilcher Arboretum was dedicated July 31, 1920. Today, it's called Pilcher Park.

On Feb. 15, 1970, a young man wielding a shotgun climbed into a car, raping and brutally torturing a teenage girl who went to Pilcher Park with her boyfriend after spending the day at the Brookfield Zoo.

U.S. Route 6 in Joliet where a gunman pulled alongside Theresa McKeen, shattering her window as she drove home from the EJ & E railroad yard.

Two older sisters who lived along Rosalind Street in rural Joliet became the first murder victims during Joliet's summer of terror in 1983.

The killings on Rosalind Street began when someone broke into Zita Blum's house. Although her blood was on found on the walls, her body was found inside the burning bedroom of her sister Honora Lahmann's house next door.

*Just weeks after getting married, Will County Sheriff's
auxiliary deputy Steven Mayer was gunned down during
a police ambush in rural Will County, Illinois. Mayer was
only twenty-two years old.*

*Around 5:30 a.m., Ray Tusek was driving along Route 53
heading to his favorite fishing spot when he thought he saw
a human hand in the grassy median. A teenage girl was
fighting to stay alive.*

Rookie Illinois State Police Trooper Doug Brown approached the gold Plymouth along the shoulder of Interstate 55 south of Joliet with his gun drawn.

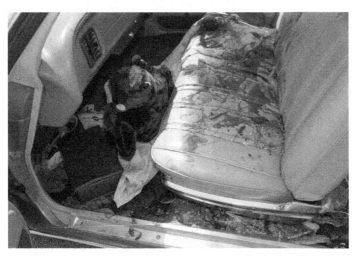

A Tasmanian Devil stuffed animal found in the car of murder victim Tony Hackett would become an enormous clue in the I-55 killing south of Joliet.

Marilyn Baers owned the ceramic shop along Joliet's busy Route 30. In 1983, she and three customers were slaughtered by a madman wielding a knife.

David Smith was riding his bicycle past the ceramic shop on Route 30 when he heard a muffled scream from one of the women being stabbed inside.

The ceramic shop killer climbed inside Pamela Ryan's red Chevy Blazer and drove her vehicle to a car wash along Route 30 where he left it.

Joliet resident Milton Johnson lived with his parents in this brick house at 1215 Luther Avenue, in the Forest Park Neighborhood Area.

Milton Johnson served out his 1970 Pilcher Park rape sentence at the Pontiac Correctional Center in Pontiac, Illinois.

The rape of Tonya Little is believed to have happened on the outskirts of the sprawling Exxon-Mobil Joliet Refinery along Interstate 55.

The 1977 Chevy Scottsdale truck driven by Milton Johnson during Joliet's summer of terror was actually owned by his stepfather, Sam Myers.

While driving south of Joliet along Route 53, motorist Ray Tusek thought he spotted an arm in the grassy median so he went back to check it out.

The sales receipt for the Tasmanian Devil stuffed animal purchased at Great America by murder victim Tony Hackett was recovered by police from the truck driven by Milton Johnson during his summer of terror.

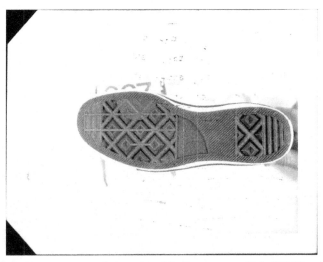

Shoe impressions from size 11 Converse ALL-STAR gym shoes were found by police at multiple murder scenes during Joliet's summer of terror.

Four women inside Joliet's Greenware by Merry ceramics were all fatally stabbed just before noon on Saturday, Aug. 20, 1983.

Joliet ceramic shop owner Marilyn Baers was forty-six when she was fatally stabbed about a dozen times inside her business. She is buried at Joliet's Elmhurst Cemetery on East Washington Street.

Joliet serial killer Milton Johnson turned 71 years old in May 2021. Authorities believe he committed 14 homicides during the summer of 1983.

PART 2

CHAPTER 18

TRUCK

After more than six hundred people attended the downtown Joliet prayer vigil seeking God's help to bring the psychopathic killer to justice, the investigation began to heat up.

On Sept. 4, 1983, *The New York Times* published a short news story headlined, "Man, 51, Arrested In Joliet Area Slaying." Donald Lego, a handyman, was charged with first-degree murder in connection with the Mills Road killing of Mary Mae Johnson, the eighty-two-year-old widow. She was bludgeoned and stabbed. Eyewitnesses saw Lego's truck parked at the widow's house around the time of her weekday killing.

Will County Sheriff's police concluded that her killing was not connected to any of the remaining unsolved murders across Joliet.

Lego, the evidence showed, broke one of Mary Mae Johnson's basement windows and a window well to gain access to her house. The elderly woman kept large sums of money in her house and after her killing, her purse and a doctor's bag went missing, prosecutors revealed. Lego used the doctor's bag to hide his blood-stained clothes from the killing, but he left his shirt behind underneath a pillow. Lego changed clothes in her house using a shirt and trousers belonging to the widow's late husband. Lego's fingerprints were also found at the crime scene.

But perhaps the most damning physical evidence was an envelope he dropped in her house. The envelope with Lego's name and address contained photographs of Lego's family. Lego had done roofing work for Mary Mae Johnson in the past, and she had paid him several thousand dollars cash for that work.

When Lego was a teenager in the late 1940s, he was convicted of an armed robbery in Missouri. Six years later, in the 1950s, he was convicted in Iowa of robbery and jail break.

In 1984, Lego was convicted of first-degree murder at a Will County trial where the Joliet handyman served as his own lawyer. In 2010, *The Chicago Tribune* reported that Lego remained mentally unfit to stand a second trial after his initial murder conviction was overturned in 1995 by the Illinois Supreme Court. The court found that Lego suffered from organic brain syndrome making Lego incapable of making rational decisions as his own lawyer during his first murder trial, Chicago's newspaper noted. But because Lego remained a danger to society, he was transferred from the state's prison system to the care and custody of the Illinois Department of Health where he remained in in-patient hospitalization decades after his initial murder trial took place in Joliet. Lego died in 2011, Will County court records show.

During the fall of 1983, Joliet's East Side residents were pleased with the news of Lego's arrest for the senseless slaying of the eighty-two-year-old widow who lived alone on Mills Road.

However, the Will County Sheriff's Office realized that much more work remained as investigators hoped to identify the killer responsible for the slew of summertime murders that remained unsolved near Joliet.

**

By mid-September, Illinois State Police pulled up to an older two-story in Joliet's Forest Park Neighborhood. Sam and Dolly Myers, a middle-aged couple, owned the house at 1215 Luther Ave. When police approached the door, they encountered Dolly Myers' son, Milton Johnson, age thirty-three.

Johnson had been granted parole from the Illinois Department of Corrections six months earlier. He spent the previous thirteen years locked away from society housed at the Pontiac Correctional Center after drawing a prison term of twenty-five to thirty-five years for committing the Feb. 15, 1970, torture rape at Joliet's Pilcher Park.

In 1983, convicted sex offender registries did not exist. Consequently, even the best and brightest detectives at the Joliet Police Department and the Will County Sheriff's Department were unaware that Illinois prison bureaucrats had let Johnson pack his bags and return to his hometown of Joliet in March of 1983.

But after three consecutive months of nonstop random murders, Illinois State Police investigators John Beck and Randy Kucaba arrived at Milton Johnson's house on Sept. 12. They asked about the black pickup parked out front. "I asked him if he ever had drove a pickup truck, and he said he'd driven the one outside often," Illinois State Police Investigator John Beck recalled. Johnson's stepfather owned the Chevy Scottsdale truck, a 1977 model that bore license plates 889930B.

During the brief interview on Luther Avenue, the two investigators made note of Johnson's features. He was five-foot-nine, 220 lbs., with a stocky, muscular build. Johnson told the police he had had the goatee the past thirteen years.

Beck and Kucaba asked Johnson about the recent string of Will County murders and "Johnson stated that the only information that he knew of was that information given out over the news."

During the face-to-face interview on Johnson's property, the state police asked if he knew of anybody who might be involved in the unsolved killings. He did not know of anyone, he responded. From there, the state police went on their way. They did not have a search warrant, and they didn't come armed with an arrest warrant.

Still, their presence at the brick house on Luther Avenue had a profound effect on the multiple murder investigation and Milton Johnson. From that point forward, the trail of terror abruptly ended.

Another noteworthy event transpired after the Illinois State Police left that day. Sam Myers' truck, the one Milton Johnson admitted he drove often, disappeared from plain sight.

The black truck would no longer be visible on Joliet's streets and roads as police stepped up patrols and beefed up efforts to identify the serial killer.

Sam Myers convinced a friend, Ernest Ulmer, to hide the six-year-old truck on the friend's property on Dellwood Avenue, about a mile and a half away. At the time, the truck did not have any major engine or transmission problems, nothing that made the truck inoperable.

That did not matter. What mattered most was that in the spur of the moment, Sam Myers' stepson was now being questioned in connection with the summer slayings. Sam

Myers did not want this recently paroled stepson to emerge as the prime suspect for these killings.

By the fall of 1983, Ernest Ulmer was not in the best of health. He was on a kidney machine. Knowing that Ulmer's health was in decline, Sam Myers turned to him, seeking a favor, an important favor. Would Ernest Ulmer let him hide his truck inside the garage?

The answer was yes.

"Sometimes he paints cars just for a little bit of side money," Mrs. Ulmer explained.

Sam Myers "wanted my husband to fix some rust and holes and repair it and repaint it back the same color," she added.

When Sam Myers dropped off his truck on Dellwood Avenue, he never came back to get it. The 1977 Chevy Scottsdale remained in a handyman's garage that October, November and December.

When 1984 arrived, the truck remained out of commission. January and February passed. March marked the sixth full month since Myers dropped off his truck. Whatever work was supposed to be done, wasn't finished.

"Considering how this vehicle was supposedly being used by all members of the family on a regular basis, it does strike one as a bit strange that a vehicle, which for all other intents and purposes is operating normally, is suddenly stashed in a garage away from the Myers' residence in close proximity to the time that questions are asked about that vehicle in September of 1983," Petka explained.

When Mrs. Ulmer was asked if the truck stayed in her husband's garage from September 1983 until March 1984, she answered, "yes."

"He was going to start on it, but didn't get to it," she said of her husband.

Mrs. Ulmer was asked whether Sam Myers visited her house between September 1983 and March 1984 to get his truck.

"Well, he came in, I think it was October or November when the weather started getting cold," she remembered. "My husband was sick. He was on dialysis, and we'd put it in the garage. And he told him he was unable to work on it because he wasn't feeling well and so it sat in the garage. He said he was in no rush for it. He came back before Christmas questioning again, was the truck ready or anything. His wife's car had gone out and something. It had to be repaired or something."

After Christmas 1983, Sam Myers became a no-show.

Never once did he visit the Ulmer property, which was just a four-minute drive from his house on Joliet's Luther Avenue. Sam Myers remained content to have his family's main source of transportation out of service.

"No, I didn't see him," Mrs. Ulmer confirmed.

As the Illinois State Police pursued Milton Johnson as a possible suspect in the I-55 murder of Tony Hackett, the Will County Sheriff's Office was unaware of Johnson's regained freedom.

All the while, the Will County Sheriff's Office focused on tying the Homer Township massacres to Milton Johnson's stepfather, Sam Myers.

A sales receipt for a fishing reel repair with Sam Myers' signature turned up under the body of Will County Auxiliary Deputy Steven Mayer. For a host of reasons, Will County aggressively went to great lengths to investigate whether Sam Myers was the July 16 killing machine.

**

Sam and Dolly Myers were hundreds of miles away from Joliet on that terrible weekend when Denis Foley, Steven Mayer, Cathy Norwood, Richard Paulin, George Kiehl, Laura Troutman, Tony Hackett and Tonya Little were killed or badly wounded.

While the Myers vacationed in Mississippi, their recently paroled son, Milton, tended to their house and garden on Luther Avenue. They also gave him the set of keys for their black pickup truck.

Their two other grown sons lived elsewhere. Louis Johnson worked as a prison security guard at Stateville Correctional Center, and his two sons attended Providence Catholic High School in New Lenox.

The Myers' other grown son, James Johnson, lived in Gary, Indiana.

"When I left, I talked with all of my kids, and I told (James) and Milton to stay home and tend to what needed to be tended to and tend to their garden," Dolly Myers recounted.

While she and her husband visited relatives for more than a week in Mississippi, the bloodbath back in Will County left a half dozen more people dead. Newspaper articles about the Homer Township rampage and the next night's I-55 murder described a dark-colored pickup truck and a Black gunman as being responsible.

But if Sam Myers had an ironclad alibi putting himself and his wife in Mississippi during the weekend killings of July 16-17, the middle-aged Joliet man had to be crossed off the suspect list.

The question remained unanswered, why was the Walt's Bait & Tackle Shop sales receipt made out to Sam Myers discovered in the roadside ditch underneath Auxiliary Deputy Steven Mayer's body?

CHAPTER 19

NEW CLUES

The Will County Sheriff's Department remained committed to closing the seemingly random killing spree, but as the leaves changed colors and blistering summer days gave way to a cool autumn breeze, there was not a clear consensus on a prime suspect.

Meanwhile, over at Illinois State Police area headquarters, just north of Joliet, investigators remained intent on solving the shooting death of teenager Tony Hackett near the Wilmington exit along I-55.

After all, police had a survivor, Hackett's girlfriend.

Back on July 17, 1983, Illinois State Police Investigator John Meduga sped to the Saint Joseph Hospital in Joliet as surgeons operated on Tonya Little.

"She was lying on a table in one of the rooms with her arms outstretched, with tubes in each of her arms and a tube in her nose," Meduga said. "She could barely talk."

The next day, Meduga enlisted a police sketch artist.

"We felt it was a good idea to have him draw a composite, not knowing if she would live or die," Meduga remarked.

Investigators learned that her assailant was a Black man, perhaps six-foot-tall to six-foot-two, medium to heavy set. He had a pot belly and strong body odor. Tonya Little thought he wore low-cut white gym shoes, blue jeans and a blue plaid flannel shirt, even though the heat was in the 90s that day.

A week after her attack, the teenager's condition improved. As a result, the Illinois State Police brought her a book containing 1,500 photographs to review.

"I told her if she observed the offender to identify him and also any other similarities of offenders that she could pick out and pick them out," Meduga explained.

The eighteen-year-old studied every photo. She did not believe the man who killed her boyfriend and tried to take her life was among those first 1,500 photographs. About forty photos contained general features that bore some resemblance to her assailant, she advised.

For the next several weeks, Little rested and recuperated at her family's downstate farm. That fall, two state police agents made the three-hour drive to the farm. This time, they refined their mugshot files. Inside her living room, the teenager reviewed a total of one hundred thirty-seven police mugshots.

"None of those photographs talked," Will County State's Attorney Ed Petka pointed out.

Petka, of course, was the keynote speaker at the downtown Joliet prayer rally that drew at least six hundred people. To this day, Petka strongly believes that God watched over Joliet that afternoon.

In the days and weeks following the community prayer rally, the tenacious detectives moved closer and closer to catching the killer.

And another thing happened.

"There were no more murders," Petka said. "After the prayer rally, the police talked to Mr. and Mrs. Myers and then the vehicle was hidden. We did not have a long delay in getting our prayers answered. I said my prayers were answered in a hurry. With everything, it took six months to arrest him. I believe we had divine intervention in this case. I believe in the power of prayer. To me, there is no such thing as coincidence."

**

By February 1984, Will County Sheriff's Investigator Charles Malinowski had meticulously reviewed the evidence files related to the previous year's summer of terror. Efforts to mobilize a police task force to solve the killings had not paid dividends. Indeed, the Joliet area killing spree came to a screeching halt, but area police remained puzzled why that was the case, given the absence of arrests.

As Malinowski dusted off reams of files for new leads, he stumbled across an intriguing police report from the previous July. A young woman named Ann Shoemaker was followed on the backroads of Homer Township by a suspicious black pickup truck. Malinowski realized the frightful encounter occurred in practically the same area of the Homer Township massacre the following weekend.

During the summer of 1983, Shoemaker's tip fell through the cracks. It did not generate any immediate follow-up investigation, perhaps because there were so many phone calls from other well-meaning citizens trying to help police take this madman off the streets.

Taking a fresh approach, Malinowski tracked down the young woman from suburban Darien. The Will County detective asked whether she could still describe the driver of the truck.

"She told me she could do better than that," Malinowski remarked years later. "She said she could give me the license plate, which she wrote down on a piece of paper that was in her purse since then; seems that no one ever asked her for that."

The Will County Sheriff's Office was in luck.

Ann Shoemaker had saved her scrap of paper. The license plates she wrote down registered to the truck of Sam and Dolly Myers.

In the coming days, Detective Malinowski spoke with his peers at Illinois State Police. He wondered whether they had investigated Sam Myers in connection with Joliet's rash of unsolved murders from the previous summer.

To his surprise, state police had not opened a case file for Sam Myers. The file surrounded the activities of his stepson, Milton Johnson. The discovery of Milton Johnson's recent freedom was an epiphany for the Will County detective, who already knew of Johnson's wicked, abhorrent acts of evil within Joliet's Pilcher Park forest from 1970.

Even hardened detectives would not forget the sheer viciousness and savagery inflicted on the teenage rape victim trapped in her backseat as her boyfriend heard her screams from the floor of the front seat. Johnson bit her body and burned her vagina with a cigarette lighter.

Thirteen years afterward, when the summer of terror began, members of the Joliet police and Will County Sheriff's Office had not been made aware that the Illinois Department of Corrections had sent back Milton Johnson to his hometown years earlier than anyone imagined. The realization that

Milton Johnson regained his freedom just three months before the Joliet area's murder spree began sent shivers down the spines of seasoned investigators at Will County.

While Sam Myers could be eliminated as a suspect, Will County police had strong forensic evidence tying his black truck to the area of Gougar Road and 147th Street, where the Homer Township massacres happened. That evidence was the sales receipt made out to Sam Myers to repair his fishing reel at Walt's.

Myers claimed his fishing receipt blew out of his window during one of his many fishing excursions to the Lemont area. But with a cunning serial killer still on the loose, Detective Malinowski was not about to take Myers' account at face value. Armed with the newly discovered license plate tip, Malinowski set out to learn the whereabouts of the pickup truck. In addition, the Illinois State Police recovered several fingerprints from Tony Hackett's shot-up car on I-55 while Will County obtained several fingerprints from the ceramic shop murders.

Would these be the fingerprints of Sam Myers, Milton Johnson or somebody else?

CHAPTER 20

PONTIAC

Milton Johnson was born May 15, 1950, in the Deep South. His family lived in tiny Millry, Alabama, a town of less than a thousand in Washington County. The region was about sixty miles north of the Gulf of Mexico. Nearly ninety percent of Washington County consisted of forest and pine plantations. Johnson was the middle child of three brothers. At age four, his parents split up. By 1956, his mother Dolly remarried, prompting the family to move to Joliet, Illinois. Since Johnson's stepfather worked for a traveling construction company, the family moved often during his youth. By 1958, the family relocated to Toledo, Ohio. After Ohio, they moved to Baltimore, where his mother found work at a fashion shop. But by 1962, the family was back in Joliet, this time to stay.

The frequent moves weren't easy for Johnson. He failed one grade and wasn't good at school. He struggled to make friends, and some kids regarded him as a school bully.

A first cousin advised police he knew Johnson since he attended grammar school in Fairmont "and considered him to be an individual who always stayed to himself. All throughout the school years ... to his knowledge, he had been a loner and that he never really had any close associations with either boys or girls."

Although Johnson completed eighth grade, high school at Joliet Central was rough. During freshman year, Johnson complained of headaches. He spent three weeks in the hospital in 1966. Four back teeth were removed. When Johnson returned to high school, he fell way behind his classmates, and not long after that, the Joliet Central teachers went on strike. Johnson chose to drop out of high school. In 1968, Johnson joined the Job Corps program and traveled to Sparta, Wisconsin, to learn the art of welding. Later that year, he found welding work at a company in Michigan. He stayed in Detroit and lived at a YMCA, but the job did not last long. During the latter part of 1969, Johnson returned to Joliet to work at the Ceco Steel plant in nearby Lemont.

At the time of his 1970 prison placement, Johnson, then twenty, was asked if he had any history of sleepwalking, exhibitionism, voyeurism, fire setting, animal cruelty, homosexuality or sexually deviant practices. He denied all of them. However, prison officials uncovered that when Johnson was fifteen, he got arrested in nearby Lockport for assault and battery against a woman. Johnson told prison officials the charges were dropped due to a lack of evidence.

Johnson described his relationship with his mother and stepfather as beautiful. None of his brothers had any problems with the law. Johnson insisted he had no juvenile criminal record and didn't get into trouble at school.

"The inmate states it was difficult for him to date because he worked midnights although he claims he did date," a State of Illinois prison psychologist wrote in his intake evaluations of Johnson.

The prison psychologist pressed Johnson about the Pilcher Park rape that put him in prison.

"It was a mistake, and we're going to get an appeal bond," Johnson answered. "I had nothing to do with it. When the police department stopped us, she didn't say it was me, and we got to the hospital, and she still didn't say it was me."

The prison psychologist made the following assessment for Johnson: "The inmate through denial and repression has managed to discount the serious situation in which he presently finds himself. Should the inmate become depressed after repeated appeals, a repeat psychiatric consultation should be considered. Placement will be left to the sociologist. He is trying to avoid a Pontiac shipment because he wishes to be in the area close by for appeal purposes. The inmate's institutional plans all revolve around his appeals pending. This young man is somewhat manipulative, trying to stay in the local area for appeal purposes and regards the institution as a stop-over until he is released to the free community."

Incidentally, Johnson referred to himself as a gym teacher during his intake interviews with the Illinois Department of Corrections psychiatrist. Johnson talked about being hired by the principal of Forest Park School, prior to leaving Joliet for the Job Corps program.

"Actually, he was not a certified gym teacher," the prison psychiatrist pointed out.

At the time of his placement, Johnson predicted he wouldn't spend much time in prison, despite his sentence of twenty-five to thirty-five years for rape, burglary and aggravated battery out of Joliet.

"I don't plan to be here that long, and I expect to get cut loose on my appeal," Johnson asserted.

Johnson focused on appealing his case to the Illinois Supreme Court.

"There are some mistakes in the trial and I feel I can be cut loose," Johnson declared.

The prison psychologist surmised that Milton Johnson, at age twenty, had a need for increased self-esteem and self-worth and "at times does feel somewhat inferior."

A medium-security prison was determined the best place to put Johnson based on his sentence and the aggressiveness of his crimes.

Johnson refused to take responsibility for the crimes that put him in prison. A prison sociologist noted that a girl and her boyfriend were parked in a Will County area park when Johnson approached and tapped on their car window. When the boyfriend rolled down the window, Johnson put a shotgun to his face and told him to look down on the floor.

Johnson ordered the girlfriend into the backseat with him and during the next hour, the girl was viciously beaten about her face and raped. The victim's boyfriend escaped by running from the car.

"Apparently, Johnson took the female victim to the hospital and when he arrived at the emergency room, he was identified, and it was noted that he had blood all over him," his prison records show. "According to Johnson, he was going to work that night and driving through the park and saw a young girl holding on to the side of the car. He states that he then took her to the hospital in his car.

"He indicated that she was wearing a sweater coat and wanted her clothes, but that he could not find them. He claims that he flagged down a police car and told them he was taking her to the hospital."

The prison sociologist concluded Johnson was not mentally retarded and not in need of mental health treatment nor was he a sociopath. Johnson was classified as having a low average intelligence, putting at the level of between seventh and eighth grade.

Astonishingly, Illinois prison officials concluded Johnson was not a sexually dangerous inmate. His torture rape deep in the woods was deemed a "situational reaction of a young adult life," their reports show.

"Although it is noted in the psychiatric report that this person may be somewhat manipulative, however, this does not appear to be greatly significant at this time," advised Dennis Jennings, the Stateville Correctional Center sociologist who evaluated Johnson. "He is desirous of obtaining his G.E.D. diploma, and it is felt that he is capable of obtaining this goal."

**

After Johnson went to the Stateville for prisoner intake, the Illinois Department of Corrections put him at the Pontiac Correctional Center. At Pontiac, Johnson was assigned to the kitchen as his prison job.

Along I-55, one hundred miles southwest of Chicago, was the small city of Pontiac, population 11,200. Pontiac was nestled along the Vermilion River and served as the Livingston County seat.

Johnson was classified as a first-time offender, who had limited schooling in Joliet. Upon his eventual prison release, Johnson said he wanted to return to Joliet, to live with his mother and stepfather.

"He has employment plans with Caterpillar Tractor Company on Caterpillar Road in Joliet, Illinois. He will be employed as a welder," his prison records noted.

Counselors at the Pontiac Correctional Center had hopes Johnson would resume his studies after dropping out of high school and getting convicted of a horrific violent crime.

However, Johnson's time at Pontiac would be marked by chaos and turmoil within the prison population.

On July 22, 1978, Pontiac drew infamy for having one of the worst prison riots in Illinois history. Three prison officers were killed and three more were injured as prisoners set fire to several institutional buildings. More than 1,000 inmates participated in the one-day rioting. Large clouds of black smoke filled the sky.

"It was just full of smoke, fire and mass confusion," a member of the SWAT team that stormed the prison later told the central Illinois newspaper for Bloomington and Normal, *The Pantagraph*.

In 1979, Johnson began to focus his attention on getting out of Pontiac. He wanted to get paroled. By 1980, the prisoner review board considered Johnson for parole. They noted he received ten family visits the previous year, indicative of moderate concern from family. "He has no employment plans at this time and states that he does not plan to attend school. He does not have his GED."

Dating back to 1971, Johnson received thirteen minor disciplinary reports and six major ones, prison records show. In the end, Johnson's parole hopes for 1980 were dashed because his release would depreciate the seriousness of his offense, prison officials concurred.

He tried for parole again in 1981. By that time, Johnson was in his eighth year of being assigned to the inmates' kitchen.

"According to his supervisor, he is an excellent worker who keeps pretty much to himself and has posed no adjustment problems," his 1981 parole report reflected.

From 1980 to 1981, Johnson received four prison visits from his mother plus three visits from his brother and sister.

"Resident has no definite employment plans ... He has job skills as a welder, which may help him," a prison counselor wrote.

Although Johnson was regarded as a well-behaved prisoner during his first decade of incarceration, that was no longer the case in 1981.

That spring, Johnson spent a week in the segregation cell for possession of contraband medicine. Days later, Johnson received fifteen days of segregation for possessing marijuana.

Not surprisingly, the prisoner review board rejected Johnson's 1981 parole bid, citing the seriousness of his crimes. Afterward, Johnson stopped working in the inmate kitchen. By summer, Johnson was on unassigned status.

Between 1981 and 1982, Johnson had eight more family visits. Of particular note, he received sixty days of meritorious good time credit at the end of 1981.

A 1982 parole report noted, "He denies gang affiliations and he denies drug abuse. He has received several disciplinary reports for contraband drug possession in the institution which leads to some question as far as the possibility of his having perhaps lapsed into drug abuse or trafficking. He has no history of escape. He has shown a significantly improved adjustment at Pontiac Correctional Center and has a reasonably good work record."

On the other hand, prison officials expressed doubt as to whether Johnson would find a job and use his welding skills, if paroled.

"Resident Johnson's employment plans are currently somewhat unsettled. This resident's very serious offense leads to some reservations about possible release at this time."

In April 1982, the Illinois prison review board denied Johnson's parole, again citing the seriousness of his crime. A few months later, he sought a transfer to the pre-release program, which was one step closer to regaining his freedom.

Prison counselor Diane Rockett indicated Johnson "has no vocational skills and little job experience," but he was encouraged and motivated to complete his education in the medium security unit's school. She indicated Johnson hoped "to eventually become a gym teacher."

Rockett determined a change of scenery might be good for Johnson after spending the 1970s at Pontiac and being there during the notorious prison riots. "It is fair that it would be in the resident's best interest for this transfer from Pontiac's Medium Security Unit to give him an opportunity to take part in programming in a new setting," her summer 1982 report stated.

With Rockett in his corner, things continued to go his way.

Johnson received sixty more days of meritorious good time credit on July 8, 1982, plus another thirty days that Oct. 6. "Resident denies excessive drinking or illegitimate use of drugs. He denies glue sniffing," his prison records reflect.

Johnson got another sixty days of institutional credits that Oct. 26. By 1983, Johnson made it nearly two years without any discipline.

"To date, resident has had a commendable institutional and program adjustment," his January 1983 records read. "Resident's institutional plans all revolve around his appeals pending. Resident claims he did not commit his current offense.

"Resident Johnson is somewhat manipulative but harmless at this time. Resident wants to become a gym teacher. Resident's overall assessment is satisfactory."

The letter ended with one final recommendation: upon his parole, Johnson should get counseling in an outpatient mental health program "due to the seriousness of his current offense."

In advance of his 1983 parole hearing, counselor Diane Rockett recommended Johnson for sixty more days of institution credits, expediting his hearing to February rather than April.

Her input weighed heavily into the parole board's decision. And on his fifth attempt, parole was granted on March 9, 1983. His time at Pontiac was over. Now, two months shy of turning thirty-three, the convicted rapist was heading back to Joliet.

It should be remembered that in 1983 Illinois had no public sex offender registry. Moreover, the Joliet Police Department and the Will County Sheriff's Department were not notified of Johnson's re-acclimation to society. As long as he lay low, Johnson would not spark interest from Joliet area police and prosecutors already familiar with his ability to terrorize unsuspecting victims, often at night, in remote areas of wilderness.

So who was the prison counselor who helped propel Johnson's early release from his twenty-five to thirty-five year rape sentence?

Diane Marie (Marion) Rockett was one year younger than Johnson. She began her counseling career at Pontiac Correctional Center and married a correctional lieutenant at the same prison in 1980. She went on to spend twenty-three years with the Illinois Department of Corrections, eventually becoming clinical services supervisor at the Henry C. Hill Correctional Center in the western Illinois community of Galesburg, where her husband became a prison captain.

She died in 2002, at age fifty one. Her obituary described her as energetic and spirited, dedicated to doing things the right way.

"She was as beautiful as she was opinionated and faced difficult challenges daily in the male dominated environment of the late 1970s," her obituary reflected. "A lifetime of employment in the prisons is a challenging career but often shortens the lives of those dedicated to serve."

Besides Rockett, Mary Jo Hillyer was another Pontiac prison employee who had a profound effect on Johnson.

Hillyer was raised in the central Illinois prison town of Pontiac and became a dietary manager secretary at the Pontiac Correctional Center just before the 1978 riots. Because of her job, she often visited the prison kitchen to talk with inmates assigned there. This was where she first encountered Milton Johnson. Her impressions were that he often stayed to himself. He did not talk with others. He never smiled.

Hillyer tried to cheer him up, but this proved difficult. But by the time she left Pontiac in October 1979, the twenty-five-year-old woman felt she had made strides. She developed a friendship with the convicted rapist and torturer. She stayed in contact with him after she moved to Milwaukee. She began writing letters to him. He wrote back.

The long-distance pen pal exchange developed into something more. Following Johnson's release from prison in March 1983, Hillyer invited Johnson to visit her in Milwaukee for a romantic rendezvous.

During the second weekend that April, Johnson made the two-hour drive to Milwaukee's South Side, booking a two-night stay at the Red Carpet Hotel, which later became the Grand Milwaukee Hotel and then Wyndham Milwaukee before being demolished in 2013.

Other times, Hillyer booked a room at the Joliet Holiday Inn along I-80 and Larkin Avenue when her job required her to travel. Staying in Joliet was a special delight. She could meet up with Johnson to share their affection. She booked hotel rooms in Joliet during the second and fourth weekends in May. She returned to Joliet during the third Sunday and Monday in June and July. Her fifth and final stay at the Joliet Holiday Inn occurred on the weekend of Sept. 30-Oct. 1.

"Mary Hillyer stated that during the time spent with Milton Johnson, she considered him a very loving, sensitive and responsive mate with no deviant tendencies," Will County Investigator Dave Simpson wrote.

In July of 1983, a few days after Hillyer stayed with Johnson in Joliet, he called her at 1 a.m. He was in Milwaukee and needed money.

Hillyer got out of bed and dressed. She cashed an $80 check in the middle of the night as she drove to Milwaukee's North Side to find him. When he rolled up in his stepfather's black pickup truck, he parked and got inside her car. He carried a Crown Royal pouch with a bulky object inside.

What had Johnson concealed inside his Crown Royal pouch? His girlfriend did not know. He did not tell her or show her. Three months earlier, Johnson made a cryptic comment, advising his long-distance lover he would not be very available at all times until the end of August because "he had some business to take care of."

"Mary Hillyer stated that he did not elaborate any further than that," Investigator Simpson wrote.

CHAPTER 21

BREAKTHROUGH

Growing up on Joliet's East Side, Albert Williams and Milton Johnson became friends in seventh grade at Gompers Junior High on Briggs Street. During their twenties, the Illinois Department of Corrections became a big part of their lives for drastically different reasons.

Johnson was serving a rape sentence at the state pen in Pontiac. Williams worked as a prison guard at Stateville where Williams worked with Johnson's brother, Louis.

And that's how Williams learned his childhood friend was getting out of prison and returning to Joliet, in March of 1983. A couple weeks after Johnson's parole, Williams and another former Gompers schoolmate, Gerald "Jerry" Edwards, invited Milton Johnson out for drinks at Big D's Tavern in Lockport. Johnson drank Budweiser beer while his two friends ordered Courvoisier Cognac.

Afterward, the three drove to the Fairview public housing projects off Woodruff Road to visit some of the women who lived there.

Later, they agreed to get together the following weekend.

Back on Luther Avenue, Johnson moped around and did not seem motivated to find a job. He was fortunate that his parole officer did not keep tabs on his progress. Johnson's brother, Louis, the state correctional guard, began to wonder about his older brother's road to rehabilitation. In fact, Louis

Johnson later told Sheriff's Investigator Simpson "that there was a time right after Milton Johnson was sent to prison that Milton Johnson advised him that he was having problems with his emotions, and that he was feeling extremely bitter and hatred for being sent to the penitentiary and ... eventually Milton turned to the Lord and that after finding religion he was able to cope with his emotions easier."

However, Louis Johnson worried his brother was leading a secluded life after being paroled from Pontiac. Louis Johnson tried to get his brother out to the bars to introduce him to new people, but that did not go well. "Milton Johnson quickly came to a point and time where he came to the conclusion that he no longer wished to go out in public due to the fact that he felt the police were watching him, and that he had a strong feeling that they were attempting to pin some type of crime on him so that his parole would be revoked and he would be sent back to the penitentiary," his brother told police.

Something else his older brother said stuck with Louis Johnson.

Expressing his anger and resentment for losing thirteen years of his life to the state penal system, Milton Johnson told his brother "that he, Milton, would get the last laugh."

**

In 1983, Jerry Edwards worked near Joliet at the Willowbridge apartment complex. At the Crest Hill apartment complex, Edwards opened a video arcade room, and one of his most regular visitors became Milton Johnson, his childhood friend who was reacclimating himself to society. Edwards enjoyed the chance to reconnect with his childhood pal. They shared laughs and stories talking about the old times, when they grew up in the Forest Park area of Joliet's East Side.

Johnson began visiting the video arcade sometimes twice a day. Edwards began to leave Johnson in charge of the arcade room as he handled other matters at the apartment complex. That summer, Edwards remembered one time when Milton Johnson brought a young white woman to the arcade to introduce her. It was his girlfriend Mary Jo Hillyer, the former Pontiac prison employee.

Other than himself and Albert Williams, Edwards was positive Johnson did not have any other close acquaintances, white or black.

Like Johnson, Edwards did not have a squeaky clean background. Edwards had several criminal convictions on his record, and Edwards also acquired and sold guns. On one such day, Edwards claimed that a man he only knew by the name of Pumpkin showed up at the video arcade asking if Edwards wanted to buy a new .357 Magnum gun. Edwards agreed to pay $100. He gave "Pumpkin" $50 up front. Pumpkin supposedly told Edwards he would return later with the gun.

That particular day was June 24, 1983.

That afternoon, Edwards visited the Service Merchandise retail store about a mile up the road in the Hillcrest Shopping Center where he bought a box of .357 caliber Magnum bullets, with Lubaloy outer coating made of zinc and copper.

Will County Sheriff's investigators subsequently obtained a copy of the sales receipt that showed Jerry Edwards signed his name to buy the box of Lubaloy bullets from Service Merchandise on June 24, 1983.

After buying the box of Lubaloy bullets, Edwards returned to Willowbridge apartments and put his bag of bullets behind his game room counter. Then, a series of strange events supposedly transpired.

First, this fellow Edwards only knew by the nickname of Pumpkin purportedly returned and gave Edwards back his $50, saying he already sold the gun to someone else.

"Jerry Edwards stated that he then later in the day relayed this story to both Albert Williams and Milton Johnson," police reports reflect.

If you take Edwards at face value, the box of bullets, which were stashed behind the arcade counter went missing and apparently was stolen.

Illinois State Police Investigator Marty McCarthy suspected Edwards fabricated the story about the bullets being stolen. When questioned by police, the arcade manager denied buying the Lubaloy bullets at Service Merchandise to give them to Milton Johnson. Edwards insisted he had not bought a gun or given any gun to Milton Johnson, either.

"Jerry Edwards denies ever having any guns inside the game room or outside in front of the game room or concealed in any vehicle that he ever drove to the game room," McCarthy's police interview reflected. "Jerry Edwards stated that after the agreement with 'Pumpkin' was broken and that he received his $50 from him, the .357 Magnum Lubaloy bullets, which were purchased at Service Merchandise, were placed in a larger bag behind the counter at the game room and that he forgot all about them."

Was Edwards the victim of the theft or was his story a smoke screen to cover his tracks? Will County and state police intended to find the true answer.

Edwards agreed to undergo a polygraph test given by state police in Joliet. The test consisted of the following five questions:

"Did you purchase those .357 bullets for Milton Johnson?"

"Did you give or sell a .357 handgun to Milton Johnson?"

"Do you know who got those .357 bullets you bought at Service Merchandise?"

"Did Milton Johnson ever tell you he did any of the killings in Will County?"

"Do you know Pumpkin's real name?"

Edwards answered no to all five questions.

The examiner concluded Edwards was untruthful and had failed his polygraph exam. "Upon being confronted with the results of the tests, Edwards continued to maintain that he had answered the questions truthfully."

Edwards bought the box of Lubaloy bullets on Friday, June 24. Will County's killing spree began with the Blum sister slayings at their house on Rosalind Street, on June 25. Lubaloy bullets were recovered from the Blum sister slayings in Joliet Township. In fact, over and over, these same bullets were recovered from practically all of the Joliet area's summer of 1983 slayings.

After flunking his first polygraph exam, Edwards agreed to take another one. The follow-up test included a sixth question asking if he made any false statements regarding this case in any way.

Edwards answered no to all six questions, and the second polygraph examiner concluded Edwards was untruthful again with his answers.

Back on July 17, 1983, when crime scene technician Melvin Trojanowski approached the gold Plymouth Gran Coupe Fury on July 17, 1983, Tony Hackett's blood drenched the front seat and broken glass littered the inside the car.

The eighteen-year-old's body was stretched across the floor, with his head near the passenger door. The crime scene analyst also found several red-brown fibers outside the passenger door. The trail of fibers led north along I-55 back to where the killer had parked his pickup truck before killing the teenager and abducting Hackett's girlfriend.

At the time of his death, Tony Hackett wore a white and blue mesh shirt, blue swimming trunks, underwear and white socks. Five bullets went through his skull, chest, both thighs and right arm.

The fibers recovered by the state police evidence technician were from a pillow or seat cushion. About eight feet behind the victim's car was a piece of duct tape near the I-55 shoulder.

Four latent fingerprints were lifted from the trunk and another thirty fingerprints were recovered from the front and back fenders, passenger door, handle, window and windshield molding.

Additionally, two samples of red and brown fibers were collected from the front seat, between the passenger door and floor.

The abundance of fingerprints opened up possibilities. The killer may have run his hands across the car while abducting Hackett's girlfriend. On the other hand, the teenage couple spent the previous day at Marriott's Great America.

Thousands of amusement park guests surely walked past their car while coming and going from the gigantic parking lot. Any number of visitors could have touched the car.

For police and prosecutors, there was great anticipation for the fingerprint analysis. Then, came the letdown. None of Milton Johnson's fingerprints matched the Plymouth Gran Coupe.

The absence of Johnson's fingerprints did not mean he was cleared as a prime suspect. After all, Tonya Little never saw her abductor touch the Plymouth during the overnight attack at the I-55 Wilmington exit.

Even though authorities were deflated by the fingerprint analysis in the I-55 slaying, several fingerprints remained unaccounted for in the ceramic shop murders. And those fingerprints were far more meaningful. After all, the killer had climbed into murder victim Pam Ryan's Chevy Blazer and drove her vehicle to the car wash along East Cass Street where he left it.

Besides the fingerprint evidence, Will County police recovered several bloody footprints inside the ceramic shop plus at the car wash.

Fingerprints were taken from dozens of possible suspects, including David Baers, Todd Lewandowski, the Bryant brothers who were the painters, bicyclist David Smith and many more.

None of those fingerprint comparisons panned out.

One person who had not been subject to a fingerprint comparison in the ceramic shop murders was Milton Johnson, even though police already had his prints on file from the 1970 Pilcher Park rape right up Route 30. At the urging of Investigator Malinowski, Johnson's fingerprints were submitted in March 1984 for comparison in the ceramic shop murders.

Illinois Department of Law Enforcement forensic scientist Joseph Ambrozich compared Johnson's set of prints to the latent fingerprints recovered from the door handles of Pam Ryan's Chevy Blazer that the killer drove minutes after the bloodbath.

"The latent print partial secured from the left front door handle of the Blazer is identical to the left little finger on the inked fingerprint card marked Milton Johnson. The remaining latent fingerprint partial was compared with no identification being made. If you should obtain Milton Johnson's inked palm prints or inked prints containing the tip of the fingers section, submit them to this agency and they will be compared with the unidentified latent print secured," Ambrozich's findings showed.

Separately, Ambrozich focused his attention on evidence Item 58, the gear shift knob from the same Chevy Blazer.

"One latent print partial that can be used for comparison purposes was found to be contained in a blood-like substance on this item," he advised Will County. "This latent print was compared to the inked fingerprint card marked Milton Johnson. This latent print is identical to the right index finger on the inked fingerprint card marked Milton Johnson."

Two different fingerprints put Milton Johnson inside the red Chevy Blazer of the murder victims on their last day alive. The work of Will County evidence technician Lynn West was invaluable. West had meticulously recovered the fingerprints at the time of the quadruple murders seven months earlier.

Without his effort, Will County would not have had useful fingerprints from the vehicle driven by the killer.

Now retired, former Will County Sheriff's Investigator Nick Ficarello said that Lynn West's contributions to cracking the ceramic shop murders cannot be overlooked.

West was in his mid-thirties at the time.

"He was very meticulous, people called him Captain Alaska," Ficarello remembered. "He was ahead of his time and very interested in computers, he had a whole computer program … very mathematical, very analytical, and very precise. He always came up with some insight that other people could not see."

Ficarello, who joined Will County in 1978, said West had a quiet demeanor, but people in the department held West in high regard. West was also qualified as an expert courtroom witness on the subject of fingerprint analysis.

"If he showed up at a crime scene, you knew that the job that he would do would be very detailed," Ficarello said. "Lynn was very tenacious."

**

Illinois State Police investigators John Meduga and Ed Miller sped south on I-55 toward Hartsburg to again interview the survivor of the previous summer's roadside attack. Hartsburg was barely a dot on the map. The central Illinois town consisted of four hundred people.

The seasoned investigators met with Tonya Little and her parents in the family's kitchen.

For the most part, they remained tight-lipped about the latest developments in their homicide investigation. Miller and Meduga had narrowed their suspects and wanted Little to review a number of mugshots they had brought along.

"I laid them on the kitchen table from left to right in a number sequence," Meduga explained. "I numbered them on the back of the photographs on the way I laid them down."

The teenage survivor starred at the photos in front of her. Was one of these the man who stabbed her and left her for dead in the median of the four-lane state highway?

"She observed the photographs for several minutes and picked up number two, and she made several statements," Meduga recalled. "She said it's possible it's him. Looks pretty right, my gut feeling is it's him, but I can't be sure. His side view looks right and his hairline seems right."

Who was the photo she selected?

"Number two, Milton Johnson," Meduga said.

With her parents sitting in the room for moral support, Little assured the state police she could positively identify the perpetrator if she heard his voice and smelled his body. She always brought up the fact that he had a low, growly voice and a terrible smell.

On March 9, 1984, the Illinois State Police brought the Hartsburg teenager to the Will County Adult Detention Facility to review a photo lineup of six Black men. Their height and weight fluctuated. Some were five-foot-eight while others stood six-foot-two.

"Four subjects had mustaches and beards or one of them, because Milton Johnson had a mustache and goatee, and also we were not sure when she observed the offender if she did observe any facial hair or not," Meduga explained.

At Will County's Jail, Meduga summoned the five other participants to enter the viewing room. He told them to stand against the wall, and he let them pick where they wanted to stand.

"Milton Johnson was brought in and he was told to stand and pick any place in the lineup, and he chose the number four position," Meduga said.

The teenage survivor was not allowed into the viewing room yet.

Finally, when she entered, Meduga told her she could stand anywhere, but not to say anything. The viewing room was small, about ten feet by twelve feet.

Was she standing in the presence of her fiancé's killer?

She approached the glass. She gazed at each of the six men. She looked into their eyes.

Next, Meduga had the men in the police lineup repeat a number of statements burned her into Tonya Little's brain by the madman who harmed her.

"Get on the ground and crawl on your belly to the truck."

"Stay low and stay down."

"Get in the truck."

"Stay on the floor."

When the six finished repeating the phrases, Meduga had them repeat the question, *"You got your eyes closed?"*

Lastly, they repeated the command, *"Keep your eyes closed."*

When the process finished, Meduga told the six to remain in their stationary positions. He left to speak with the survivor.

The investigator asked if she wanted to be in the same room as the men in the photo lineup. He offered to make the men turn and face the wall so she could smell them for that foul, lingering stench.

But that was not necessary, she informed Meduga.

"She says, 'No. There's no need to go in the other room. It's number four. There's no doubt. There's no doubt about it. He did it.'"

Man number four in the police lineup was Milton Johnson.

CHAPTER 22

RIGHT TRACK

March 9, 1984, became an epic day in the murder investigations. Not only did Tonya Little identify Milton Johnson in a photo lineup as the I-55 killer, but the prime murder suspect underwent direct questioning for the one and only time.

In the days leading up to Johnson's contentious interview, Illinois State Police Special Agent Paul Ferbend visited the parole offices north of Joliet along Airport Road and Route 53 to review the convicted rapist's files. A case agent was expected to contact the parolee at least every ninety days. A testing process was in place to determine the level of supervision for parolees. Johnson was put on low supervision status since July 9, 1983, his files showed.

A few days after his release from Pontiac, Johnson met with his original case agent on March 11, 1983. By March 28, the case agent helped Johnson with job service offerings. On April 4, Johnson requested a permit to travel. On April 7, Johnson requested a travel permit to visit his brother in Milwaukee for the weekend of April 8-10.

On April 28, Johnson spoke with his case agent about jobs. But in May, June and July, Johnson had no contact with parole officials. On Aug. 3, Johnson told his case agent he was trying to get hired at Johns Manville in Rockdale. On Sept. 1, Johnson informed the parole office he got a speeding ticket and had to appear in court in two weeks. On Sept. 9, Johnson was transferred to a different agent.

The new case agent assigned to monitor Johnson's parole informed the state police "that he really cannot tell us too much information in regards to Milton Johnson due to the fact that he has recently received Milton Johnson's file and has really had no contact with him to speak of."

The new parole officer assigned to Johnson refused to show the actual entrees to Special Agent Ferbend and Will County Sheriff's Investigator Simpson during their personal interview.

"It should be noted that Larry Hemingway did not show the assigned officers the entries themselves," their interview reflected.

Hemingway told them Johnson visited the parole office on Nov. 7 and advised he had gotten a landscaping job. Other than that, Hemingway said he tried calling Johnson's house, but had negative results on Jan. 20, 1984.

On March 5, 1984, Simpson and state police Special Agent McCarthy interviewed a neighborhood letter carrier on Johnson's street to learn more about their mass murder suspect's movements. According to the postal worker, four people often stayed at the house: Sam and Dolly Myers, Milton Johnson and another of their sons, possibly in his early twenties. Sam Myers worked at Joliet's Caterpillar plant and got a lot of mail from them, the postal worker told police. He described Milton Johnson as Black, medium complexion, 200 to 225 lbs., short type Afro hairstyle and mustache. Ordinarily, Johnson or his mother retrieved the mail. The letter carrier told homicide investigators "Milton Johnson is receiving some type of State of Illinois check in that there is mail which is addressed to him which comes in a white envelope with a plastic window on the envelope with his name being reflected ... he recognizes these envelopes, which are used by the state of Illinois to send checks out to people."

**

After showing up at the parole office for what he thought was just another routine visit, Johnson found himself face to face with Marty McCarthy and Dave Simpson on the afternoon of March 8, 1984.

Unbeknownst to Johnson, his time was up. Simpson and McCarthy broke the news: he was under investigation for the previous summer's murders. They reminded him that he previously told the state police on Sept. 12 that all he knew about the Will County murders came from what he read in the newspapers.

During the follow-up interrogation, Johnson told McCarthy and Simpson he drove past the ceramic shop around 2:30 p.m. on his way to Highland Liquors. Johnson said a policeman was in front of the shop directing traffic. When he saw several police cars in the parking lot, he realized something had happened.

As to his whereabouts on that tragic day for Joliet, Johnson said he had just come from the city's south side. Johnson, however, refused to divulge any more details than that. All he would say was that he was "seeing some people." Johnson refused to reveal any names when pressed by police.

In any event, Johnson said he bought seven lottery tickets at the Highland Liquors after driving past the heavy police presence at the ceramic shop. That particular Saturday marked one of the biggest Illinois Lotto jackpots in state history. People all over Joliet hoping to become the next multi-millionaire visited their neighborhood liquor stores, gas stations and convenience stores to purchase lottery tickets.

At the time he bought the lottery tickets, Johnson said he had his stepfather's pickup truck and was by himself. He parked the truck on Luther Avenue and stayed home the rest of the day and night, he told investigators.

Johnson described the black 1977 Chevy truck as being "in damn good shape." The pickup had a red interior, semi-chrome wheels, metal trim rings, chrome around the wheel wells and a brown camper top.

"When asked where this vehicle was now, he said it had been in a repair shop in Lockport for six or seven months. He said it needed body work because it was rusting through on the passenger's side door. He didn't know where the truck was in Lockport and that the person working on it was frequently ill," Johnson's interview reflected.

McCarthy and Simpson inquired when Johnson had left his house to head to Joliet's south side on the day of the ceramic shop murders. Johnson insisted he did not recall the time he left. As for his travel route, Johnson said he left the Forest Park area of Joliet by heading west on Woodruff Road to Collins Street. Then, he drove south on Collins and over to the city's south side.

Again, Johnson refused to discuss any further details about his movements that day when the pair of homicide investigators tried asking him a second time.

"He could not recall anyone he saw or spoke to on the south side," McCarthy wrote. "When he left this area he drove to Cass Street and headed east toward Highland Liquors. He arrived at the liquor store at 2:30 p.m. and only slowed at the ceramic shop for a minute or two."

The next day, Johnson recalled driving his stepfather's Cadillac to the Lockport car wash along Route 171 and Nobes Avenue. Johnson said he washed the Cadillac every other Sunday. As for the truck, Johnson said he washed it at the house on Luther Avenue.

Since Johnson was a violent ex-convict, he was not supposed to have any weapons. He insisted there were no weapons at his parents' house. He remembered that his stepfather used to have a shotgun, Johnson maintained it was stolen. One time, an aunt brought a two-shot Derringer to the house, but she left with the gun, Johnson told police.

Being extremely cautious, McCarthy and Simpson chose not to divulge too many details of their evidence trail that led to Johnson. For example, they did not tell him about the fishing reel receipt with his stepfather's signature that turned up at the Homer Township killings.

The receipt fell out of the pickup Johnson drove and turned up under the body of Auxiliary Deputy Steve Mayer at 147th Street and Gougar Road.

"He said he had no knowledge of those murders and that he has never been in that area before. The only part of Gougar Road he was familiar with was an area just north of Route 6 by a bridge and a creek where he has fished," investigators noted in their interview of Johnson.

Along those lines, Johnson denied having any knowledge of the I-55 murder of Tony Hackett from July 17, 1983. "He said he was more interested in national news and didn't pay much attention at the time to the news of the murders," McCarthy's interview showed. "He said if something doesn't affect him directly, he doesn't concern himself with it."

With no advance warning, Simpson and McCarthy put Johnson on the spot. They told him they knew he committed the four ceramic shop murders because his fingerprints were at the crime.

"He said if the police had his prints, someone else must have put them there," Johnson's interview reflected.

By 6 p.m., Will County State's Attorney Ed Petka gave the go ahead to arrest Johnson on first-degree murder charges.

"He was arrested on the basis of information that was given to us by the survivor of the attack on I-55," Petka told reporters. "She had picked him out of a photo line-up, and he was then placed in an in-person lineup and positively identified as the person responsible for that crime."

Petka would not divulge to reporters covering the major developing story why Johnson was put into a photo lineup and in-person lineup.

"I can simply tell you as a result of a Crime Stoppers tip that was received several weeks back that within the last fourteen days, investigators interviewed a number of women who claimed to have been harassed by an individual in a dark pick-up truck," the Republican State's Attorney remarked. "As a result of those interviews and as a result of getting a license plate number, information was then developed that the pickup belonged to the stepfather of the person who now stands accused, who will be charged with the offense of murder on Monday afternoon."

Meanwhile, Johnson's girlfriend in Milwaukee later told sheriff's detectives that at no time since Johnson's arrest in his boyhood home of Joliet has he ever made any admissions or statements of participating in the killings to her.

Johnson would frequently call Hillyer from the Will County jail as he waited to stand trial. During one of his calls, Johnson told her that he would write her a long letter explaining everything to her.

**

Thousands of people who didn't normally subscribe to Joliet's daily newspaper ran out to their neighborhood convenience stores, gas stations and supermarkets on Sunday, March 11, 1984. Practically everybody in Will County was eager to devour the blockbuster headline stripped across the front page: "Suspect Linked to 10 Murders."

Herald-News photographer Steve Sumner captured an image of Milton Johnson in handcuffs being escorted into the Will County Courthouse by several Will County Sheriff's deputies. Milton Johnson was formally charged with the July 17 killing of Tony Hackett on I-55.

"Based on evidence which we have processed, he is a prime suspect in the ceramic shop murders and the Homer Township murders," Petka informed the press.

Petka credited Will County Sheriff's Investigator Charles Malinowski with uncovering crucial evidence that led to a breakthrough.

Malinowski was not one of the original investigators handling the 1983 homicides, but at a later point he was brought into the case to review all of the original reports, tips and leads that arrived at the Will County Sheriff's Office since the killing spree began.

In February 1984, Malinowski became the first Will County sheriff's investigator to interview Ann Shoemaker because of a tip involving a dark pickup truck. Once Malinowski learned the license plates of the menacing truck traced back to the stepfather of Milton Johnson, the murder investigation came together rapidly.

"Everything clicked," Petka said. "All the evidence that was gathered then began to make sense."

"We have put thousands of man-hours into these cases," Will County's Sheriff John Shelley remarked at the time. "We have had a lot of ups and downs. A lot of times we felt we were on the right track and the track ran out."

Johnson's arrest stirred considerable outrage within the Joliet area, mostly toward the Illinois Department of Corrections.

After all, Johnson got paroled after serving only thirteen years of a rape sentence that carried twenty-five to thirty-five years imprisonment. Unknown to Joliet law enforcement, Illinois prison officials quietly turned Johnson loose on March 9, 1983, and let him slip back into Joliet under the radar.

During the summer of 1983 terror, three separate murders bore striking similarities to Johnson's 1970 torture rape inside Pilcher Park: young couples parked in their cars on a lonely dark road only to be caught by surprise when a stranger wielding a loaded gun tapped on their window.

In the follow-up newspaper stories chronicling the ex-convict's arrest on murder charges, bureaucrats with the Illinois Department of Corrections tried to downplay Johnson's early release.

State of Illinois prison spokesman Nic Howell told reporters Johnson earned seven-and-a-half days of good behavior credit for every month he spent institutionalized. For Johnson, his continuous good behavior allowed him to go before the prison review board to petition for parole starting in August 1979. According to Howell, the Illinois Prison

Review Board denied Johnson's first four attempts, but his fifth parole attempt was granted.

While Howell tried to soften the uncomfortable news of Johnson's early release from prison, there was no denying that Joliet's summer of terror began just three months later.

Here's a look back at the key timeline:

June 24, 1983: Jerry Edwards, Johnson's childhood friend, went to Service Merchandise to buy a box of Lubaloy bullets. Months after the fact, he claimed the box was stolen from the Willowbridge apartment arcade he ran with the help of Milton Johnson.

June 25: sisters Zita Blum, sixty-six, and Honora Lahmann, sixty-seven, were stabbed, fatally shot with Lubaloy bullets and set on fire inside their Joliet Township house on Rosalind Street.

July 1: Kenny Chancellor, thirty-three, and Terri Lynn "Athena" Johnson, twenty, were fatally shot with Lubaloy bullets while parking in a remote area of Orland Township, just outside Will County.

July 9: College co-eds Ann Shoemaker and Cindy Shepherd encounter with a menacing pickup truck on the backroads of Homer Township. Shoemaker wrote down its license plates and noted the truck was a blue or black Chevy. A friend, Todd Walsh, told police the driver was a Black man, five-foot-eight, 170 to 180 lbs., no hat, having a short Afro and wearing a red and blue flannel shirt. The license plates matched the truck owned by Johnson's stepfather.

July 16: Six people were gunned down on 147th Street in rural northwest Homer Township. A fishing reel repair receipt made out to Johnson's stepfather was discovered under Auxiliary Deputy Steven Mayer's body. Police find several shoe impressions from size 11 Converse All-Star high tops. Witnesses described the shooting suspect as a black man in his mid-thirties with short hair, a dark shirt and reported seeing a blue pickup with a white camper top.

July 17: Emden, Illinois, teenager Tony Hackett was fatally shot as he slept in his car near the I-55 Wilmington exit. His girlfriend was kidnapped, assaulted, stabbed and dumped along Route 53 south of Joliet. She described the attacker as a Black man with a pot belly, short black hair and wore a long sleeve, blue flannel shirt. He smoked cigarettes and drove a dark or blue pickup.

Aug. 20: Four women are fatally stabbed inside the Joliet ceramic shop on Cass Street. One victim was shot in the neck with Lubaloy bullets. Fingerprints and shoe impressions from Converse All-Star high-top gym shoes were found at the crime scene.

Sept. 12: Two Illinois State Police investigators showed up unannounced at Johnson's house asking questions about the rash of Will County murders and whether he drove the black Chevrolet truck registered to his stepfather.

March 9, 1984: Johnson is confronted with the fact that his fingerprints were left at the ceramic shop murders. The survivor of the I-55 shooting identified Johnson from a photo lineup as the perpetrator.

One of the biggest questions for police surrounded the whereabouts of Sam Myers' missing truck. Where did he put it?

Coinciding with Johnson's arrest, investigators learned the truck was stashed away inside the cluttered detached garage of Lockport Township resident Ernest Ulmer.

The truck had been there seven months ever since Illinois State Police detectives showed up at Johnson's house, asking whether Johnson drove the truck on occasion. At the time of the initial interview, police did not have a search warrant to impound the truck. In March 1984, they did.

The truck was towed to the Illinois State Police District 5 headquarters where crime technician Melvin Trojanowski examined the Chevy Scottsdale. In the cab, he retrieved reddish-brown fibers from behind the seat-belt retractor. A light colored hair was under the passenger seat as were several more reddish-brown fibers.

"The seats were in fairly good condition with the exception of the left front area of the driver's seat, which had a rip along the left side near the door," Trojanowski recalled.

Five Illinois lottery tickets were found in the front cab. Two were dated Sept. 22, 1982. Two others were from Aug. 29, 1983. The fifth was dated Sept. 21, 1982. Trojanowski used metal tongs to take them as physical evidence.

In the back corner of the truck bed, Trojanowski found a steak knife. Then he found another slip of paper that confirmed police were on the right track.

A sales receipt surfaced behind the driver's seat. The receipt came from Marriott's Great America in Gurnee, Illinois. It was dated July 16, 1983. The receipt was for a Tasmanian devil Looney Tunes stuffed animal.

When Tony Hackett was shot to death while sleeping in his car along I-55, he was holding the Looney Tunes stuffed animal.

As he shattered their window, the overnight creeper reached inside and opened the passenger door of the Grand Coupe Fury.

CHAPTER 23

CONNIVING SLIME RAT

In the early 1980s, Bill Swano was a hard-working and win-at-all costs lawyer who practiced criminal defense law in one of America's busiest halls of justice: Chicago's Cook County courts. Skillful and scrappy is how other lawyers described him.

A tireless advocate for clients, Swano came prepared to court.

Swano got his start in the 1970s with the Cook County Public Defender's Office, a great place for young ambitious lawyers to gain experience. There was no big money to be made working crazy hours as a Cook County public defender, so Swano eventually went into private practice where he could get rich and lead a luxurious lifestyle.

Swano worked hard, partied hard and in the 1980s his private practice flourished. He made a boatload of money though some of it went to waste as Swano indulged in cocaine.

It was only a matter of time before Swano engaged in the dark side of the law: public corruption involving bribes. He would not be the first lawyer in Chicago dishonoring the profession.

Back in 1981, a different Chicago lawyer was representing a mob hitman named Lenny Chow and two others for the shooting death of William Chin in Chicago's Chinatown district. One of the mobsters made it clear he wanted a not-guilty verdict. The hitman's lawyer realized Cook County Judge Thomas Maloney, who had a reputation as a tough-as-nails, no-nonsense judge, could be bought in certain circumstances. In the Chinatown mob hit, the judge received a portion of the $100,000 bribe, and the defendants were all acquitted at trial. Judge Maloney ruled that Chin's dying statements identifying his killers was unreliable evidence, a damning blow to the Cook County State's Attorney Office.

In 1982, Swano began his own regrettable relationship with the crooked Chicago judge. That year, Swano was hired to represent a white-collar criminal charged with forgery. Swano's client already had one conviction, so he feared a prison sentence was inevitable. Luckily, Swano came to his rescue. The Chicago defense lawyer arranged for his client to pay a so-called $5,000 fee of which half was handed to the judge at Chicago's McCormick Place lounge.

Sure enough, Swano's client got what he wanted, a sentence of probation, not prison.

Also in 1982, Swano paid another bribe to Judge Maloney with the expectation that murder defendant Owen Jones would not be sent away to prison for decades as the defendant's mother feared. Cook County charged Jones with beating a man to death during a burglary. To secure a lenient sentence Swano instructed the mother to raise the extra money to pay off the judge.

Once again, Swano had another success. His client was not convicted of murder, but rather, the much lesser crime of involuntary manslaughter. Jones drew a nine-year prison sentence. Judge Maloney made $4,000 to $5,000 for fixing that one, according to a Chicago newspaper expose.

Turns out, not all bribe and court-fixing rackets last forever, even in Chicago. By the mid-1990s, Swano and Maloney each went to prison. Their legal careers ended with a terrible stain that would never be washed away.

**

In the 1990s, Swano's days of practicing law were through. He got a four-year federal prison sentence for arranging bribes through the once-respected-but-morally bankrupt Chicago judge. To minimize his own culpability, Swano became a state's witness. His testimony played a huge role in Thomas Maloney's bribery and extortion convictions as part of the notorious Operation Greylord scandal.

During the 1980s and 1990s, Operation Greylord made major newspaper headlines, resulting in criminal indictments for seventeen judges, forty-eight lawyers, eight police officers, ten deputy sheriffs, eight Cook County court officials and one state lawmaker.

According to the FBI, nearly all the people were convicted and most pleaded guilty. "It was an important first step to cleaning up the administration of justice in Cook County," the FBI declared.

Most of the judges convicted in Operation Greylord were guilty of fixing lowly misdemeanor crimes and traffic tickets. Judge Maloney went down as one of the most egregious examples of Chicago's broken justice system. It was proven he fixed at least three murder cases.

The Chicago Tribune branded Swano as one of Chicago's most corrupt lawyers. In 1991, Swano pleaded guilty to federal racketeering charges and agreed to turn federal witness, pointing the finger at some of Chicago's dirtiest judges.

At his 1995 sentencing in federal court, Swano declared, "In some regards, this is a good thing that has happened. I'm free of the secret I kept for many years."

In addition to Judge Maloney, Swano testified he was involved with paying off other Cook County judges including Judge Adam Stillo Sr., who got sentenced in 1993 to four years in prison related to bribery allegations. Furthermore, Swano claimed he fixed cases with Cook County Judge Maurice Pompey, including a date rape case, as well as a fourth judge whose identity had not been made public, *The Chicago Tribune* reported in 1995.

Not all the bribes went smoothly.

In 1986, Swano had handed off a bribe intended for Judge Maloney during the murder trials of two Chicago El Rukn gang members, only to have the money returned. Maloney realized the FBI was onto his bribery scheme. The judge panicked during the middle of the El Rukn murder trial and chose not to accept Swano's $10,000 bribe.

That year marked the slide down the slippery slope for Swano. In the men's bathroom at Chicago's Criminal Courts Building at 26th and California, Swano encountered another crooked criminal defense lawyer. Unbeknownst to Swano, the other lawyer wore a hidden tape recorder for the FBI, *The Chicago Tribune* reported. During their recorded conversation, Swano began swearing, asking what's the worst thing that could happen to someone. When the lawyer answered having someone steal your girlfriend, Swano told him it was having a judge take a bribe in a case but give the money back.

By 1994, Maloney was sentenced to nearly sixteen years in federal prison of which he served thirteen years in a federal prison in Lompoc, California. Maloney called Swano "a conniving slime rat" at the discredited judge's sentencing.

The federal judge who sentenced the former Mount Carmel High School graduate told Maloney that "releasing dangerous criminals is atrocious. I personally agree 100 percent with the jury verdict."

In 2008, the eighty-three-year-old Thomas J. Maloney died at a nursing home in suburban Westmont, Illinois, one year after finishing his sentence.

His newspaper obituary called him "arguably the most corrupt judge in state history."

As for Swano, he originally faced up to ten years of federal prison time for his own moral failings in Maloney's courtroom. Fortunately for Swano, his deal with the federal government resulted in a four-year sentence with an expectation of parole after serving one-third to two-thirds of imprisonment.

By 1995, Swano was forty-nine, a broken man, a disgraced former lawyer, ready to atone for his many sins.

Swano knew his shameful actions brought outrage toward him and stained Chicago's legal profession. He would never be allowed to practice law again.

However, several years before his law career imploded, Swano was hired as Milton Johnson's criminal defense lawyer in Will County.

**

In 1984, Johnson's mother and stepfather had every reason to fear their 34-year-old son would die at the hands of the State of Illinois, strapped to a gurney at the Illinois Department of Corrections. Lethal injection was the state's capital punishment method.

Sam and Dolly Myers did not want their son represented by the Will County Public Defender's Office. They had been down that road once before, when their son was pronounced guilty and sentenced to prison in 1970. This time around, Johnson's stepfather made good money at the Caterpillar factory in Joliet.

The middle-aged couple scraped together $15,000, a lot of money for 1984, to retain Swano, a thirty-nine-year-old high-energy criminal defense lawyer based in Chicago with no ties and no connection to Will County's prosecutors and judges.

"He initially asked for $8,000, then $7,000 and then $2,000 more," Sam Myers wrote in a letter to court officials. "I gave him $15,000 altogether and told him that I would not give him anymore. Mr. Swano told me that this case would be expensive because he would have to hire some people to help him."

Johnson's upcoming murder trial would involve the I-55 killing of downstate teenager Tony Hackett, plus the rape and attempted murder of Hackett's teenage girlfriend, who survived the attack.

"Mr. Swano told me that the police did not have any evidence on Milton, and that Milton would be back on the streets after trial, and I took his word for it," Mr. Myers reflected. "Years after the trial, I heard about Mr. Swano's legal troubles. I also heard that they called him the 'Drug Man' in Chicago. I was not surprised to hear this."

Sam Myers maintained that his son was being unfairly demonized in the Joliet and Chicago area newspapers.

"I have known Milton for most of his life, and he has never been a problem to me or his mother," Myers wrote . "He was a very good stepchild and did everything I asked of him.

I have never known him to be violent or be a disciplinary problem. He was a very big help around the house and made his mother and I very happy."

Following his parole for the Pilcher Park torture rape, Johnson moved back to his family's house. He began participating in Joliet's Job Corps Center, a federally funded program administered through the U.S. Department of Labor. The vocational training center had taken over the old Joliet East High School campus along Mills Road.

"After Milton's first incarceration, which I believe was very questionable, he got a job and had no problems while living at home with us until he went to Job Corps," Myers wrote. "When he returned from Job Corps, he got another job. Milton always worked and took care of himself."

Even though Johnson was disciplined several times at the Illinois Department of Corrections during the 1970s related to drugs, his stepfather claimed Johnson never used them.

"I never had a problem with Milton as far as drugs and alcohol were concerned," Myers remarked. "Nor have I seen him act violently toward women or anyone else."

Johnson's mother agreed her son was not the violent type.

"Milton was a good child," Dolly Myers wrote in one letter. "He was very respectful and very helpful. I have never had any trouble out of him at home or school. He helped around the house in any way he could.

"Milton went to school regularly until he dropped out in the ninth grade when he found a job. He was always working one way or another. He was never involved in gangs or drugs and got along with everyone."

Of the fourteen Will County area murders authorities suspected of Johnson, none of the victims involved people he knew.

"He has always treated everyone he knew very well," his mother said. "Milton got along with everyone. After Milton's first incarceration, which I do not believe he did, he came to live with us in Joliet. He always took care of himself and never asked anyone for help. Milton would help many of the older people in the neighborhood. No one believes that Milton would hurt people around here."

Starting in 1984, Johnson's life was in the hands of the scrappy though unsavory criminal defense lawyer from Chicago. Would Swano's overly aggressive posture be an advantage or a disadvantage at his client's forthcoming capital murder trial?

Joliet and the surrounding Chicago region eagerly awaited the daily news coverage. The murder trial, however, would not occur at the Will County Courthouse in downtown Joliet.

Swano convinced Will County Judge Michael Orenic that Johnson would not get a fair trial in Will County because of the intense pretrial publicity. Virtually all of the print, television and radio coverage painted Johnson as a deviant monster.

Orenic moved Johnson's murder trial out to the boondocks, in Iroquois County, a region of 33,000 citizens along the Indiana border. The county seat was Watseka, a town of 5,500 about seventy miles southeast of Joliet.

Unlike Joliet residents who devoured the pretrial coverage, the citizens of Iroquois County knew next to nothing about Johnson and the I-55 murder of Tony Hackett.

While Johnson and his attorney were satisfied the trial was moved away from Will County, the selection of a farm region that was 96 percent white, was hardly a victory. Swano petitioned Judge Orenic to reconsider. The Chicago defense lawyer preferred a jury from Cook County. However, Orenic ruled that the Chicago and Joliet news organizations had had the least impact in terms of tainting or prejudicing a jury pool within Iroquois County, so the trial would take place in Iroquois County whether Johnson and his lawyer liked it or not.

A guilty verdict would move everything to a secondary sentencing phase where the question of life imprisonment with no parole or death by means of lethal injection was the only two outcomes.

For the trial, the prosecutor's table would be manned by two prominent Eds in the Will County legal community: State's Attorney Ed Petka, a forty-one-year-old Republican politician from Plainfield, and thirty-three-year-old First Assistant State's Attorney's Attorney Ed Burmila.

CHAPTER 24

EYES

Milton Johnson, thirty-four, was on trial for his life in a small farming town of five thousand people near the Indiana border. Surrounded by thousands of acres of black dirt and plenty of green-painted John Deere combines and tractors, Watseka seemed a world away from the rough and tough blue-collar industrial city of Joliet where he called home.

As anticipated, the lawyers needed a couple days to impanel a jury of citizens from Iroquois County who agreed to fulfill their civic duty faithfully and impartially. The people of this sparsely populated region didn't pay much attention to the news from Joliet. Johnson was not a bogeyman to them. He was not a notorious monster. He was not a danger to society. The people picked for jury duty didn't know anything about Johnson's past. All this jury knew was that he stood trial on charges of first-degree murder for the previous summer's I-55 deadly shooting of a teenager in a parked automobile. Additional charges included attempted murder, sexual assault and kidnapping of the victim's girlfriend. She overcame miraculous odds, and Johnson's lawyers realized her forthcoming testimony would influence the trial's outcome.

The jury trial got underway during the last week of July in 1984.

"The people are going to call several witnesses in this case and they are going to describe to you how a trip to Great

America brought us to this courtroom," prosecutor Burmila announced.

Tonya Little, the jury heard, was abducted at gunpoint and forced to perform sex against her will. Later, she was blindfolded, stabbed and tossed out of a truck. Her attacker expected her to die.

Now, a year afterward, the nineteen-year-old would be the trial's star witness.

"She's going to tell you that the description of this individual that did this to her was a Black male with a pot belly," Burmila revealed. "She's going to further testify that later in March of 1984 ... she made a tentative identification that she saw an in-person identification or an individual, by face and voice, and the evidence is going to show that that individual is the defendant, Milton Johnson."

Burmila spoke how Johnson's pickup truck came to the forefront of the murder investigation. The truck, however, was owned by his stepfather, who "took that truck to a garage to have it painted and that truck remained at that garage for approximately seven months."

When the truck in question was finally impounded, police recovered brown and red fibers similar to ones found outside murder victim Tony Hackett's car on I-55 as well as brown and red fibers where Hackett's girlfriend was left for dead on Route 53.

"You are also going to hear from a person from the crime lab who is going to testify that not only were the fibers located on the roadway, in the vehicle and on (the victim's) clothing similar to fibers located in Mr. Johnson's truck, but that there were other items, fibers, parts of feathers, some animal hairs that were also found on (her) clothing that were linked to the inside of that vehicle.

"We believe that after you hear all of the evidence in this case that you will return a verdict of guilty against the defendant. Thank you," Burmila told the jury.

The defense jumped at the chance to put forth its arguments.

Swano and one of his law firm partners, Eugene O'Malley, maintained the case was about misidentification. Swano asserted that Tonya Little had misidentified his client as well as the physical characteristics of the 1977 Chevy Scottsdale owned by Johnson's stepfather, Sam Myers.

The defense argued the truck owned by Myers had a cracked windshield at the time of the murder and rape along I-55. Little had not told police that her kidnapper's truck had a busted windshield.

"This truck, at the time of the crime in July of last year, had a defective muffler which caused loud sounds to emanate as it was being operated. And you will also hear that this truck had no cigarette burns on its seat nor on the floorboard. This truck also had a visibly significant cracked windshield," Swano's co-counsel declared.

O'Malley alerted the jury that the I-55 rape victim did not indicate her attacker had a goatee and facial hair.

"Last July," O'Malley began, "Mr. Johnson had that goatee. He has had that goatee for the past thirteen years of his life. And Mr. Johnson is a man five-feet-nine inches tall. He's also a man approximately 225 pounds on this date, but in last July he weighed 240 pounds."

The victim believed the rapist looked to be six-foot to six-foot-two, no mustache, no beard, and between twenty-five to thirty years of age.

On the subject of fingerprints, Illinois State Police lifted fifteen sets off the homicide victim's car.

"And you will hear that no fingerprint of Mr. Johnson is on that vehicle," O'Malley asserted.

Furthermore, police never found the gun used to kill Hackett.

"You will see that the gun, a gun, was used to kill Mr. Hackett. There is no association between Mr. Johnson and the gun," O'Malley assured jurors. "There is no association between Mr. Johnson and a knife that was used in stabbing" Tonya Little.

As for the sales receipt found inside the truck Johnson frequently drove, O'Malley told the jurors they will need to weigh that in their mind as they contemplate their verdict.

"Somehow, eight months later, incredibly, that receipt is among a number of papers in the cushion of the seat of Mr. Myers' truck," O'Malley said. "Essentially, ladies and gentlemen, this case you will hear is a question of identification. It's a question of misidentification.

"I believe the evidence will show this, visible evidence that at least links the crime scene with Mr. Myers' truck and that truck is used by numerous people, and you have a weak identification," the defense lawyer argued. "It will fall woefully short of the evidence you need to prove, for the State to prove beyond a reasonable doubt, that Milton Johnson is the perpetrator of these crimes."

The opening day of the trial resulted in a newspaper story from *The Herald-News* headlined, "Identification Of Killer Questioned."

Still, it stood to reason that Johnson's lawyers got sloppy in their trial preparedness. On one hand, despite claiming the rape victim misidentified the truck by overlooking the cracked windshield, Johnson's defense appeared willing to concede the truck was used in the commission of the overnight crimes.

As the trial moved forward, Swano would point the finger at one of his client's siblings in hopes of proving Milton Johnson's innocence.

Was this a gutsy defense or a reckless ploy? Iroquois County jurors had to soak up all the testimony like a sponge and then render its decision.

**

Nobody has a perfect memory, but Tonya Little tried her best to remember the intimate details of her kidnapper's truck. She thought his truck had automatic transmission, a chrome bumper, hubcaps and big mirrors. Since she was taken in the middle of the night, she could not see the colors of the vinyl seat. She guessed they might be dark blue. Inside the cab, she saw a one gallon jug of distilled water and a white Styrofoam cup. Her captor had a duffle bag that may have concealed his knife.

The man who kidnapped her listened to music on the radio.

She also noticed he wore low cut, white gym shoes, that he smoked cigarettes, he had a terrible smell. She was not sure of his height. It was possible he stood at least six-foot-tall. His hair was a half-inch to an inch in length, but not an Afro. Areas of his face exhibited roughness.

He was several years older than her, perhaps in his mid-twenties. He wore blue jeans, a sleeveless tank top and a long-sleeve, blue plaid, flannel shirt. He did not wear jewelry. He did not have an accent, but his voice was low. She did not notice any obvious facial hair.

He carried a shiny revolver; it had a white handle, and the barrel was four to six inches long. His truck was dark or blue, from 1975 to 1979. She thought it was a Ford.

Burmila handled the delicate yet direct line of questioning for his main witness. Her living nightmare from the previous July was now on display for everyone gathered in the Watseka courtroom. On Saturday, July 16, she and her fiancée arrived at Great America in his two-door, hardtop Grand Coup Fury at 2 p.m. They stayed eight hours.

"And now, during that time that you were at Great America, did you have an occasion to purchase any souvenirs?" Burmila inquired.

"Yes," the witness testified. "We bought some shirts and stuffed animals."

"Now, regards to that stuffed animal, what type of stuffed animal was it?"

"A Tasmanian devil."

"Is that a cartoon character?"

"Yes."

"Who purchased the Tasmanian devil?"

"Tony."

"How did he pay for it?"

"Cash."

"Did he get a receipt when he bought that Tasmanian devil?"

"Yes."

Burmila asked if she saw what Tony did with the Great America receipt.

"He put it in his billfold," she testified.

After leaving Great America, which is north of Chicago, the pair of downstate Illinois teenagers did not drive home. Since they were just a few miles short of Wisconsin, Hackett and his girlfriend drove across the state line to purchase a six-pack of bottled beer.

"He drank half of one bottle and put the rest in the back seat," the teenager testified.

At that point, Hackett drove for the next hour, but he made a wrong turn, sending them into Chicago. "We got back on Interstate 55 and drove on down towards Kankakee," Little testified.

Around 1:30 a.m., the teens were too tired to keep driving.

"We pulled off on the shoulder of the interstate," the survivor testified. "I got in the back seat and slept and Tony was sleeping in the front. I had on shorts and a guy's cutoff shirt."

As Little fell asleep, Hackett stretched his legs across his front seat, resting his head against the passenger door. The furry stuffed animal he bought at Marriott's Great America served as his pillow.

Early that Sunday morning, as the teens drifted off to sleep, a stranger pulled behind them. He tapped on their window to startle them awake.

It was all part of his routine.

"I heard a tapping on the passenger side window," Little told the jury.

"What, if anything, did you hear after you heard the tapping?" Burmila inquired.

"Heard gunshots and glass breaking," she responded.

"Approximately how many gunshots did you hear?"

"Two or three."

"Could there have been more?"

"Yes."

A pathologist testified Hackett suffered five distinct gunshots with the deadly shot being the wound that penetrated the right side of his head.

Hackett's parents were in the courtroom during this testimony, and when the boy's mother began crying, Judge Orenic briefly excused the jury. After Hackett's parents left the courtroom, the trial resumed.

When Hackett's fiancée testified, Burmila asked what noises she heard after the bullets shattered the glass.

"I was told to get Tony's wallet and his watch and my purse," she replied.

"Now, is that the same wallet that you had seen Tony put the receipt in?" Burmila followed up.

"Yes."

"Now, did you hand these things to the person that the voice came from?"

"Yes."

"Could you see any part of the person's face at that time?"

"No."

"Could you see his hand?"

"Yes."

"Was the skin on the hand white or black?"

"Black."

"Did you see any part of the clothing that this black hand had on?"

"Yes."

"And what was that?"

"Had a flannel shirt on, long-sleeve, flannel shirt."

"This person say anything else to you at that time?"

"Told me to get out of the car and crawl on my belly to the truck."

"Did you do that?"

"Yes."

The highway killer had parked his truck about ten feet behind Hackett's gold Plymouth.

"The passenger side door was open, and I got in the truck," the victim testified. "I was told to get in the truck and stay on the floor and keep my eyes closed."

As she crouched on the killer's floorboard, the man in the long-sleeved flannel climbed behind the steering wheel and shifted out of park.

"Did you have an opportunity at this that time to see his face?" Burmila wondered.

"Yes."

"Now, you testified that you'd been told to keep your eyes closed. Did you do that?"

"No."

"Did you stare at this person?"

"No."

"How was it that you looked at him?"

"I took small, quick glances."

"Now, the voice that you heard say give me the wallet, the watch and the purse, is that the same voice that said crawl to the truck on your belly?"

"Yes."

"Is that the same voice that said get on the floor and don't look at me?"

"Yes."

"Is he here in the courtroom?" Burmila wondered.

"Yes."

"Could you point to him and say something that he's wearing?"

Little pointed at Johnson and announced, "Light blue shirt."

Burmila asked the judge to take note that his witness identified Johnson as her assailant.

Suddenly, Johnson's lead attorney spoke up.

"May the record reflect Milton Johnson is also the only male black seated at the counsel table?"

"Record may show both," Judge Orenic announced.

Over the next couple hours, the teenager recounted how she was forced to perform numerous degrading sexual acts upon the man who just killed her boyfriend.

The Joliet area was unfamiliar territory to her since she lived in a tiny central Illinois town between Springfield and Bloomington, another ninety minutes away.

She remembered being driven to an isolated spot with scores of pink lights off the highway. She saw a white building and a wired fence.

"I could hear voices," she testified.

Besides hearing sounds of people talking in the distance, Little believed she heard car doors opening and closing. However, she kept her head down as her rapist demanded. The man who killed her boyfriend right in front of her eyes threatened to shoot her if she looked up at any point.

Will County Sheriff's investigators believe he drove her to the mammoth ExxonMobil Joliet Refinery along I-55. Forty miles southwest of Chicago, the Joliet refinery with a chain-link fence around the perimeter was built in 1972 and processed crude oil delivered by pipeline.

In any event, Burmila asked the witness what happened after being driven to this remote spot in the wilderness, in the middle of the night.

"I was raped," she testified.

"Did the defendant place his penis in your vagina?"

"Yes."

"Was that with your consent?"

"No."

While she was being violated, she remembered how the rapist spoke up.

"He asked me why I was crying and if I hadn't ever done that with my boyfriend," she testified.

"Did he ejaculate?"

"I don't know."

"What, if anything, happened after the five or ten minutes went by?"

"He leaned back and wiped me off and wiped himself off with a rag."

She remembered asking the time.

He told her it was 4:30 a.m.

"Was it still dark out when you left the scene where you were raped?" Burmila asked.

"Yes."

After driving momentarily, the rapist made a sudden stop.

"He stopped along the shoulder of the highway and put a rag in my mouth, not a full rag, and he covered my eyes with the rest of it," the victim remembered.

Now blindfolded, Little estimated the man drove around with her for another ten to fifteen minutes.

Then, he pulled off the road along Route 53 a half-mile south of Huff Road near railroad tracks.

"He stabbed me. I lost consciousness. I remember sitting in the middle of the median of the highway," Little testified.

Little spent ten agonizing days hooked up to monitors and machines fighting for her life from her bed at St. Joe's Hospital in Joliet. The love of her life, Tony Hackett, was gone.

Now, a year later, Burmila approached and handed her People's Exhibit 99. It was a crime scene photograph.

"That's the Tasmanian devil we bought at Great America," she replied.

"And where is that Tasmanian devil depicted as being in People's 99?"

"In the front seat of the car on the floor," she testified.

"After you'd given the defendant Tony's wallet, did you ever see the wallet again?"

"No."

"While you were in the truck and you had the opportunity to glance at this individual, was there any particular feature on his face that you paid note to?"

"Yes."

"What was that?"

His eyes, she answered.

CHAPTER 25

WINDSHIELD

Johnson's lawyer Bill Swano engineered a crafty defense centered on potential flaws in the eyewitness testimony from Tonya Little as she recalled being kidnapped.

Swano aimed to convince the jury that his client's family truck already had a huge crack in the windshield by the time of the I-55 shooting.

By then, Dolly and Sam Myers left Joliet in one of their other vehicles for a two-week family reunion and vacation in Mississippi. They left their pickup truck back in Joliet, along with the keys.

"You were not at your house?" prosecutor Burmila inquired.

"No," Dolly Myers responded.

During their vacation, Milton Johnson watched their house.

"Now, ma'am, you talked about the windshield on your truck. When did the windshield on your truck become broken?" Burmila asked.

"I don't know exactly," Dolly Myers testified. "I really don't. Can't say exactly but I know it were broke bad."

"It was broke real bad?"

"Yes it was."

"When you got back from your vacation in Mississippi, you had it repaired?"

"My husband."

"Do you know where it was repaired?"

"The man fixed it in front of the house."

"Did you see him do that?"

"Yes."

"Do you know where the man was from?"

"No I can't say right off because I didn't pay any attention. I didn't ask no questions."

Burmila asked if she reported the broken windshield to her insurance company.

"My husband did everything like that," she responded.

"So he filed a claim in regards to the broken windshield?" Burmila inquired.

"He sure did," she agreed. "I believe Montgomery Ward, he tend to do all that. I believe it was. He tend to all of that. He paid the bills and he tend to it."

Trials are often won by the lawyers who do the best research and are the most prepared. Johnson's lawyer claimed the existence of the cracked windshield proved Tonya Little misidentified her abductor's truck.

The table of the Will County State's Office was hardly ready to concede that point. Burmila produced an employee of Montgomery Ward who testified about the true events regarding the broken windshield.

The employee's testimony, in essence, shattered the defense's contention.

"It was made to me on August 1st," the insurance claims adjuster testified.

"And was a date of loss reported to you?" Burmila asked.

"Yes it was. July 27, 1983," she testified.

"And was the time of loss reported?"

"Yes, approximately 12 p.m."

"Was the location of the loss reported?"

"Located at Route 6 in Marseilles, Illinois."

"And was a description of the loss reported?"

"The cause, he was not sure at the time, but he thought a rock had cracked the windshield."

"Did Montgomery Wards' insurance pay that claim?"

"Yes we did."

"Does the policy reflect an address on the policyholder?"

"Yes it does, 1215 Luther Avenue, Joliet, Illinois, 60432."

With that, Burmila established that a rock broke Sam Myers windshield ten days after the I-55 murder.

"I have no further questions," Burmila announced.

At a later period in the trial, lead prosecutor Petka reminded the jury how Dolly Myers told the jury that the truck's windshield sustained a giant crack prior to going to vacation in Mississippi.

"Whether you want to call it fib, or a lie, or a mistake, it simply doesn't matter in this case," Petka said. "You will recall that (Tonya Little) was examined over a period of time about a crack in the windshield of the pickup truck, a crack that she said she did not recall seeing. The last witness you heard from said that the date of the loss report, the date that that crack was placed on the windshield was July 27, 1983, which just happens to be about ten or eleven days after the incidents that have been described."

Additionally, Dolly Myers told the jury how everyone in her family borrowed the truck.

"Her words," Petka said. "She said there was a lot of noise in the vehicle, her word. But something that we could go to check on the accuracy of her description of when that windshield was cracked, bring in a third party, eleven days off."

**

Burmila went to great lengths to find people to corroborate the testimony of even his most solid witnesses. He paraded into the courtroom, Anna Longo, a training supervisor in the merchandise department at Six Flags Great America, formerly Marriott's Great America.

She told the jury how the amusement park's souvenir stand worked.

"Most of the stuff in our stores at Great America have the same cash register, NCR 280, and they operate the same way," Longo testified. "You have to ring the stock number and a price, and it gives you a total and then when the guest gives you money, you punch in the amount tendered. It's all the same in all the stores."

Burmila raised a question about the souvenir merchandise.

"Every different piece of merchandise in the park has a different stock number," she testified.

The prosecutor handed Longo People's Exhibit 125A.

"If you could examine that, please, and tell me what it is," Burmila instructed her.

"It's a typical receipt that comes out of one of our cash registers," she answered. "OK, every merchandise shop in the department has a different number, and this unit number happens to be 1211, which is Merry Menagerie, one of the stores in our park."

"So by that number, you can tell the particular shop that the receipt came from?" Burmila wondered.

"Yes," the Great America supervisor replied.

Longo was then asked what the number 7-16-83 corresponded to on People's Exhibit 1.

"That is the date of the sale," Longo told the jury. "The date is put in by the opening supervisor in the morning. It's part of the opening procedure and also every time a different cashier goes, signs in on the register, they have to enter their ID number so we can keep track of who's on the register, and at that time the date also goes in."

Burmila drew her attention to the numbers 4348 in the middle of People's Exhibit 1.

"OK, 4348 stands for the amount of transactions that that register has had up to date," she explained. "I mean, it turns over after a certain amount of time."

"And what did the numbers 404 that follow it correspond to?" the prosecutor followed up.

"OK, 404 are the number of transactions that there's been that day," she replied.

Burmila questioned whether Great America could determine the time of day sale number 404 occurred.

"Well, it's a number which is very high," she answered. "So I would guess that it would have to be at least late afternoon."

In the middle of People's Exhibit 1, the prosecutor informed the courtroom, was the number 32201089. Did that number hold any importance to the witness?

"OK, that's a stock number for an eighteen-inch Tasmanian devil plush," Longo responded.

"Is there any other item that Marriott's carried in July of 1983 that had that identification number, other than an eighteen-inch Tasmanian devil doll?"

"No, that's impossible," she replied.

Burmila approached and showed his witness People's Exhibit 94. The photograph showed an object near the slain body of Tony Hackett in the front seat of his car.

"What's there appear to be in People's Exhibit 94 for identification?" he wondered.

"It looks like our Tasmanian devil plush that we sell in the park," Longo responded.

"I have no further questions," Burmila announced.

Judge Orenic turned to Johnson's defense able.

"May I have a moment, please, judge?" Swano asked.

Swano and his client huddled momentarily. How would they refute the testimony regarding the Tasmanian devil sales receipt found in the cab of the Johnson family's truck?

"We have no questions, thank you," Swano informed the judge.

CHAPTER 26

HERO

As the two-week murder trial unfolded, Burmila and Ed Petka presented several Illinois State Police officers, evidence technicians, pathologists and emergency room surgeons who saved Tonya Little's life.

From Petka's standpoint, Ray Tusek, the Lockport man driving to the Kankakee River as part of his summertime fishing ritual, was the hero of the case. The middle-aged man saw the badly injured and barely conscious teenage girl along the four-lane stretch of Route 53 highway south of Joliet on his way toward Wilmington.

"He can't tell you what brought his attention to (her)," Petka told the jury. "He was driving to go fishing on Sunday morning. He simply did not know, but one thing he did say he saw a hand. A hand that appeared to be coming literally out of the weeds from the median strip, he made the inquiry.

"Find out what this was about, and there is no question that his help and the summoning of help in the nick of time saved the life of (Tonya Little). There is no question that the quick action of the Wilmington rescue squad and the quick trip up to Joliet went a long way towards insuring that someone was going to be here to describe the stark terror on Interstate 55 in the early morning hours of July 17, 1983," Petka continued.

One of the biggest arguments during the trial concerned whether Judge Orenic would let Ann Shoemaker testify for the prosecution. The college co-ed had the harrowing experience of being chased around the backroads of Homer Township by a man driving a pickup. The incident happened one weekend before the Homer Township massacre and the I-55 murder. Shoemaker planned to testify she wrote down the license plates, which matched the truck Johnson often drove during Will County's summer terror.

"The prejudice far outweighs the relevance," Swano argued. "There is no indication that the driver of the truck was Milton Johnson. To my knowledge, there's never been a lineup in which she identifies Milton Johnson as the driver.

"It's Sam Myers' truck," Swano conceded. "Other people have access to the truck. We object that it's irrelevant and prejudicial to Mr. Johnson's case on trial here."

Burmila told the judge that Tonya Little identified the I-55 perpetrator as being a heavy-set Black man, with a round belly, wearing a flannel shirt and blue jeans.

"Now, the significance of that is that because there are not too many people who wear heavy flannel shirts in the middle of summer," Burmila pointed out. "Second of all, the license number comes back to Sam Myers' truck, the truck in which evidence linking Milton Johnson further to our crime by way of fiber evidence …

"Thirdly, the circumstantial nature of the description of the person, flannel shirt, heavy set, which is not the description of Mr. Myers, will show that Milton Johnson, on the weekend prior to this, and our crime happened on the weekend, in the late evening hours of a Saturday into the early morning hours of a Sunday, is out prowling around in that pickup truck," Burmila asserted. "A person can drive up and down on the street in front of other citizens' houses as much as he wants, but it's certainly suspicious.

"So, I think the fact that Mr. Johnson circumstantially is linked to that pickup truck on the preceding weekend, acting in a suspicious nature, utilizing the truck in the late evening hours, and the truck belongs, again, to his stepfather, indicating he uses it when his stepfather could possibly be at home or asleep or not using the truck for work, lends reliability to the admission of that evidence."

Swano pleaded with the judge to keep the young woman's forthcoming testimony out of the jury trial altogether.

"All they're trying to do is throw fear in the hearts of the jury that Milton Johnson is out harassing young women, that he's tailgating them, or following them, that he's a cur in the night, with a different set of circumstances than what their allegations are in the instant case," the Chicago defense lawyer suggested. "And what it's showing is that Milton Johnson was out that night, and he had targeted two other potential victims that he was going to kill that night but for the fact that these girls jumped in the weeds and but for the fact that these girls found their boyfriends and turned it around and they followed him."

Swano wrapped up his arguments by declaring it would be a tragic mistake to let this evidence go in against Johnson.

"Is there anything that conclusively shows that this is the truck that was used for the Hackett murder?" the judge asked the lawyers.

"Well, I don't know what you mean by conclusive," Burmila replied.

"Well, I shouldn't use the word conclusively," Judge Orenic said. "Is there any convincing evidence that this is the truck?"

"No one saw the truck on the day of the killing and said, 'There goes Sam Myers' truck,'" Burmila answered. "We believe the fiber evidence will link the truck to the killing on the day of the killing, if that's what you're asking me."

Swano's law partner, Eugene O'Malley, reminded the judge that no license plate identification was made in the I-55 murder.

"No license plate was taken?" the judge inquired.

"No one took the license plate down on the day of the murder," Burmila acknowledged.

With that answer, the judge issued his ruling on whether to let Ann Shoemaker testify.

"All right, then, I think that evidence should be admissible, so I am going to deny your motion," Orenic told Johnson's lawyers.

"You think that it's relevant to the trial at hand?" Swano responded.

"Yes, I do," the judge told him.

As the trial continued, Johnson's parents began having second thoughts about paying Swano $15,000 to defend their son.

"During trial, I noticed that Swano was very passive," Sam Myers recalled. "I mentioned that he should make more objections, and he started to do this the next time in court. Swano would look at me in court as if he was objecting just to please me.

"Sometime during the trial, Swano told me not to come to trial and to stay at a motel because he did not want me to testify. I did exactly as he said. That was just for one day.

Mr. Swano came to the motel at lunch time and asked me for $2,000. I told him that the $15,000 was all he was getting. Swano mentioned he needed the money to pay someone to bring something into court. He did not get any more money from me."

In the end, Swano did not let Johnson testify in his own defense.

As the trial drew to a close, Swano praised the seven men and five women for their attentiveness. They were the most patient jury he had ever seen, he told them.

From there, Swano launched into a history of the American jury system and how it traced back to the 12th century, King John's tyranny and the Magna Carta. "That Magna Carta traveled a long way across the Atlantic to the United States and was embodied in our Constitution by the founding fathers," Swano declared. "It's codified the rights of every individual to be proven guilty beyond a reasonable doubt. And that as any defendant sits in court, he is presumed to be innocent until such time as the prosecution has overcome that presumption and proven him guilty beyond a reasonable doubt … it is not Mr. Johnson's rights, it is all of our rights."

Reflecting on the trial, Swano said the jury heard testimony from nearly two dozen witnesses. "Some of the testimony bears on Mr. Johnson's guilt or innocence. I submit a lot of it doesn't. The issue in this case is not that a horrible tragedy occurred on July 17th off I-55. There is no dispute Anthony Hackett was murdered. There is no dispute that (Tonya Little) was raped, and somebody tried to kill her. There is only one issue in this case. And there is only one issue that you ladies and gentlemen of the jury must deliberate upon and that is whether or not the state has proven beyond a reasonable doubt that Milton Johnson was the perpetrator of that crime. I submit that after careful analysis of the evidence they will have not met their burden and that you will render a verdict of not guilty." The knife found in the back cab of the truck had no relevancy to the case, argued the defense.

"They brought out that the knife was found in Mr. Myers' truck," Swano said. "I submit that that stab wound was consistent with any steak knife that any one of us have in our kitchen drawers."

The defense reminded jurors how the prosecution did not call David Sims to testify. Sims was the black motorist who stopped to help Ray Tusek render aid to Tonya Little as she lay in the Route 53 median.

"Mr. Sims was a black male and that … would explain some of the Negroid head hairs that were found on her person at the hospital," Swano suggested. "Why didn't the prosecution bring Mr. Sims? Because it is reasonable to infer that head hairs from him may have landed on (Tonya Little). They only brought Mr. Tusek."

Then, there was the empty beer can found near the rape victim along Route 53. "There were no fingerprint lifts from that beer can," Swano reminded the jury.

"The prosecution has tried to make a big deal out of the fact that Sam Myers decided that his rusted-out, old truck was in need of some body repairs so they called Mrs. Ulmer.

"There was no testimony that Mr. Myers was asking to stash the truck away. As a matter of fact, Mrs. Ulmer's testimony was that the truck was blocking the way of various other vehicles at their house and her husband put the truck in the garage. Mr. Myers came over to the home several times during the fall and winter months to find out where his truck was."

Swano argued the Great America sales receipt for the stuffed animal by defied logic, since the find happened after eight months after the homicide.

"And lo and behold, the find of the century, and it is a receipt from Great America," Swano remarked. "There is no wallet, there is no purse. But the receipt is found."

On the other hand, several fingerprints were lifted from Hackett's car and none linked back to Johnson.

"There is no weapon recovered that's linked to the shooting death of Mr. Hackett," Swano stressed. "Now, there were guns found at Mr. Myers' house, but none of those guns were the guns that were used to fire the bullets into Mr. Hackett's body.

"I submit that not one iota of physical evidence in this case points guilt at Mr. Johnson. I would submit that at best the physical evidence links the truck to this crime but you must decide beyond a reasonable doubt whether or not Mr. Johnson was the driver of that truck that evening. And I submit after careful analysis of all the evidence the state has not met their burden in that regard."

As for the rape victim, she was in a state of trauma. She was scared. She was told to stay down, crawl on her belly, not to look up. It was dark.

The man she identified as the killer and rapist was a Black man, closer to six-foot-two, with no mustache or beard, Johnson's lawyer said.

"She told you that it was a blue Ford. This is a black Chevy," Swano told jurors. "She told you that it had hubcaps. There are no hubcaps. She told you that it had a white wide stripe. There is no white, wide stripe. She told you had blue interior. There is no blue interior. She told you that there was a gallon milk jug. There was no gallon jug recovered from Mr. Myers' vehicle."

With that, Swano implored the jury to find his client not guilty.

"The law is not that you must have fifteen reasonable doubts or fourteen reasonable doubts or ten reasonable doubts or five reasonable doubts. If you have a reasonable doubt as to the identity of the assailant as to the identity of Milton Johnson, you must find Milton Johnson not guilty. And we are asking you to do that. Thank you."

Burmila would handle the prosecution's rebuttal.

He would start his remarks by telling the story of a ship captain and the captain's second mate.

CHAPTER 27

VERDICT

A graduate of De Paul University Law School in Chicago, Ed Burmila was on the fast track for success upon joining the Will County State's Attorney's Office. In 1977, Burmila began prosecuting misdemeanor crimes. Seven years later, he was prosecuting the most notorious mass murderer defendant in Will County's history.

Known around the Will County Courthouse as Eddie B, Burmila was unconventional. At one moment during Johnson's trial, Burmila got on his hands and knees to illustrate for the jury at how difficult it was for Tonya Little to estimate the height of the rapist who kidnapped her in the middle of the night along the interstate. The only time the victim ever saw her attacker stand was when he ordered her to crawl on her belly back to his truck and not look up or he would shoot her dead.

Burmila also maintained that the downstate teenager's inability to notice Johnson had a goatee was insignificant, given that it was dark outside as well as inside the kidnapper's truck.

The first Illinois State Police reports from the case reflect that Little did not see any noticeable facial hair.

"I'd like to begin by telling you that listening to Mr. Swano's argument reminded me of a story that I heard a long time ago," Burmila told the Iroquois County jurors seated in the small-town courthouse. "It was a story about a ship that was going to be put to sea and stay out at sea for a very long time. And the second-in-command on that ship showed up the night this ship was to leave dock, and he had been drinking, and he had been drinking quite a bit because he wasn't going to see his friends, his family, for a long time. And he went on to the ship, and the captain wrote a notation down in the logbook and said, 'First day of journey, second mate drunk.'

"The whole rest of the journey, he performed marvelously. The captain told him as they neared the end of the journey, 'You know, you are the best second mate I have ever had on this ship' and he said, 'Well, I will never be able to get a ship of my own if you leave that on the record. They will see that that has to be explained,' and the captain told him, no, a fact is a fact, I leave it in the record," Burmila told the jury.

"So, when they got in port the captain happened to be sleeping on the last day, and the first mate was in charge, and he wrote in the logbook, 'Returned to port, tonight the captain is sober.'

"Now, what does this story tell us?" Burmila asked the jury. "Never accept a fact without an explanation. Nothing stands by itself. An explanation."

All the facts mentioned by Swano had an explanation, including the empty beer can found in the area where the rape victim was left for dead, Burmila pointed out.

"Has there ever been any connection whatsoever, any connection whatsoever, of this beer can to the offender in this case?" Burmila asked. "Did (she) say there was a beer can in the trunk? Did she say the man who did this touched a beer can? Did she say when he threw me out of the truck, he touched a beer can? That is an attempt to divert your attention from the true facts in this case."

Indeed, police recovered thirty-two fingerprints from Hackett's car. Almost all of them belonged to the Hackett family or the two victims.

The two unidentified fingerprints came from the fenders, Burmila told jury.

"Did (she) ever tell you that the person who did this touched the fenders of that vehicle? Do they have any relevance whatsoever in this case, unless it is to divert your attention from the true facts? There is no known way to tell the age of a fingerprint. How many hundreds of people passed that car in the parking lot at Great America that day? The fact that those fingerprints are not the defendant's means absolutely nothing."

Burmila also scoffed at Swano's contention that one of Johnson's two grown brothers, James or Louis, drove the family's truck when Ann Shoemaker was being chased along the backroads of Homer Township the weekend prior to the Homer Township massacre on 147th Street and the I-55 slaying.

"Don't leave your common sense outside in the hallway when you go in that jury room," Burmila implored. "Who lives in the house? Milton. Where's Louis live? Someplace else, and James is staying in Gary, Indiana … Do you think Louis in the middle of the night came over, came into the house, just took the truck in the middle of the night, not the person who lives there? … Louis works for the State of Illinois, two kids in a private school, married, lives in another place, maybe it is him," Burmila remarked sarcastically.

As far as being wrong about Johnson's height, Burmila said the survivor was only off by two inches.

"The truck," Burmila persisted. "She said it was a dark-colored truck. She thought that it was a Ford. I submit to you that most nineteen-year-old girls would be lucky if they knew Ford made trucks. She talks about hubcaps. You look at those pictures, chrome-trim rings around the wheels, chrome lug nuts, chrome hub covers, that won't look like a hubcap to somebody crawling on the street when she passes by it?

"She is sound asleep. Sound asleep and within five minutes time, look what happens to her: Gunshots. Her fiancé is killed. She is armed robbed. Her hair is pulled ... I think the description she gave of that truck is pretty darn close under those circumstances."

On the middle of July weekend of the Homer Township massacre and the I-55 killing, Johnson's parents were down South.

"Milton, who stayed home from the trip to Mississippi, alone, keys to the truck," Burmila said. "We know this is the truck. There is no question about the truck. The fibers are there, the red and brown ones, the lilac-colored fibers, the smoky-gray fibers, the feather parts, they are all there. We know this is the truck.

"That truck couldn't have been in any better of a preserved state if we had put it in a block of ice," Burmila declared.

Then, on Sept. 12, 1983, Illinois State Police Investigator "John Beck shows up at the house and suddenly the truck takes the Deep Six. We don't have the gym shoes because he got rid of the gym shoes, and we don't have the gun because he got rid of the gun, and we don't have the wallet because he got rid of the wallet. We don't have the purse because he got rid of the purse, and he thought he had the truck out of commission because it was going to be painted, and the body work was going to be done, but he didn't know the fibers. He didn't know that the receipt was in there. He couldn't get rid of that because he didn't know it was there. Where was that truck for eight months? Is it like it was driving around the street, people were jumping in and out of it? It was locked up in a garage."

Angrily, Eugene O'Malley, one of Johnson's lawyers, blurted out, "Objection again. Ulmer was sick."

"Please," Judge Orenic responded.

"Judge, he is inferring the truck was hidden," O'Malley argued.

Orenic had no problem with Burmila's insinuation.

"The objection is overruled," Orenic ruled.

Finally, Burmila brought Will County's case to a close.

He reminded the jury of the brown stuffed animal the happy-go-lucky teens bought as a keepsake at Marriott's Great America.

"Tony Hackett is the one who told us who the killer is in this case," Burmila told the jury. "Because he did something at Great America so they could remember that day. He bought (Tonya) a Tasmanian devil and he bought that Tasmanian devil to remember the day. Little did he know how good a job that Tasmanian devil would do.

"I am going to ask you to go into the jury room, and I am going to ask you to look at the verdict forms, select the ten that say guilty, guilty, guilty, guilty, guilty, guilty and sign those verdict forms because this is the man who killed Tony Hackett. This is the man that raped (Tonya Little), and this is the man that committed deviate sexual assault on her. This is the man that tried to kill her."

With that, the biggest murder trial in decades was over at Watseka's courthouse. At 4:32 p.m. on a Friday, the twelve registered voters of Iroquois County, ranging in age from their early twenties to early seventies, retreated to the jury room to begin their closed-door deliberations Aug. 3, 1984.

While American gymnast Mary Lou Retton racked up gold medals at the U.S. Olympics more than 2,000 miles away in Los Angeles, jurors in Watseka, Illinois, weighed the evidence in the I-55 murder. Tony Hackett's parents remained in the courthouse as did Sam and Dolly Myers, the defendant's parents.

At 10 p.m., the jury reached a unanimous verdict, and the news quickly spread.

"Johnson Guilty; Jury To Eye Death Penalty," declared the next morning's front-page headline for *The Herald-News*.

Will County State's Attorney was elated.

"The verdicts were certainly consistent with the evidence," Petka told reporters. "In my opinion, the evidence was overwhelming. We are going for the death penalty."

Johnson's parents fumed. They put up $15,000 to hire Swano. Now, the best they could hope for was a life sentence for their son.

"I believe that Mr. Swano took my money and just went through the motions during the trial. I do not believe that he ever really tried to win the case," Sam Myers said later.

To ensure Johnson's right to a fair and impartial trial, the jury was not told the murder defendant was a recent parolee from the Illinois Department of Corrections after serving thirteen years for a scary late-night torture rape at Joliet's Pilcher Park.

Throughout his trial, Johnson let his criminal defense lawyers control his case, but those days were over. Johnson did not want the jury deciding his fate in a capital murder case. The jury was sent home and thanked for its service.

Johnson decided Judge Orenic would render his sentence.

"You may have heard that I'm personally opposed to the death penalty but that would not alter any decision I would make," the judge told Johnson.

"I also have heard you have imposed the death penalty in some cases," Johnson responded back.

**

Born in 1924, Michael Orenic was three months shy of turning sixty as Will County's chief judge presided over Johnson's death penalty trial. Orenic had twenty years on the bench.

Orenic grew up in Joliet, graduating from Joliet Catholic High School in 1942. He enlisted in World War II, serving as a navigator in the Army Air Force, retiring as a major in the U.S. Air Force Reserves. By 1950, Orenic graduated from De Paul University Law School in Chicago. He served as an assistant state's attorney for Will County from 1957 until 1964 when he was elected a Will County Circuit Court judge. He would serve as the chief judge for the 12th Circuit of Illinois from 1976 until 1982 and again from 1984 until 1986. The 12th Circuit included Will, Kankakee and Iroquois counties at that time.

"He was a fascinating guy, a brilliant guy," remarked Joliet attorney George Mahoney III during an interview with the Illinois State Bar Association. "He was a big guy with flowing white hair. He had this physical aura about him. He looked like a judge."

When he wasn't wearing a black robe in Will County's Courthouse, Orenic played violin with the Floyd Wilson String Quartet. Orenic also played in the Joliet Junior College Community Orchestra as well as the Lewis University Symphony Orchestra in nearby Romeoville.

Besides being a member of the Illinois State Bar Association, Orenic served in the Joliet Federation of Musicians Local 37 as well as the Knights of Columbus Joliet Council 382.

One of his quirks, according to other Joliet lawyers, was that Orenic kept a spittoon in his Will County courtroom.

Now, the tobacco-chewing judge had to deliver justice for Milton Johnson. The sentencing pronouncement took place Sept. 16, 1984.

Unlike at trial, Petka could now introduce evidence and testimony from other terrorizing Joliet area crimes linked to Johnson. Petka started with the barbaric Feb. 15, 1970, attack upon the Plainfield teenage girl who was burned with a cigarette lighter as Johnson raped her inside the woods of Pilcher Park.

The crime left her so haunted that she moved far away from Illinois and chose not to return to Illinois to testify against Johnson at his capital punishment sentencing. Chandler, her boyfriend at the time of the attack, testified in the alternative.

"Back in 1970, Milton Johnson was convicted of this truly random assault on a couple that was parked in a car in Pilcher Park," Petka told the judge. "He was sent to prison and during that period of time, he accumulated a number of violations. I believe the number was twenty-four. But significantly, he was released, that being on March 9, 1983."

Then, within three months of his prison release, Milton Johnson returned to his wicked ways, the judge heard.

"And as to the theory in our opinion, Milton Johnson was about to do what he does best, and that is maim and torture people in Homer Township.

"He was once again looking for a parked couple in an isolated area, where he took a person's life," Petka argued. "A person that he had never seen before in his life … Using an analogy of the so-called hidden picture, and I'm sure, judge, that you have seen these little almost puzzle-like type of caricatures in various children's magazines, where a person is asked to take a long look and find out after looking at these pictures, whether or not they see an elephant in there or see a tiger or see a clown.

"In looking at the murder which occurred on I-55, the hidden picture became crystal clear that it was a picture of Milton Johnson."

The State's Attorney tied Johnson to the July 1983 random Homer Township massacre that left five people dead and only one survivor.

In northwest Homer Township, Cathy Norwood, in her twenties, and Richard "Dewey" Paulin, in his early thirties, parked their little car near a farm. During their romantic rendezvous, Johnson emerged and began to watch them in the middle of the night.

Paulin was fatally shot in the backseat. Norwood was shot in the grass not far from the car.

"If the court just examines the situation without a pickup truck, the situation of a couple that is parked in a field … the court will see once again, that we have a couple that is parked, an assailant who comes upon the scene and interrupts whatever the couple may have been doing," Petka told Judge Orenic.

"I think that a picture that is surely emerging is a picture that has Milton Johnson in it," Petka continued. "What this testimony tells us in corroborating what Mr. Foley said was that he was shot with the assailant's gun. I believe that the testimony clearly indicates that Deputy Steve Mayer and Sergeant Foley were shot with the assailant's gun. That the guns were taken from Sergeant Foley and from Steve Mayer and one of those guns, which we now believe to be Steve Mayer's weapon, was used to shoot Cathy Norwood and Richard Paulin, the people in the little car."

Moments later, George Kiehl and his girlfriend were shot in their approaching van. He died, and other bullets struck her in the shoulder.

Then, the next night, Tonya Little and her boyfriend were harmed in their car along the shoulder of I-55.

And there was the shooting along U.S. Route 6 that shattered Theresa McKeen's window as she drove home from Joliet's EJ & E train yard the weekend before the summer murder rampage began.

"Theresa McKeen testified here in open court that in the late evening hours of June 17, 1983, that as she was leaving Silver Cross Hospital, that a Black man in a pickup truck opened fire on her without cause or provocation," Petka pointed out. "And that a short while later, she had occasion to see this Black man who was near a pickup truck, who was yelling at her with an angry face. That he had a gun in his hand, and he fired at her again, again and again."

After Johnson was arrested in March 1984 for the I-55 murder, McKeen went to the Will County jail to view a photo lineup of suspects in her crime.

"And she identified Milton Johnson as being the person who had fired that weapon at her," Petka said. "I think that the key thing about that identification is that when the identification was made and shortly thereafter, this woman became extremely hysterical, emotional, and she required medical support."

Less than two hours after McKeen's car was shot up, Illinois State Trooper Robert Rogers located a truck parked near Cedar Road and U.S. Route 6. Johnson was the driver.

"A vehicle which was registered to Sam Myers and which was driven by Milton Johnson was seen, which, in our opinion, corroborates very closely the testimony that was given by Theresa McKeen in connection with the assault upon her," Will County's State's Attorney revealed.

As the judge heard testimony during the death penalty phase of the trial, Johnson's chair remained empty. The convicted killer chose not to be in the courtroom for a large portion of the proceedings that continued in his absence.

The killer's moody behavior left Orenic unsure whether Johnson would be in the courtroom when the judge rendered his decision.

But after choosing to stay away for several days, Johnson wanted his chance in the spotlight. He wanted to leave his mark on the judicial process regarding the I-55 murder trial.

"Your honor, I don't have a prepared statement for the court," Johnson began. "I think that a lot of things during this trial, a lot of the procedure, period, has been somewhat outrageous in my belief.

"I think that it is not only my opinion, but a lot of other peoples' opinion, also. Some of the things that they considered as evidence, some of the things that was taken as facts, that was strictly lies, and they knew about beforehand."

Johnson had more to unload on the judge.

"It's not something that I could readily at that time prove, nor now. It just seems strange and so obvious that someone could remember certain things and then forget other things that were so pertinent. Even the State made statements, the things that they couldn't prove I suppose could have hid or threw away or whatever. And the victim in this case, they stated things so far, low-cut shoes that she was positive about, that I don't own, never owned, never wore low-cut shoes."

Johnson fixated on his belief that his teenage rape victim did not recall every exact detail of his face, his clothes and his shoes at the time he kidnapped, assaulted and thrust a long knife into her belly.

He left her to die in a ditch along a lonely highway, but she lived to everyone's astonishment, including his.

"Everything they have, everything I'm saying, everything is already in print," Johnson addressed the judge. "If they can use it against me, I want them to. I want them to. So it boils back down to the same thing that I'm saying is that, if she was so positive that he was wearing low-cut shoes, and minor as it may have seemed, but yet it was something she was positive about, and the state of the fact is, I don't even own one. I don't have, never wore. The only kind I have is high tops."

Actually, a March 9, 1984, Will County Sheriff's report from the raid at Johnson's house on Luther Avenue contradicts Johnson's sentencing testimony. Deputy Sheriff Mark Tomany photographed two pairs of Converse All-Stars gym shoes: one pair high tops, the other pair low cuts, and he photographed two plaid, flannel shirts.

Johnson grew angry that prosecutors presented testimony from the rape victim suggesting he wore a blue plaid shirt.

"I don't own any plaid shirts, blue. Never wore them," Johnson suggested. "The only people that knows this is my family, friends."

Interestingly, Johnson, never once suggested he was innocent. He never suggested he was the wrong person standing trial for the I-55 murder. Rather, he used his sentencing to nitpick some of the more obscure items of evidence from his trial.

"Some of the things that I get mad about when I see them imply this, and show it and hold it up in front of a jury, knowing that they are lying," Johnson said. "So it doesn't make any difference whether it's true or not. It was implied. That's enough. I sit up there and listen to her tell about, she looked in a guy's eyes and saw that they was bloodshot. She saw his chin, which was a normal chin.

"But yet, she forgot so many things, so that they couldn't recall as to whether he had facial hair or not … I've had facial hair for a long time, even the investigators know about this. I even watched the investigators get up and say it was longer at the time, which was a lie, because the pictures proved … especially the last month of June or July, it was longer than what it is now … the fact is that I have been wearing it all along for thirteen years. The last thirteen years, at least, so there is no chance for it to be removed or anything else. The State even went as far as to imply different things as far as my family was concerned, my brothers, other things that they were wrong about."

Johnson maintained that his girlfriend from Milwaukee, Mary Jo Hillyer, came to Joliet and checked into the Holiday Inn on Sunday, July 17. Because her visit happened after, not before, the I-55 killing and kidnapping, it was hard to understand Johnson's point.

"They knew from the telephone calls and the receipts of the things that was taken, that that night, as to where I was,"

Johnson countered. "They even knew that within a few short hours after the incident with Miss (Little), after she was supposedly rushed to the hospital in a life and death situation that I was out at the Holiday Inn with my girlfriend at this time. They knew this. They talked to her. The investigators talked to her. They implied to me at a time of racial tension, but they were somewhat disillusioned when they found out the girl I was with happened to be a white girl."

Since this was Johnson's moment of limelight in his courtroom drama, the convicted killer was not going to let up.

"They told this girl not to mention that she was with me," Johnson claimed. "You understand? They had not got in touch with her. Why, you understand? So many things that they knew about beforehand, they hid. They did their best. I can understand that. My attorneys was given forty-five days from the time they took over this trial to defend me for these crimes. I've been down here in this county jail in this basement down here the last few months with guys that was in here for double murders that was in before me. But I'm sure their trial will be coming up after the election. I'm positive of that."

Johnson then scolded Judge Orenic for making his lawyers take his case to trial expeditiously.

"I didn't feel that they was prepared," Johnson said. "Unfortunately, you wasn't defending me, but you was sort of the control over everything that was done in this courtroom as far as evidence.

"It was your decision as to whether the jury would see it or not, even the pictures. The police sketch artist that the witness gave nowhere matches me, period."

Johnson believed the police composite of the I-55 killer was not a perfect match for his facial characteristics.

"Even if the fact that she told the sketch artist the face was a little bit wider, she did not tell him he had a beard or mustache," Johnson pointed out. "It was your decision as to whether the jury would see it. And you denied that also. And then again, I must admit, I wasn't surprised. And I explained it to my attorney also.

"There's a lot of things that could be said about this trial, a lot of unanswered questions," Johnson reflected. "I know, because I've been back over some of the police reports myself, even from the things brought in from the Homer Township incident to whenever this other incident was out on Route 6."

Johnson offered a scathing rebuke of several witnesses for the prosecution. He told the judge he watched police officers walk into the courtroom and lie.

"But like I said, it was admitted in evidence. And it's hard to sit up and listen to someone tell you one thing and strike it from the record. They don't strike it from your mind. I don't care who you are. There's nobody that good, not even you. You heard testimony and everything else and as to how you would accept the facts, I don't know."

Johnson pondered how his jury trial went.

"I'm definitely not pleased with it, period," Johnson complained. "My reasons for not being here in the last few days was not arrogance upon the court in a sense of this and that. I heard rumors as far as he's breaking as far as that.

"I've got news for everybody that thinks he's breaking," Johnson declared, referring to himself in the third person.

"From the day I walked in and pleaded not guilty with a smile on my face, I'll walk out this evening the same way, with a smile on my face. Because I get mad only when I see the statements that other people say, and I know they are lies, and there is nothing I can do about it. That's the only thing that bothers me."

With that, Johnson drew his comments to a close.

"Like I said there's a lot of other things I can say, but it's not going to make any difference. If it's possible, it would probably be overruled by you. So that's all I have to say."

A brief silence came over the courtroom. Then, the judge spoke.

"Based upon all of the evidence that the court has heard in the trial of the case and the evidence presented at the sentencing hearing, the court determines that there are no mitigating factors sufficient to preclude the imposition of the death sentence," Orenic pronounced.

"Under the law, the court now must and does sentence the defendant, Milton Johnson, to death."

But Johnson's trip to the penitentiary would not happen yet.

CHAPTER 28

SECOND TRIAL

Following his success in front of the Iroquois County jury, Petka immediately filed four more first-degree murder charges against the Joliet killer for the Aug. 20, 1983, ceramic shop slayings.

Again, Petka sought the death penalty. Not long after Will County Circuit Judge Robert Buchar was assigned to the case, Swano's days of defending Johnson drew to a close. His client's family did not have the funds to retain him for a second trial.

In late 1984, the judge appointed the Will County Public Defender's Office and assigned lawyers Sam Andreano and Richard Orloff to Johnson. At that time, Johnson told the judge he "would be more than satisfied" to have Andreano as his lead criminal defense lawyer.

Then, on the day of the Sept. 30, 1985, trial, Johnson revealed a change of heart. He wanted to get rid of Andreano and Orloff as his lawyers. The next day, Johnson filed a pro se motion, meaning he drafted his own legal filing as a lay person. He wanted the judge to remove his public defenders and assign him brand new lawyers from outside the Will County Public Defender's Office and outside Will County in general.

Johnson was supposedly furious Andreano and Orloff did not share all the police and prosecution files with him.

Furthermore, they refused to track down everyone Johnson insisted they interview and call as trial witnesses.

Because of the last-minute chaos, the judge delayed Johnson's trial in the ceramic shop murders.

At this juncture, Johnson changed his mind again. This time, he told Judge Buchar he would take Andreano back along with public defender Kathleen Kallan to replace Orloff. The judge agreed to the switch.

One week later, more pretrial shenanigans happened.

Johnson told the judge he was firing Andreano after a dispute over stipulated testimony from a medical examiner's pathologist who would not be available to testify in person at trial.

Johnson opted for self-representation. He would stand trial in a quadruple murder trial as his own lawyer.

Not wanting the high-profile multiple murder case reversed on appeal, the judge ordered Andreano and Kallan to remain in his courtroom at all times during the jury trial as standby counsel.

In other words, Johnson could consult with them at any point during his trial once the jury was seated.

The Illinois Supreme Court would eventually be asked to render a legal decision on the matter.

The ruling went in favor of the judge.

"We recognize, of course, the importance of a defendant's right to counsel," the Illinois Supreme Court wrote. "However, we cannot countenance use of that right in a manner which appears calculated to thwart the administration of justice or to otherwise embarrass the effective prosecution of crime."

Illinois Supreme Court justices agreed "a defendant should not be permitted to frustrate the trial court's efforts to conduct an orderly, fair and expedient trial, and then benefit from an alleged error by the court which he invited through his own conduct. In addition to the foregoing, we believe the admonishments defendant received in this case were sufficient since, although he represented himself, he had the benefit of standby counsel 'for advice and consultation at all times during the course of the trial.' Whether or not defendant actually chose to avail himself of their services, and the extent to which counsel in fact participated in the proceedings is not, as defendant suggests, the relevant inquiry."

It would be a Will County murder trial like none other. The burly mass murder defendant could walk the courtroom and approach detectives and family members of the four slain women with his own line of questions.

Johnson embraced the chance to be his own lawyer. He constantly referred to himself in the third person during trial proceedings.

The Herald-News carried the headline, "Johnson Gets Passing Grade As Lawyer." The article began: "While he was no Clarence Darrow or F. Lee Bailey, Milton Johnson wasn't inept as an attorney during his trial."

Will County Public Defender Kathleen Kallan told the newspaper that she gave him a letter grade of C as during his two-week murder trial. The article quoted Johnson's other standby public defender Sam Andreano as saying, "There are lawyers who would have done worse."

All eyes were on Johnson. He was both the mass murder defendant and the master of his domain. He commanded everyone's attention as his own lawyer.

It was a sight to see.

**

When Johnson's second trial began Jan. 3, 1986, State's Attorney Petka was no longer in the courtroom. He paired Burmila with Assistant State's Attorney Stephen White. Johnson directed his own defense. After picking a jury of Will County citizens, testimony got underway a week later.

"Now, what do we know about the killer of Marilyn Baers, Barbara Dunbar and Anna Ryan and Pam Ryan?" White informed the jury. "He left footprints. Where did he leave them? He left them by the body of Anna Ryan and Barbara Dunbar. Where? On a piece of paper and that paper was examined by the forensic scientist, forensic expert, and the footprint, footprints, the same footprints are seen in the shop. They are seen in the doorway. They are seen on the concrete walkway just outside of the ceramic shop. They are seen on the driveway, right by where the Blazer was parked, and that is where they ended, and they did not pick up again and they were not observed again until in the car wash, not under the Blazer, but around the Blazer, around the perimeter in its final resting position."

The shoe impressions were all the same.

"But on August 20, 1983, there are no shoes to compare to the prints," White pointed out. "They are consistent with a size 11, and they are all made by a Converse All-Star gym shoe."

The killer handled a rag found near the bodies of Dunbar and Anna Ryan. The rag contained two hairs from someone of African-American origin, the jury learned.

A bullet tore through Anna Ryan's neck and lodged in the ceramic shop wall.

"And the killer, the murderer, took the purses and the money and then dumped the purses in Hickory Creek off of South Chicago Street on the south side of Joliet," White announced.

Three victims rode in Pam Ryan's Chevy Blazer and parked in front of the ceramic shop shortly after 11:15 a.m. Less than thirty minutes later Helen Allen pulled into the parking lot. However, she chose not to enter. Instead, she drove away.

"Helen Allen stated that at 11:40 that morning, that she arrived and saw a figure of a person in the window, walking from one side of the ceramic shop to the other," White remarked. "The Blazer is out in front of the door and that is the exact location to where footprints are later found. At twelve noon, approximately, at the car wash, seen by Sherri Walters, who lives next door to the car wash, is the Blazer in its final resting position in that stall."

When Joliet resident Edna Hauck pulled into the business lot around 12:05 p.m., the Ryan's Blazer was not there.

"She enters," White said. "She sees no one, called for Marilyn Baers, she gets no response. She goes back out to her vehicle. She is there with her daughter-in-law and grandchildren. She goes in. She discovered the bodies and called the police, and the police arrived and take control of the ceramic shop."

By 12:46 p.m., Will County evidence technician Lynn West went to 1405 East Cass Street, the building that used to be a grocery store. In 1983, Greenware By Merry contained molds and clay. The four slain women were all found in the backrooms, and none of them had identification.

The Joliet business had three entrances all on the south. The main door used by customers was the middle door, a full length Thermopane glass door.

"There were indications of an attempted entry through the number 1 exit door furthest west," the evidence technician noted. "These indications were observed in subsequent processing."

West videotaped the scene, including the four victims, and the overall conditions of the building. While processing the crime scene, West photographed the shoe impressions.

Barbara Dunbar was found in a backroom converted from a refrigeration cooler into a space to make the Greenware clay. Dunbar's head pointed north, and she was on her back.

"The amount of blood at this location was massive," West wrote. "I observed multiple punctures/lacerations about Barbara Dunbar's chest and neck. She was fully clothed. Her wrists were under the small of her back and adjacent to this I found a mold strap."

Made of canvas, the straps had metal buckles to hold the Greenware molds together. "I observed a number of mold straps on the floor at the feet of Barbara Dunbar," West wrote.

Dunbar's glasses remained on her forehead. Her skin showed discoloration from bruising. The circular marks around her left eye indicated a blunt object hit her, "propelling the glasses against the eye area or that it was incurred in a fall."

West estimated Dunbar suffered twelve stab wounds to her chest and three to her throat. As he analyzed her wounds, West cut her blouse and her brassiere to examine her puncture marks and to attempt to recover fibers and latent fingerprint residues.

The second victim, senior citizen Anna Ryan, was closest to Dunbar. Ryan's head pointed east and she was on her back.

"The amount of blood at this location was massive, and there was an additional pool of blood north of her body," West advised. He found another mold strap on the floor between the two bodies.

Anna Ryan suffered multiple punctures and cuts to her throat, neck and chest. She was fully clothed, and her lower false teeth protruded out of her mouth. A fake pearl necklace and a set of eyeglasses were found near her body. Anna Ryan suffered ten stab wounds to her chest and two to her neck.

At the gory scene, West found a purse from one of the victims on a shelf between a cooler and the bathroom. The purse blended into the ceramics and appeared to the naked eye as being part of the ceramics. There were no drag marks near the two bodies of Ryan and Dunbar.

The third victim, Pamela Ryan, was found in the southeast corner of the bathroom. Her right leg extended toward the north wall between the toilet and sink. Her right knee was up in the air, and her left knee was spread in a westerly direction. Dried blood appeared on her inner thigh, and blood flowed toward the top of her body. Pamela Ryan was fully clothed in her red tube top, no bra, blue denim shorts, underpants and sandals.

A pair of glasses was under her right hand on the floor near the bathroom sink. Molding straps were tied around both of her wrists with a square knot. The killer stuffed a small towel into her mouth. West, the crime technician, found a puddle on the floor indicating the victim discharged her bladder. There were also splatters in the puddle that resulted from the killer urinating on her or from water dripping from his hands. The splatters were in front of the sink.

West gathered the tube top, molding straps and towel as evidence. Pamela Ryan suffered six stab wounds to her chest, one neck wound, plus three other injuries he classified as suspicious.

The fourth dead woman was shop owner Marilyn Baers. Her body lay east of the bathroom in a small aisle inside the loading docks. She was found between a refrigerator and a set of double doors.

Baers was on her back. Her wrists also bound behind her back with a molding strap. Unlike the others, she was not gagged. She was fully clothed, in a blue blouse, bra, cloth shorts, shoes and underpants.

The Joliet store owner suffered four puncture wounds to her throat and seven to her chest.

The simulated necklace found on the floor was the only indication jewelry may have been involved in the crime. Aside from that, Deputy West did not believe jewelry was a factor in the killings.

After an exhaustive search, sheriff's deputies did not locate the store's key. "The key is suspected to be in the possession of the perpetrator," West wrote.

That day, West processed as many areas as possible for fingerprints. He recovered two from the main door frame above the lock. Additionally, West saw a metal cash box on the floor behind the counter. The open metal box contained utility bills, a $10 bill, a $20 bill and $19.82 in coins. West saw no shoe impressions in this area, leaving him to surmise the killer did not go behind the counter.

"A visible shoe impression known to be a Converse-style gym shoe was observed inside and outside the store," West noted.

Several of these Converse shoe impressions led out the exit door in a southwestern direction. The trail of shoe impressions ended at the sidewalk.

In all, West found shoe impressions in at least seven locations at the ceramic shop.

Back in the bathroom, West found blood spray near Pamela Ryan's body plus a blood stained bottle of Joy dish washing detergent. The nozzle for the bottle was in the open position.

Meanwhile, no fingerprints were left on the hot and cold water taps of the sink.

"No rags were found in the bathroom, which may have been used to dry the perpetrator's hands, as he apparently did wash his hands in the sink," West observed.

The most revealing information from the autopsy findings was the discovery of the gunshot wound to Anna Ryan's neck. The lone gunshot went through the right side of her neck, near her collarbone, and exited through her left shoulder.

Of major importance, West and Joseph Ambrozich from the state crime lab recovered several latent fingerprints from the Ryan's Chevy Blazer.

Those and many other crime scene fingerprints were compared to dozens of potential suspects of all ages and races. When the fingerprints were finally compared to those of convicted rapist Milton Johnson, an exact match was found.

At the time of his arrest, Johnson denied being at the car wash on the date of the multiple murders.

"He also told Marty McCarthy that he was on the south side of Joliet until approximately 2:30 in the afternoon," prosecutor Stephen White reminded the jury. "What happened after March 9 when Milton Johnson tells him that he is on the south side? They interview someone from the south side as to whether or not the defendant was there on August 20, 1983. Now, what does that person tell him?

"Obrie Trotter says that he was with the defendant. The defendant had approximately $500, a wad of $20 bills. He lost a total to himself and another individual, of approximately $350, and that he left," White revealed. "All on August 20, 1983, as the helicopters were flying overhead."

One of the murder trial's most interesting moments came when Johnson, as acting as defense counsel, questioned Trotter, his old pal.

Trotter told jurors he shot craps with Johnson for a few hours after the ceramic shop murders.

"Why did you talk to the police about the defendant?" Johnson asked, referring to himself in the third person.

"They questioned me about you, I don't know," Trotter testified.

"Are you an informant for the police department?" Johnson then asked.

"I don't know," Trotter answered. "You know more about me than I do. What do you think?"

"I think you turned stool pigeon," Johnson snapped.

As he prepared his case, Johnson cherry-picked from the reams of police reports to present a mistaken identity defense.

He hoped to convince his jury that eyewitnesses saw a young white man driving the Ryan's Chevy Blazer in the aftermath of the murders.

**

On the day of the ceramic shop killings, Daniel Jones drove back to Joliet after attending a community festival in the nearby village of Channahon. At the traffic light near Jefferson Street and Stryker Avenue, Jones thought he spotted Bob Ryan's distinctive red and white Chevy Blazer. The Blazer featured fancy wheels and tires plus optional lights. Jones considered it "decked out."

Jones met Bob Ryan eight years ago through Jones' job as security guard at the Dresden Nuclear Station south of Joliet, near Braidwood.

"Did you know what type of vehicle Mr. Ryan drove?" the murder defendant asked his witness.

"Yes I do," Jones responded.

"And can you describe that vehicle?" Johnson inquired.

"It was like an orangish red and white Blazer, Chevrolet Blazer."

"Was there any other characteristics about that Blazer that you recall?"

"Guess you'd say it's sort of decked out," Jones answered. "It's got fancy wheels on it and tires. It has, I believe, optional lights in the front, things like that."

Johnson asked the power plant security guard to recall his whereabouts from around noon on the day of the homicides.

"I believe I was out in Channahon ... there was supposed to be a fair out there, or like a homecoming-type thing where they have a carnival and things like that."

Jones wasn't sure when he returned to Joliet. It could have been as early as 1 p.m. or as late as 3 p.m.

"Mr. Jones, between the hours of 2 and 3 p.m. do you recall if you was in the area of Stryker Avenue?" the murder defendant inquired.

"Yes, I was," Jones agreed. "I was driving on Jefferson Street."

"While you were driving on Jefferson Street, did you see the Ryan's vehicle?"

"Yes, I believe that that's the vehicle I saw as far as I can recollect on, that's what I saw," the witness agreed.

On the date in question, Jones was accompanied by his two children and a woman he described as "a lady friend of mine."

"I, just offhand, after the vehicle had passed, I had made a comment to the lady friend of mine that I thought that was Bob Ryan's vehicle, and the reason why I made that comment was that she had seen me, I had started to beep the horn and wave, but then it wasn't Bob driving the vehicle. So, I didn't."

The driver had blondish, dishwater ruddy hair, Jones testified.

"That's basically what I remember," Jones remarked. "He wasn't a real big guy because you'd see somebody sit up on the seat if they're a good-size person."

While parts of that encounter faded from his memory, Jones was certain Bob Ryan was not driver.

"No, it looked nothing like Bob," Jones testified.

"And this was on August 20, 1983?" Milton Johnson asked.

"Yes," Jones replied.

When the prosecutor had his chance to ask questions, Burmila wanted the jury to realize the witness, although well-intentioned, was wrong about everything.

"OK, now, you made a statement that you'd never made a mistake in beeping and waiving at him," Burmila asserted. "So, you've never had an occasion where you beep and wave at him and then saw him and say, 'Hey, I beeped and waved at you and then he said, yeah, it was me.' So, you don't know if you ever made a mistake in beeping and waiving, do you?"

"No, I don't," the Joliet motorist agreed. "I wouldn't know that."

Burmila asked if Jones remembered the weather on the day of his supposed sighting of the victims' Blazer on the opposite side of Joliet from where the killings happened.

"Not really," Jones answered. "I know that it wasn't raining at the time."

"OK," Burmila followed up. "Do you remember speaking to an investigator from the sheriff's office by the name of Diane Seeman?"

"Yeah, I think I do."

"OK, did you tell Diane Seeman that the windows were rolled up in the Blazer because it was raining that day?"

"I don't remember that, no."

The Saturday of the ceramic shop killings was hot and humid. It did not rain in Joliet.

The witness acknowledged he came forward and after seeing a photo of Bob Ryan's Blazer in the newspaper several days after the murders.

"So, it wasn't until you saw the newspaper that you thought anything about this incident of beeping and waving?" Burmila inquired.

"Yeah," Jones agreed.

"After you knew Mr. Ryan's wife and mother had been murdered?"

"No, just when I saw the picture," Jones insisted. "I didn't even read the article. I very rarely read the newspaper."

Burmila did not ask any additional questions nor did Milton Johnson.

Interestingly, Daniel Jones was not only person around Joliet believing they saw the Blazer within hours of the grisly murders.

A Ridgewood neighborhood-area resident insisted she saw the vehicle with the license plates RR650 on the far east side of Joliet a couple of hours after the killing spree.

Sandra Killman lived on Harwood Street, just up the hill from the ceramic shop murders. She was thirty-nine, divorced and had two daughters, ages thirteen and six. She worked at Joliet's Sunny Hill nursing home.

She became Milton Johnson's star witness for his defense.

Killman remembered taking her daughters to downtown Joliet's Public Library on Ottawa Street, staying about ninety minutes.

After leaving downtown Joliet, Killman drove to New Lenox where Trinity School had a big, summer garage sale on Gougar Road.

"Miss Killman," Johnson began, "as you was on East Cass Street, were you in the vicinity of East Cass Street Car Wash?"

Yes, she agreed.

Killman believed she saw a Black man washing a white Cadillac, but no other vehicles.

"Miss Killman, as you passed the car wash," Johnson began, "are you familiar with an establishment known as Merry's Greenware?"

Again, she answered yes. She remembered several mini-cams, police cars and lots of people outside as she drove past.

"At that time, did you stop there or anything?" Johnson wondered.

"No."

"You proceeded on Cass in an easterly direction?"

"Yes."

Killman told the jury that she and her oldest child often played a game of spotting unusual license plates during their travels.

"Miss Killman, at that time, in reference to the games you and your daughter play," Johnson began, "were there any vehicles that caught your attention at that time?"

"Yes. It was a red Blazer," she answered. "It resembled the paramedic truck that my neighbor drives. The color is what caught my attention. It's red and it has black lettering on it and white."

And something else caught her attention.

"What was that?" Johnson asked.

"The RR," she responded. "My husband worked for the railroad and RR for railroad."

"And the other three numbers of the vehicle you saw?"

"Six, five, zero," the Joliet woman replied. "It's red. It's a red Blazer."

Killman told the jury she caught a glimpse of the driver along Route 30 as he was turning off Washington Street heading away from Joliet toward New Lenox.

Hitting his groove, Johnson kept asking probing questions.

"Can you describe the person that was driving it?"

"He was white, sandy-blond hair, about shoulder length and in his early twenties."

Killman testified the man remained a couple car lengths ahead of her after he pulled onto Route 30.

"Did you have on that occasion to see this person's arms, side of face, or anything?" Johnson followed up.

"I thought he was familiar," she responded, "but I thought I had seen him over at my other neighbor's once before."

"Was the person that you saw on this day in that vehicle there a white male?"

"Yes, he was."

Next, Johnson presented a photo of the license plate for the Ryan's Blazer.

"That is the license plate of the vehicle that you saw, RR650?"

"Yes," Killman answered.

"No further questions," the murder defendant announced.

Will County's prosecution table now faced the daunting challenge of overcoming Killman's testimony, which was crucial to the defendant. If the jury believed the witness saw a young white man with long hair driving away from Joliet toward New Lenox in the murder victims' sports utility vehicle, how could Johnson be the ceramic shop killer?

CHAPTER 29

TAPE MEASURE

Sandra Killman was one of several people who called the Will County Sheriff's Department after reading about the ceramic killings in the Joliet newspaper. But investigators concluded that her tip, while well-meaning, was worthless.

But Killman persisted. She convinced herself that the newspaper photo was the very same vehicle she saw several hours after the killings.

Prosecutors Burmila and White decided to combat Killman's testimony by calling big Dave Simpson to the stand. The six-foot-six Will County Sheriff's sergeant worked in the investigations unit and had a lead role investigating several area murders linked to Johnson.

Simpson was one of the only detectives who interviewed Johnson.

"There was a small group of people he really did not like at all, and I was one of them," Simpson remembered. "I had the authority. I had the power over him, and I was part of this group.

"He was a big guy, stocky, good-sized guy, but I still towered over him, and he did not like that. I was six-foot-six, so I had a good six to eight inches over him. He knew I was not intimidated at all."

On Sept. 18, 1985, two years after the ceramic murders, Simpson again interviewed Sandra Killman.

"She mentioned that there was one vehicle in front of her," Simpson told the jury. "She described it as a location while driving eastbound on Route 30, passing a trailer court, which is on the south side of Route 30 … and she went over the hill crest and after she went past the trailer court and over the top of the hill crest, that's where she stated that she first seen the vehicle on Washington Street. It was a red and white Blazer."

Simpson explained that she supposedly saw the Blazer at the intersection of Washington Street and Route 30.

Later, Killman showed Simpson where she saw the vehicle in Joliet Township. Will County Sheriff's Investigator Jim Cardin brought along a tape measure that stretched one hundred feet.

"We used a warning sign which warns the east bound traffic on Route 30 that they're approaching Washington Street as a mark," Simpson testified.

Simpson was asked to tell the jury the distance from the warning sign along Route 30 to Washington Street.

"It's approximately five hundred and eighty feet," Simpson revealed.

Burmila also inquired whether Simpson measured the distance from Washington and Route 30 to the end of the left-turn lane on Gougar and Route 30. That was the other location Killman insisted she saw the license plates.

"Yes, sir, I did. It's approximately eight hundred and fifty feet," Simpson revealed.

"Mr. Simpson, how large is a letter on a license plate?"

"It's approximately three inches in height."

"I have no other questions judge," Burmila announced.

Thanks to the tape measure, Burmila hammered home his point: how could Sandra Killman see the license plates of the murder victim's Blazer from a distance of at least five hundred feet away, let alone eight hundred fifty? One is the distance of nearly two football fields. The other was almost three football fields away.

As the trial drew to a close, White raised his voice in anger as he made the prosecution's closing arguments.

"What you heard in this case was how five people became involved in Greenware By Merry, the ceramic shop on East Cass Street on August 20, 1983. Four of those people were butchered by an animal, and that animal is among us today, and he sits right there," White hollered, pointing directly at Milton Johnson.

"Marilyn Baers, Barbara Dunbar, Anna Ryan and Pam Ryan received forty-three stab wounds to the chest, heart area and throat by Milton Johnson and Anna Ryan received a gunshot wound at the same time. One person left that ceramic shop and that was Milton Johnson.

"Pamela Ryan, Anna Ryan and Marilyn Baers," White declared, "their purses are all taken from the ceramic shop and the Blazer is moved. And it is moved to the car wash which is a short walk, a half of a block away from the ceramic shop."

White urged the jury to disregard the testimony from Johnson's two witnesses who claimed they saw the Ryan family's Blazer in different parts of Joliet hours after the killings. After all, Will County police had identified several other witnesses who were sure they saw the Blazer backed into the car wash shortly after the killings.

"At twelve noon, approximately, at the car wash, seen by Sherri Walters, who lives next door to the car wash, is the Blazer in its final resting position in that stall," White stressed. "Sandra Killman is supposed to have seen the Blazer in New Lenox. She first saw the Blazer at five hundred eighty feet, as it were measured, and then saw a license plate from a distance of eight hundred fifty feet.

"Now, the letters or the numbers on a license plate are two inches, three inches high. From eight hundred fifty feet, if you take the standard print, approximately one-eighth of an inch in a magazine print … if you work that proportion out, it would be similar to reading a magazine from a distance of 35.4 feet. And you can hold a magazine at 35.4 feet, and it is literally impossible to read, absolutely impossible to read that magazine.

"You can't read it from six hundred feet," White assured jurors. "A license plate, which would be the same as twenty-five feet, if you take it even to three hundred feet, that's reading a magazine from twelve-and-a-half feet. And that, too, is impossible."

To drive home his argument, White explained that two more eyewitnesses saw the Blazer at the car wash at 3 p.m. and 3:30 p.m. respectively.

"The Blazer is moved to the car wash by the murderer. Inside of the ceramic shop, we also learn through the questioning of both the prosecution and defense that a rag is handled by the killer. The rag which is by Barbara Dunbar and Anna Ryan, and what does that rag have on it, but two hairs, two hairs which are of Negro origin."

White addressed the shoe prints from the bloody murders.

"Milton Johnson wears a size eleven. We heard that. Found at Milton Johnson's home are size eleven Converse All Star gym shoes, in March of 1984. Now, that's seven months after the murder. They are in worn condition. They, too, are here for you to examine."

The March 1984 police raid of Johnson's house recovered .357 Lubaloy ammunition with the copper outer coating while "the killer used a .357 Lubaloy ammunition bullet that is found in the wall in direct line with Anna Ryan, from her neck, going into the wall and is recovered there by the police," White reminded jurors.

But besides all that, Johnson's fingerprints proved he committed the murders, White declared.

"We also know that the defendant's fingerprints of his left little finger is found on the driver's door handle at the very end, inside that Blazer, found inside that car wash on the driver's door. Anyone who opens that car door, after that individual, would destroy that print. He opened that door and that's not the only print that is found, but one of blood, not in blood, but of blood.

"There was blood on his finger when he touched it and placed it on the gear shift. The right index finger, and whose print is that? His. Inside that Blazer, inside that car wash, in the final position, where each and every one of those people saw it in exactly the same place with the shoe prints around it that are exactly the same shoe prints that are in the driveway, by where the Blazer was parked."

As he wrapped up his arguments, White told the jury they were here for a reason.

"You have heard that evidence. You can't take that evidence away. That is there. His prints are there. The shoe prints are there, and he killed them all. I'm going to ask you to go back and deliberate this case, to return a verdict of guilty for each count of murder against Marilyn Baers, Barbara Dunbar, Anna Ryan and Pamela Ryan, both as to murder, and to felony murder, because he took those purses from them, and he took that money."

When White ended his remarks, Judge Buchar turned to the defendant.

"Mr. Johnson?" the judge asked.

"Your honor, at this time, the defendant waives closing argument."

Johnson, acting as his own counsel, also waived his chance to present an opening argument at the start of his quadruple murder trial.

With the trial over, the jury retreated behind closed doors to deliberate. As White and Burmila remained in the courtroom, Johnson turned to his prosecutors and asked them a question.

He was focused on gaining their affirmation of his performance in the courtroom as his own lawyer.

"How did I do?" he asked.

Decades later, White laughingly recited how Burmila turned to Johnson and in a complimentary tone responded "Just good enough."

In the end, the jury pronounced Johnson guilty of all four murders. He received another death penalty for those killings.

Two separate trials equaled five murder convictions.

Then, to the dismay of some, Will County State's Attorney Ed Petka decided he was through.

No more murder trials against Johnson. The five-time convicted killer would not stand trial for the Homer Township massacre that took the lives of auxiliary deputies Foley and Mayer along with Richard Paulin, Cathleen Norwood and George Kiehl.

Instead, Petka let the Illinois Department of Corrections take custody of Johnson to begin his Death Row sentence.

One of the biggest factors in Petka's decision concerned the statements of the lone shooting survivor, Laura Troutman. She was interviewed by Will County deputy Pat Lombardo just minutes after her dying boyfriend crashed their van into a bean field.

In the haze of the chaotic shooting, Troutman saw Mayer, the young auxiliary deputy, running toward her boyfriend's van that was driving into the ambush.

In a state of hysteria, Troutman told the first responders that she and her boyfriend were shot by the officer.

Petka said the investigation proved that Johnson removed the guns from both auxiliary deputies after shooting them, and then he used their guns to kill some of his victims.

Had there been a third trial, Troutman's eyewitness statements would have been problematic for the prosecution, Petka conceded.

Therefore, it was not worth the risk of proceeding to trial, knowing Troutman's testimony would be far more beneficial to the defense and detrimental to the prosecution. Petka did not want to risk the jury returning a not-guilty verdict, which would have bolstered Johnson's appeal efforts for his two other murder trial convictions.

But even though Johnson did not stand trial for the Homer Township massacre, Petka was able to present evidence pointing to Johnson's culpability during the death penalty sentencing arguments for the I-55 homicide of Tony Hackett.

Looking back, Petka said his decision not to charge Johnson with the Homer Township killings was one of his most difficult decisions as State's Attorney. He drew fierce criticism from high-ranking Will County Sheriff's Sgt. Ed Mayer, father of the slain auxiliary deputy.

Petka, however, was a devout Christian and a man of deep faith. He said he spent considerable time weighing the pros and cons of putting Johnson on trial for a third set of murders before making the decision not to do it.

"In Homer Township, we had conflicting testimony," Petka admitted. "Why open up that route? In the I-55 murder, we had the Great America sales receipt, the fibers from the pillow and (Tonya Little's) testimony. Laura Troutman said the person who shot her was a white deputy. Well, we know, that did not happen."

Petka was a firm believer and strong advocate for the death penalty. On May 10, 1994, Petka watched the lethal injection behind the walls of the Stateville prison near Joliet for John Wayne Gacy, one of America's most notorious serial killers. During the 1970s, Gacy dumped four of his murder victims in Will County's section of the Des Plaines River after running out of room to bury his bodies in the crawl space of his Norwood Park Township home near Chicago.

Gacy was convicted of thirty-three Chicago area murders during the early to mid-1970s.

As for Milton Johnson, Will County prosecutors and police connected him to fourteen murders during a three-month-span in 1983.

Simpson, one of the lead sheriff's investigators on the case, said he is certain Johnson committed the slayings in Homer Township, plus the two older sisters whose bodies were burned beyond recognition, and the romantic couple whose bodies were dragged from their car and dumped in the tall weeds near Route 6 just outside Will County.

On Oct. 28, 1986, the Cook County Sheriff's issued a report announcing the double homicide of Kenny Chancellor and Terry Lynn Johnson was being classified as a closed investigation.

"Since February 1984, Milton Johnson has been the prime suspect ... along with four other multiple homicide cases from Will County. In the Cook County case as with the Will County cases numerous similarities were present. The similarities on the spent projectile removed from the body of Kenneth Chancellor and compared to the Will County cases, that Assistant State's Attorney Edward Burmila, Will County, used each in aggravation in the two murder convictions he gained on Johnson."

The Cook County supplemental police report from three years after the slayings of Chancellor and Terry Lynn Johnson, no relation to Milton Johnson, listed the Homer Township slayings of five people, the four ceramic shop murders, the double murder and arson on Rosalind Avenue and the I-55 murder of Tony Hackett and the Chancellor/ Johnson slayings in remote Orland Township as "the murder cases linking Milton Johnson as the offender."

Cook County Sheriff's Investigator James Houlihan noted in his report that he shared this information of Assistant Cook County State's Attorney Robert Clifford, 6th District Supervisor, and that "after reviewing this information, Clifford related that prosecution of Johnson on the Cook County case would serve no practical purpose since the suspect is waiting the death penalty on two multiple murders already."

For those reasons, Houlihan wrote, the June 1983 slayings of Chancellor and Terry Lynn Johnson were being "cleared by exception and closed, naming the offender as Milton Johnson."

From Simpson's perspective, so many of these random crimes all fit the same pattern, but the one common denominator was the unusual Lubaloy bullets. The summer of 1983 killing spree always contained the same ammunition, the copper-coated Lubaloy ammunition, Simpson said.

Simpson believes that Johnson's 1970 crime, the one that put him in the penal institution for thirteen years, was a defining moment in Johnson's life because it gave him a chance to refine his deviant behavior.

The fact that Johnson committed such an unspeakable heinous crime at Pilcher Park on the verge of his twentieth birthday, helped fuel Johnson's inner monster. At the Illinois Department of Corrections, he had thirteen years to learn and refine his criminal skills from some of the best, according to Simpson. That's where Johnson got his schooling, but it wasn't in acquiring a new job skill to rehabilitate and change his ways upon his return to society.

Rather, Johnson learned from other older and much more seasoned hardened criminals what mistakes not to make in his future crimes.

By the time Johnson got out in March 1983, he had an edge. He had a chip on his shoulder. He became a know-it-all criminal. He became convinced he would always outsmart the police.

"He's a clear predator that jumps right back into crime," Simpson explained.

"He's built on rage," Simpson continued. "And he's more than just killing one man and one woman. He goes from one crime scene to another crime scene, and his crimes are getting bigger and more brutal."

Simpson believes that Johnson hated society and was deeply resentful for the thirteen years of his life he lost to the Illinois Department of Corrections for the Pilcher Park torture rape.

With little to live for, Johnson's mission and motivation in life became bringing pain and sheer terror to those he encountered. Practically all of his crimes involved the element of surprise, Simpson explained. He picked his victims at random, and his sadistic side gave him a chance to watch the agony in the eyes of his victim moments before he plunged his long knife into their necks or pumped their bodies full of bullets.

In the I-55 crime near the Wilmington exit, Johnson could have killed eighteen-year-old Tony Hackett without waking up the teenager stretched across his front seat. Instead, Johnson made the choice to tap on the passenger side window in the middle of the night. Instead, Johnson tapped his hand on the window to make sure Hackett died with a look of horror on his face as Johnson pumped five bullets into Hackett's body before taking Hackett's girlfriend hostage and raping her over the next couple of hours, before plunging a knife into her stomach.

"This was not just a matter of pulling the gun and shooting someone," Simpson said. "He's brutal."

CHAPTER 30

DEATH ROW

Practically everyone who was alive in 1983 around Will County has vivid haunting memories of the ceramic shop killings and the previous month's massacre in northwest Homer Township.

The Homer Township crime was the one that ultimately put police on Johnson's trail because his stepfather's fishing reel repair receipt was found under Steven Mayer's body in the roadside ditch. But at that time, authorities did not make the connection Johnson and Sam Myers were related or that Johnson frequently borrowed the family truck.

The Homer Township crimes were marked the one case Johnson was caught off-guard. His purpose may have been to watch the two lovers from Lemont sharing affection under the moonlit sky inside the small red Chevette parked near the farm entrance. But when the Will County squad pulled up, Johnson knew he had to react.

The 1983 newspaper articles gave various accounts of how the crimes occurred. However, the forensic evidence gives us the most accurate and reliable account.

In all likelihood, Johnson parked his stepfather's truck along the gravel road around 3 a.m. From the distance, he watched the two lovebirds in the Chevette. Suddenly, the two auxiliary deputies came up Gougar Road. Thinking on his feet, Johnson told them he needed a jump for his truck.

As the deputies stopped and got out, Johnson grabbed his revolver and wounded both of them. He immediately took their wallets and guns and approached the Chevette.

He shot Richard "Dewey" Paulin through the back, killing him. It remains unclear whether Johnson intended to abduct Cathy Norwood or whether she tried to make a run for it, but she was fatally shot in the grass just outside her lover's car.

"He's a predator, and he wants to have the upper hand and have the element of surprise and come upon people to victimize," Simpson said of Johnson. "He does not want to be rousted by the police. I got this feeling that from him going to the Department of Corrections, he knows that he wants to lay low and that's the same thing he can have with that truck."

During the death penalty portion of Johnson's first trial, State's Attorney Petka outlined the following sequence of events at 147th Street and Gougar Road that left five people dead in Homer Township:

"On the early morning hours of July the 16th of 1983, there was a small car that was parked in a field ... almost perpendicular to that vehicle was a truck which was variously described by Sgt. Foley as being a brown van and by evidence that was adduced on cross examination, as being a pickup truck, that was parked there.

"Sgt. Foley told Jim Fetzner, when he was in extreme pain, when he arrived upon the scene, he noticed a small car that was parked in a field. There was also what he described as a brown van ... a Black person emerged and stated that he needed a jump and that next thing that happened was that Sgt. Foley was shot, as we subsequently determined, two times. And that his partner, Steven Mayer, was shot multiple times.

"The next thing that was related to this court from Sgt. Foley's mouth through Jim Fetzner, was that this Black man came over and got his gun and his wallet and got his partner's gun and that the next thing that occurred after that is that the people in the car was shot.

"He doesn't recall anything else that happened after that. And I submit to the court, that he probably was starting to lapse into early unconsciousness. We also know that this person who assaulted Sgt. Foley, a police officer of quite extensive experience, even though he was an auxiliary, a trained eye, described this individual as being six-foot-tall, over two hundred pounds, and wearing a flannel shirt," Petka relayed.

"The best that we can determine on the evidence that is before us that after the people who were in the little red car were killed that Laura Troutman and George Kiehl returned up Gougar Road, up to 147th Avenue from 151st Street and at that time a person who had probably been shot, Steven Mayer, attempted to stop them, and it was at that time that the shooting started once again."

As the van reached 147th Street, the wounded Mayer made a desperate run toward the van, pleading for help. As Mayer darted toward the oncoming vehicle, several more gunshots rang out. Mayer died before he reached the van. The other bullets hit the Lockport couple, and they crashed into the bean field hundreds of feet down the road. Troutman's boyfriend died after being shot in the head. She was covered in blood, but alive. Mortified and hysterical, Troutman ran from the van to a nearby farmhouse. She screamed and yelled as she awoke the farmers in the middle of the night, to tell them of the horror she just encountered.

"He never expected a squad car to come through there," Simpson said of Johnson. "That causes him to be ever more brazen, and he becomes even more dangerous. He's going to explode, and the other person is going to die sure as hell, whether it's with a gun or a knife."

Reflecting on the case, one of Petka's most vivid memories involves his conversations with murder victim Tony Hackett's father. The man was deeply religious and opposed to the death penalty, Petka said.

"I said it's not your decision to make," Petka remembered. "Once it's a criminal matter, we will consider other reasons why we feel we should prosecute. He told me he became conflicted on his son's murder. I said, it's off his conscience totally, even though he had his religious scruples."

One of the biggest challenges involved jury selection, Petka said. He didn't know what crop of jurors he would get in the mostly agrarian region of Iroquois County. One person summoned for jury duty was a big, burly man, in his early fifties. Frank Emme was a farmer from Chebanse, who was in local Lions Club and an avid card player.

But earlier in life, Emme was convicted of theft, so he had a bad experience with the criminal justice system, Petka figured.

Petka and Burmila could have exercised one of their preemptive strikes to remove the farmer from the jury pool, but they chose not to do so. When the prospective juror told the lawyers he did not have any negative feelings toward the police, his answer surprised Petka.

"He said, look, what I did was wrong, but I paid for what I done, and I regretted that I did it. That for me was all I needed to hear," Petka said. "He was just a really big guy."

The farmer became one of the most attentive members of the jury weighing Johnson's guilt or innocence. The giant man wore bib overalls to the courthouse every day. And when Tonya Little described the awful details of her rape, the farmer often made a loud hacking noise as he turned his head and glared at the defendant. The sound showed the juror's pure disgust and contempt toward Johnson's actions. "It was a loud deep breath," Petka recalled during a 2020 interview. "He was just groaning, and he had his thumbs on the top of his overalls."

When Johnson stuck his knife into the chest of Tonya Little and dumped her along the road south of Joliet before sunrise, he never could have imagined she would live to testify against him.

Petka believes God's will kept her alive long enough for the two motorists to find her in the patch of weeds along Route 53. The nurses, doctors and surgeons at Joliet's St. Joe's hospital brought her back from the brink of death and in less than two weeks, she was able to go home to her family's farm in central Illinois.

Most importantly, she did not become Milton Johnson's fifteenth murder victim, Petka said. Her grit, determination and perseverance gave her the strength to recover.

Petka and Burmila agree that the teenager from tiny Hartsburg, Illinois, emerged as the ultimate hero in their quest to rid this world of Milton Johnson and give him a death sentence.

Indeed, Johnson went to Death Row. He drew an execution date. But unlike the clown killer John Wayne Gacy, Johnson managed to escape his date with the executioner. Johnson's murder-conviction appeals dragged on. Though never successful, Johnson's appeals kept the calendar changing. By his early fifties, Johnson caught the ultimate break.

Two days before leaving the office of Illinois governor, Kankakee Republican George Ryan announced he was ending the state's practice of capital punishment. No more lethal injections in Illinois, ever.

"You know, when you run for public office as I had, you get questionnaires every time there's an election," Ryan told Chicago television station WTTW during a 2020 interview. "Of course, there's one that comes from the death penalty people and they say, 'Are you in favor of the death penalty? And I always marked it yes and believed in it, thought it was good. But the death penalty people decided that they needed to have the death penalty so I stayed with them on it.

"But I was sitting in the (governor's) mansion watching the news from Chicago on the television when here's little Anthony Porter coming out with a big grin on his face after spending sixteen years on Death Row only to be found innocent of his charges. And I said to my wife, 'How did that happen in America?' You put a fellow on Death Row for sixteen years. He wakes up every morning and says, 'I wonder if this is the day they're going to throw the switch on me?'"

Porter spent years on Illinois Death Row after being wrongly convicted of shooting and killing Jerry Hilliard, 18, and his fiancée Marilyn Green, 19, in August 1982 during a robbery at Washington Park on Chicago's South Side.

Because of the Anthony Porter wrongful conviction case from Chicago, Ryan came to the realization "that there had been something wrong with the system, and that's when I started to change my thoughts and my attitudes about the death penalty."

As people in Illinois know, Ryan later spent five years in a Terre Haute, Indiana, prison after the United States government convicted him of wide-ranging federal corruption charges. In 2013, at the age of seventy-nine, Ryan finished serving his federal prison sentence.

Back in Will County, nobody was more than angry with Ryan's abolishment of the death penalty than fellow Republican Ed Petka.

After Petka left the State's Attorney's Office in 1986, he was not surprised that Johnson's execution did not happen in a timely manner. "The state was in no hurry to see someone in this state executed," Petka said. "Four members of the (Illinois) Supreme Court opposed the death penalty. Governor George Ryan was not opposed to the death penalty until he came under federal investigation" and realized he might get a jury more favorable to him if he opposed capital punishment.

Petka said he was a big political supporter of George Ryan in 1998.

"It was one of the biggest political mistakes I ever made," Petka admitted. A Plainfield conservative, Petka served as a state senator in Springfield from 1992 until 2006 after six years as a state representative.

"Milton to me is a person without a conscience," Petka lamented.

Petka said there was never any doubt among prosecutors, Will County Sheriff's police, Illinois State Police and members of the Joliet Police Department who put Milton Johnson in prison for his 1970 crime that Johnson turned into a serial killer upon his parole in 1983.

While there was anger and criticism leveled at the Illinois Department of Corrections for paroling Johnson in 1983, Petka said in the grand scheme of things, it only changed the time frame for his killings.

In other words, had Johnson been freed in 1990, instead of 1983, the killing spree would have taken place then, Petka said.

"There is no doubt, none, one-hundred percent, that he is the murderer of Tony Hackett and that he raped and stabbed and tried to kill (Tonya Little) and the four women at the ceramic shop," Petka reflected in 2020. "We knew we had the right guy. This was not a who done it for us."

Johnson's fingerprints were recovered from the ceramic shop victims' automobile. The Great America receipt for the Tasmanian devil doll purchased by I-55 murder victim Tony Hackett remained in the cab of the Johnson's family truck. The truck matched the license plates written down by Dolton teenager Anne Shoemaker as she and her friend were followed on the backroads of Homer Township the weekend prior to the massacre that left five people dead.

But the most incriminating sign of all, Petka said, was the decision to hide the truck at a family friend's garage in nearby Lockport after the Illinois State Police showed up at Johnson's house in September 1983.

Also, Johnson's Converse All Star high-tops matched the shoe impressions left at several murder scenes. And all the killings involved Lubaloy bullets, the same ones that mysteriously disappeared from the apartment complex arcade in Crest Hill once Johnson's life-long friend brought them back from the Service Merchandise store.

Jerry Edwards always denied that he purchased the bullets for Johnson, who was prohibited from owning a gun. Although police had suspicions Edwards may have been an accessory in that he obtained a gun and the bullets for Johnson, Edwards was never charged with any crimes.

"Jerry Edwards stated that after the arrest of Milton Johnson that he was hoping that the bullets which were stolen from his game room were not stolen by Milton Johnson and used to kill the people in the Will County area. Jerry Edwards went on to state that even though he hoped it was not the bullets used, that they probably were indeed the ones used by Milton Johnson. He also denies giving the bullets to Milton Johnson and also states that he is not the person that bought or had given a gun to Milton Johnson," Investigator Simpson's interview reflected.

During a 2020 interview, Simpson said there was enormous relief across the entire law enforcement community when Johnson was proven to be the mass murderer.

The string of killings drained many at the Will County Sheriff's Office. Some families and marriages were ruined because of the emotional toll the violent crimes had on people. The homicides hit home when two members of the sheriff's office were among the victims. Sgt. Ed Mayer's young adult son, who was just starting out his career in law enforcement, became one of the victims. Steven Mayer's life ended at age twenty-two just one month after his fabulous wedding day.

As Simpson looks back on the case, he said the recovery of the 1977 Chevy Scottsdale made all the difference.

"It's not a classic car nor is it broken," he explained. "You're hiding the vehicle because you know police want to go through it with a fine tooth comb. The truck runs. The truck is functional. It was used in a commission of multiple crimes."

Then, the sales receipt from Great America turned up.

"What are the odds of finding the stub? What a grand slam," Simpson said. "How come the stub didn't show up in somebody else's vehicle in the world? It shows up in their truck. A reasonable person has to say he has to be involved because that's very significant."

The author wrote multiple letters to Johnson, who remains in the Illinois Department of Corrections, at the maximum security prison in Menard, Illinois. Johnson chose not to respond to the author's request for an interview about his crimes. Several retired members of the Will County Sheriff's Department said they were not surprised Johnson did not want to be interviewed for a book about his crimes.

But because Johnson has chosen to remain silent, some aspects of his serial killings remain a source of mystery.

The guns stolen from the two auxiliary deputies never turned up. Police believed that Johnson used a revolver to commit most of his murders in 1983, but that gun disappeared, too.

During a 2020 interview with the author, Simpson offered his own theory what may have happened.

First, several of the older houses within Johnson's neighborhood on Luther Avenue had burn barrels. That area of Joliet's Forest Park is also known as The Hill.

"On Luther Avenue, there were a lot of burn barrels in the backyards," Simpson said. "A lot of people would burn their garbage. There's nothing that stops someone like Milton Johnson, with an arm full of stuff, to throw in some wood and some paper and burn it down. It could be that simple. He was not a real sophisticated guy, but as I was trained in law enforcement, he was trained in criminality, and he was in the advanced courses at the Department of Corrections and when he was in jail."

Overwhelming evidence suggested Johnson killed his victims with the same Lubaloy-coated bullets Jerry Edwards bought at Service Merchandise the day before the murder rampage started.

However, a number of scenarios may explain how a gun fell into Johnson's hands.

"There's guns on the street and there were four or five taverns on The Hill," Simpson explained. "I don't think it's all that difficult to walk into one of those taverns and ask, 'Hey do any of you know someone who's got a gun?'"

The fact that Johnson burned the genitals of his 1970 rape victim with a cigarette lighter shows how brutal and cruel he was, Simpson said.

"Then he gets arrested and put into the Department of Corrections and he's talking with people who have done the same crimes and worse," Simpson remarked. "Now, he's able to hone his craft."

During an interview in 2020, Simpson, who is in his seventies, began to choke up as he reflected on the hard work invested by the Will County Sheriff's Department and Illinois State Police in catching Johnson.

After the ceramic shop murders, Illinois State Police question Johnson three weeks later. His truck gets stowed away. The killings stop.

Why would Johnson stop the terror?

"The heat is on," Simpson said. "The cops are swarming The Hill. They are everywhere, and they're stopping and talking to everybody. People are constantly being brought in for interviews. It causes the criminal element to realize that they have got to lay low because they don't want to get caught up in this. It's a real scary time here, and we are really out there beating the bushes and bringing people in for interrogations, easily fifty to one hundred people.

"We were all over Ridgewood and The Hill, all stones were being unturned. We're looking for all the people that hide under the rocks and the undesirables, and we're making contact with everybody. And the beat cops, that information is being forwarded to the investigative section. He's going to be laying low because he's not stupid. He certainly stayed to himself when he got out of prison. He's not stupid to crime because that's his life … the one thing he doesn't want is contact with the police."

What gave Simpson the inner strength to remain focused and see the case through from beginning to end?

"The Boy Scout in me says you can't get away with this," Simpson said his voice cracked with emotion. "You got the entire law enforcement community involved. Nothing was easy about it. He's a criminal. He left evidence, and we were fortunate enough to make something out of the evidence. We had all these murders but nothing tied them all together. The rotten-to-the-core person that committed these crimes, if he was really good, he wouldn't be able to get caught, and the Boy Scout in me says, you can't get away with that."

Reflecting on the case decades later, retired Will County Sheriff's Investigator Nick Ficarello said that Charles Malinowski, Simpson and Marty McCarthy of the State Police were among the key people responsible for bringing Johnson's vicious killing spree to a screeching stop.

Sadly, Malinowski died unexpectedly of a massive heart attack at age sixty-seven in 2016 while on the job as the security supervisor for the Lac Vieux Desert Casino in Watersmeet, Michigan. He retired from Will County in 1998. In 1993, then-sheriff Tom Fitzgerald gave Lt. Malinowski a Meritorious Service Award for his role in the ceramic shop killings. The award recognized Malinowski for "actions that exhibited professional skill and conduct for assisting in the successful investigation of a quadruple homicide which occurred on August 20, 1983, in Joliet, Illinois."

"Malinowski was the fresh set of eyes, and when they brought in Malinowski, all he did was sit and read, sit and read, take notes and make comparisons, and Simpson was like the dog looking for the bone, he was not going to give up until he found out where that bone was hidden," Ficarello recalled. "It was personal for Dave that somebody would be that brutal and commit all these brutal acts, and Dave took it very personal that they would commit these crimes in unincorporated Will County."

CHAPTER 31

TOO OLD

The longer we live, the more we grow old as our bodies ache, and we hobble to get around. Because Illinois abolished the death penalty in 2003, Johnson's sentence got reduced to life in prison, and he's remained alive and well ever since, mooching off the taxpayers of Illinois, who pay for his living quarters, his three daily meals, his television access and the prison guards expected to constantly monitor his movements.

While prison life can take a toll on even the hardest of criminals, that hasn't been the case with the Joliet serial killer. In 2021, Johnson turned seventy-one. Johnson has now spent more than a half century behind the walls of an Illinois state penitentiary. He was incarcerated from February 1970 until March 1983 and from March 1984 to present.

That's astonishing to think about. More than fifty years in an institutionalized setting. Some men and women were born to be star athletes. Others became famous movie stars or musicians. Milton Johnson was born for prison life. That's what he knows better than anything else on earth. He follows orders and does what he's told. Prison guards and wardens do not consider him a troublemaker. He does not organize prison riots. He has not made homemade weapons to attack his guards. He has not tried to dig a tunnel through the concrete blocks of his prison cell.

Despite being an elder statesman at his southern Illinois maximum security prison, he surely commands respect within the prison yard because of his seniority and the number of people he's tortured and killed.

Even though Johnson has entered his seventies, it's seems doubtful that a hard-core, dope-dealing, carjacking twenty-three-year-old Gangster Disciple from Chicago would mess with the likes of Johnson at Menard, his southern Illinois maximum security prison that opened in 1878 overlooking the Mississippi River in Chester. The Menard prison capacity is 3,861 inmates, and the average age for these inmates remains around thirty-four years old. Johnson is old enough to be a father and grandfather to many of his fellow prisoners.

Two words come to mind when reflecting on Johnson's life in behind walls. One is repetition. The other is perseverance. While many key people responsible for Johnson's loss of freedom have long since died Johnson continues to outlive everybody.

The Joliet man first sentenced to death in 1984 continues to wake up and breathe in 2021, now in his early seventies.

The older Johnson gets, the more likely the question will be asked whether it's time to open up the prison gates and send Johnson packing.

The prospect of Johnson returning to Joliet might seem preposterous to many, but Illinois has already freed two high-profile mass murderers within the past few years, who like, Johnson, were up in their years.

On Feb. 21, 2020, Chester Weger regained his freedom almost sixty years after being convicted in the 1960 killing of three Chicago suburban women at the famous Starved Rock

State Park. Weger went to prison for the triple homicide in 1961.

The front-page headline splashed across the *Chicago Daily Tribune* in March 1960 read, "Full Confession of Killer" and the deck headline declared, "Re-Enacts His Crime in Cavern of Death, Describes Triple Killing."

At the time of the triple murders, the twenty-one-year-old Weger washed dishes at Starved Rock Lodge along the Illinois River in Oglesby. A ball of twine used to bind the hands of the victims came from a spool of twine in the kitchen, and Wager confessed to killing the women with a frozen tree branch during a robbery. The victims, ages fifty, fifty and forty-seven, had booked a weekend excursion to Starved Rock State Park to hike and birdwatch in the scenic wilderness.

In 1960, Weger took police and newspaper reporters to St. Louis Canyon to reenact how he killed the three women. In the coming days, Weger recanted and claimed the police coerced him into confessing, according to the *Associated Press*.

"The deputy already had the confession already drawn up," Weger told a Chicago television station during the 1980s. "He threatened me with a pistol. He said you either sign the confession, or I will kill you and say you tried to escape."

Weger's time in prison included Stateville, Pontiac and Menard. Weger petitioned the Illinois Parole Board a total of twenty-four times before his parole was finally granted in November 2019.

During a 2010 interview with legendary CBS Chicago television reporter John "The Bulldog" Drummond, Weger remarked, "I do a lot of reading, and read a Bible a lot and watch TV."

"Did you kill these women?" Drummond asked.

Weger began to shake head. "No, no sir, I did not. I denied it all the time," Weger told Drummond.

"Why should I feel remorse, if I never killed them? I mean, I feel sorry for the people being dead, but I'm not going to admit that I done something that I never done," Weger continued.

A decade later, as he neared his eighty-first birthday, Weger's wish came true.

On Feb. 21, 2020, newspapers across the country published the *Associated Press* article headlined, "Inmate Dubbed the 'Starved Rock Killer' Freed After 59 Years."

Incidentally, just two years before the infamous Starved Rock killer was let go, a mass murderer from Yorkville, Illinois, was granted parole in April 2018 after serving forty-five years at the Illinois Department of Corrections.

That killer, Carl Reimann, was sent home from the Dixon Correctional Center at age seventy-seven. On Dec. 29, 1972, Reimann and his girlfriend frequented two bars near the farming town of Plano, Illinois. From there, Reimann drove to the Pine Village Steak House at the intersection of Route 47 and Route 34 in Yorkville.

In 1970, Yorkville had a population of two thousand. The community along the Fox River was fifty-five miles southwest of Chicago.

Inside the Yorkville restaurant, Reimann pulled a gun while his teenage girlfriend stole money from the register. Although a family of five walked into Pine Village during his armed robbery, Reimann told them they would not be harmed if they sat down. Reimann proceeded to gun down the five people already inside: three restaurant employees and two patrons.

The dead were ages sixteen, thirty-five, forty-eight, forty-eight and seventy-four. The other family was spared because Reimann ran out of ammunition.

On Jan. 10, 2003, Illinois Gov. George Ryan sent a letter to the warden of the Pontiac prison notifying him that although Johnson was convicted of two sets of first-degree murder "it has been represented to me that said Milton Johnson is a fit and proper subject for Executive Clemency."

The governor's letter declared that the sentence for Johnson was commuted to "natural life imprisonment without the possibility of parole or mandatory supervised release."

Based on the 2003 commutation, Johnson's odds of being released into society might seem unlikely. But people need to remember, this is Illinois we're talking about, one of the country's most corrupt states, a place where back-to-back Illinois governors: Ryan, a Republican and Rod Blagojevich, a Democrat, went to federal prison for several years for public corruption in elected office.

In Illinois, rules and laws often find a way of being bent, abruptly changed or ignored altogether, so it would be no surprise in the not-too-distant future to learn Johnson has been released from the Menard prison and returned to society.

Because Johnson is now in his seventies, there are sure to be some bureaucrats in the Illinois prison system sympathetic to his plight. To them, Johnson has more than atoned for all of his horrid crimes by spending more than fifty-one years behind prison walls. Therefore, given Johnson's advanced age, the odds of him being released on a medical furlough, for instance, grow stronger and stronger every year.

But would the State of Illinois commit another giant blunder if prison officials handed Johnson a bus ticket and a leather suitcase filled with new dress slacks and buttoned down shirts?

Would Johnson, after being inside a maximum security prison since the second term of President Ronald Reagan, be able to cope in a modern-day world? Perhaps a better question is whether Johnson would want to?

Would Joliet and Will County let him move back to town after all the harm and violence he caused decades ago? It's hard to believe Jolietans would be ambivalent about Johnson returning to his childhood hometown after spending all these years in prison. After all, many Joliet residents figured he would die during his date with the state-sanctioned executioner.

"He had us all terrorized, whether he was here or not," remarked Jean Haas, the widow of Will County Sheriff's Investigator Pete Haas. The couple on Rosalind Street were the neighbors who found the burned slain bodies of Zita Blum and her sister Honora Lahmann.

During a 2021 interview, Jean Haas said that people in Joliet will never ever forget the carnage caused by Milton Johnson. "Oh, it was just random," she said. "The poor ladies at the ceramic shop, you didn't know where he was going to strike next."

When the killing spree began during the last weekend in June in 1983, there were only seven residential driveways along that stretch of Rosalind Street. Jean Haas remembered. "Seven driveways on the street and he picked that one. It actually hit home because they were so close to us," she said, referring to the Blum sisters. "And Pete worked the ceramic shop murders. That was gruesome."

With a menacing mass murderer still in the loose in 1983, Jean Haas said she and her husband installed a burglar alarm on their barns, where they kept their horses. "I would take a handgun to feed the horses," Jean Haas remembered. "That's how scared I was. I was scared here. I had all my weapons ready to go. I wouldn't let the kids play outside unless I was watching them.

"Life was just fine. You didn't have to lock your doors and then, bam. We never went back to that way even though nothing's happened ever since then. Pete would always tell us or the kids to look for things suspicious. Put a notebook in the car and write down license plates. It's just training you to be on alert."

Jean Haas is positive Joliet would be in uproar if the Illinois Department of Corrections ever turned Johnson loose and let him return to his hometown of Joliet to live out his golden years.

"That would be like reliving this whole nightmare," she said. "It still lingers. Oh, it still lingers. I don't think the community could handle that. There are so many family members of the victims still alive.

"With all that crime, that really was a year of hell, definitely a year of hell, and he finally got arrested."

Johnson has never confessed to any of the fourteen killings authorities say he committed. During the 1970s, he claimed he did not commit the Pilcher Park torture rape. At no point since his 1984 arrest has Johnson ever given a written or oral confession to his summer of terror killing spree in the Joliet area.

"I am surprised," Jean Haas remarked. "I really am."

But given how so many years have passed, the rural Joliet woman doesn't expect Johnson will confess now.

"I don't think he ever will. I don't think so. Maybe he feels the chances of him getting out of prison are better if he didn't say anything. Who knows what's in his mind?

"Criminally insane? Yes, definitely."

Nick Ficarello, the retired Will County investigator, said he hopes the day never comes when Johnson is released from prison, whether it's a medical furlough or some other technicality intended to lessen the burden on the state's prison population.

Obviously, Johnson has reached his early seventies, but is there any reason to believe he has any remorse? Isn't there every reason to believe Johnson could still terrorize and torture yet again?

As Will County police know, Johnson has spent his time and energy for thirty-plus years focused on overturning his conviction in the I-55 murder of Tony Hackett on a legal technicality. His last post-conviction ruling of any importance occurred April 2, 2019.

In an eleven-page order, the Appellate Court of Illinois Third District rejected Johnson's petition for a new murder trial. Johnson argued that an out-of-state expert witness for the prosecution gave flawed scientific testimony regarding the bullets that police seized from Johnson's family's house on Luther Avenue.

"Initially, we note that in defendant's direct appeal, our supreme court found the evidence of defendant's guilt to be 'overwhelming' without even mentioning (the) expert testimony," the Illinois appeals court wrote in 2019. "We agree with our supreme court's view of the evidence. At trial,

(Tonya Little) positively identified defendant as the man who assaulted her and murdered Hackett. Overwhelming circumstantial evidence found within the Myers' pickup truck, to which defendant undisputedly had access, corroborated her testimony … Consequently, we hold that it is not reasonably probable that the outcome of the trial would have been different had defense counsel successfully moved to bar (the expert witness) or presented a witness to rebut his testimony. For the foregoing reasons, we affirm the judgment of the circuit court of Will County."

With the mass murderer's chances of post-conviction success now standing at slim to none, it seems logical Johnson will try to use his health and advanced age as his best ammunition for a get-out-of-jail-free card in 2021 and beyond.

But can he prevail?

Is he destined to follow the path of two other notorious Illinois mass murderers, Chester Weger and Carl Reimann? Years ago, nobody would have predicted the terrorizing Starved Rock Killer would regain his freedom, able to come and go freely in Illinois. And now he does. And who would have expected that the man who randomly gunned down five people inside a roadside diner in Yorkville would also be sent home from the Illinois penal system?

And who would have predicted the governor of Illinois, a Republican, would end his state's death penalty and move everyone off Death Row and commute their capital punishment to life imprisonment?

Citing those examples, one can't help but wonder if the day in Illinois is looming when Johnson will meet up with Weger on a gorgeous summer day for a game of checkers or chess at a small-town neighborhood park. Or, in the alternative, Johnson may meet Reimann for a cup of steaming coffee and a hearty breakfast sandwich at a Chicago area McDonald's where the two killers can reminisce about their time together in prison.

Simpson, the retired Will County investigator, said Illinois must never release Johnson from prison under any under circumstances, including medical. If the day comes when Johnson's health rapidly declines or he becomes terminally ill, then Johnson should die in a prison infirmary.

"His head is just kind of wired in a manner that says, 'You know what? I kind of get a kick out of killing some people,'" Simpson replied.

During a 1996 interview with the *Chicago Tribune*, Burmila, the prosecutor at both of Johnson's murder trials, reflected how the 1983 murders unnerved the entire Joliet region.

"He was completely amoral," Burmila told the Tribune. "He was a stone-cold killing machine."

Simpson and Petka are convinced that Johnson would return to his old wicked ways of murder and mayhem, if given another chance at freedom.

Sure, he's a lot older, but why would anyone believe Johnson's days of bringing harm to unsuspecting people are all but a thing of the past?

Simpson, like Johnson, is now in his seventies. He can't envision Johnson becoming the type to take an avid interest in growing a garden or taking a part-time job as a greeter at a Joliet area Walmart store.

Ficarello termed Johnson a sociopath. Like Simpson, Ficarello does not want to see Johnson back in society. He fears Johnson would revert back to the one thing he's good at doing, which is slaughtering people.

"With killers, there's planned and unplanned, so he was an unplanned criminal, however, it appeared that his targets were random," Ficarello said. "They were not targets where he had done any victimology on them as far as studying their habits.

"The organized sociopathic killer will watch their victim and plan the attack. The unplanned person is more of a random target."

Ficarello, who investigated the ceramic shop murders on the day of the killings, said Johnson may have been scoping out the ceramic shop for his next kill, knowing most of its customers were women.

Johnson may have had his eyes on one of the women who arrived in the Ryan family's Chevy Blazer. Ficarello pointed out that the Joliet business was known for offering pottery classes to customers.

"It's a very strong possibility he observed the females entering the shop and that caught his attention, whether or not he knew every Saturday there would be ceramic class there," Ficarello remarked.

As for the Homer Township killings that took the lives of five people, Ficarello suspects that Johnson was lurking around the area because it was a haven for parkers. To his satisfaction, the young man and woman from Lemont showed up.

"He probably knew that people would park there at the corner for lovemaking, sex, whatever, but that's probably as far as his plans," Ficarello theorized. "No connection with him and his victims at all."

Some true-crime readers may scoff at the theories of the retired Will County police and prosecutors fearing that

Milton Johnson would kill again, if he's ever released from prison.

After all, how many senior citizens are roaming the streets murdering people? Most killers are in their twenties, thirties and forties. Murder is not an old man's crime.

While that may be true, prison officials in other states have learned the hard way that setting a convicted killer on the road to freedom can lead to more murders.

Just take the July 18, 2019, headline: "Killer Released Prison, Dubbed Too Old To Be Dangerous, Kills Again."

The *New York Post* reported that a jury in Maine needed less than an hour to find seventy-seven-year-old Albert Flick guilty of the 2018 murder of a homeless mother. Flick stabbed her at least eleven times while her twin boys watched.

In 1979, Flick went to prison after stabbing his wife to death in front of their daughter. In preparation for his 2018 killing, Flick began stalking his future homicide victim, a forty-eight-year-old woman, as she dined at a local homeless shelter.

Flick came to the conclusion that "If I can't have her, I will kill her," the *New York Post* reported.

Back in Johnson's hometown, a fifty-six-year-old woman became the city of Joliet's first homicide of 2021. The man arrested in connection with her shooting death was Ben Rockett age sixty-nine. Thirty years earlier, Rockett committed a murder in Will County.

Approaching his late seventies, retired prosecutor Ed Petka's mind remains sharp. The retired Illinois state senator can still recall obscure trial facts and names of the jurors even though thirty-seven years have passed since Petka convicted Johnson of the I-55 killing.

Petka wanted the death penalty for Johnson. After weighing arguments, a judge who morally opposed the death penalty agreed death was warranted. Nineteen years later, a governor who supported the death penalty, but was on the verge of being indicted on federal corruption charges, decided to make a name for himself by abolishing capital punishment in Illinois. George Ryan's controversial decision spared Johnson's life.

At the time of John Gacy's arrest, there were serious discussions that Will County, not Cook County, should take the lead in prosecuting the clown killer's murders because Gacy discarded four bodies in Will County. In the end, Cook County took the lead, but Petka was intimately involved in the Gacy case, and that's why he was invited to be one of the witnesses for Gacy's 1994 execution at Stateville.

And yet the one killer Petka worked so hard to convict, so hard to bring justice to the families of Tony Hackett and Tonya Little, still lives, even though a death sentence was pronounced by the judge.

As the room of spectators watched from the other side, Gacy died after a poisonous needle ended his life at age fifty-two. Johnson, convicted of five murders, but the prime suspect in fourteen killings, remains alive and well, twenty-seven years after the state of Illinois ended Gacy's life with a lethal injection.

"As far as I'm concerned, both were terribly savage people," Petka remarked during a 2020 interview. "The big difference is that Gacy got executed, and Milton did not."

Petka can't imagine Illinois will turn Johnson loose for any reason, medical or otherwise. In Petka's mind, Johnson must only leave the Illinois Department of Corrections prison at Menard by a hearse.

"All I can tell you is that him and society don't mix," Petka said.

Petka has a scrapbook that includes countless newspaper articles of the Milton Johnson case. Above all, Petka does not want the memories of Johnson's victims to fade away and become forgotten. Reading the haunting articles years later does not diminish the raw pain and fear that Johnson brought to his victims.

A Plainfield teenager at the time, Mary West unknowingly became Johnson's first victim in 1970.

She and her boyfriend Lee Chandler met up with another teenage couple for a Sunday afternoon at the famous Brookfield Zoo near Chicago. The four planned to attend a drive-in movie theater later that night, but the parents of West's friend made her stay home. In the alternative, West and her boyfriend chose to visit the Pilcher Park forest after dark.

Fourteen years after that horrific night, *Joliet Herald-News* columnist John Whiteside interviewed West, then thirty-two years old, by phone. She did not want anybody knowing her identity nor the state where she relocated. Whiteside's column was headlined: "Night of Terror Has Changed Her Life Forever."

"I've been living my own hell. I can tell people about it, but they will never fully understand," she told Whiteside, after learning Johnson was being charged with multiple Will County murders after being paroled for raping her at Pilcher Park years later.

"His arrest has brought it all back," she said. "I can smell my flesh burning again. I can hear his voice talking to me."

West became the first of Johnson's many random victims. She survived, but her life was ruined by her random encounter with Johnson in the woods of Joliet on Feb. 15, 1970, a freezing Sunday night.

She spent six weeks in the intensive care unit at Silver Cross Hospital. She lost almost fifty pounds as she recovered from her broken jaw. Then, in the summer of 1970, she made the decision to take her own life. She drove into a garage and left the engine running. At the last second, Whiteside wrote, she jumped out of her car and ran from the garage.

One night in Pilcher Park changed the course of her life. But West always knew the day would come when Johnson got released from prison.

"I knew he would do it again if they let him out," she told Whiteside fourteen years after being raped and beaten beyond recognition.

"Not one day of my life has gone by when I didn't think about him. He changed my life. It tore my family apart. I can see a car, hear a voice or see someone resembling him. Then it all comes back. I'll never stop looking over my shoulder, behind bushes or feeling unsafe when out from behind an unlocked door. I feel it could happen.

"With all this now, it's like it happened to me two weeks ago. I can still hear his voice. I can smell my burning flesh. I've had vomiting spells ever since I heard he was arrested. I've been dragged back to it all, again."

For More News About John Ferak,
Signup For Our Newsletter:

http://wbp.bz/newsletter

Word-of-mouth is critical to an author's long-term success. If you appreciated this book please leave a review on the Amazon sales page:

http://wbp.bz/terrortowna

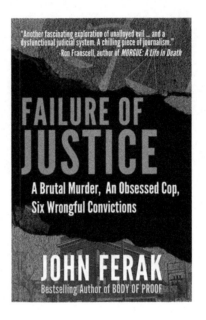

Made in the USA
Las Vegas, NV
11 September 2021